'Free Trade' and Moral Philosophy

'Free Trade' and Moral Philosophy
Rethinking the Sources of Adam Smith's
Wealth of Nations   Richard F. Teichgraeber III

Duke University Press   *Durham 1986*

© 1986, Duke University Press
All rights reserved
Printed in the United States of America
on acid-free paper ∞
Second printing, 1988
Library of Congress Cataloging in Publication Data
Teichgraeber, Richard F.
'Free trade' and moral philosophy.
Bibliography: p.
Includes index.
1. Smith, Adam, 1723–1790. Inquiry into the nature
and causes of the wealth of nations. 2. Free trade and
protection. 3. Capitalism—Moral and ethical aspects.
I. Title.
HB161.S6694   1986   330.15'3   85-25408

Contents

Acknowledgments   vii

Abbreviations   ix

Preface: The Problem of Adam Smith   xi

I   Introduction: Free Trade and Moral Philosophy   1

II   Francis Hutcheson   29

III   David Hume   75

IV   Adam Smith   121

V   Epilogue: The Man of "Public Spirit"   170

Notes   171

Index   207

Acknowledgments

A number of scholars have read all or part of this book and have made valuable suggestions. Donald Winch, James Moore, Thomas Horne, and Joyce Appleby offered helpful responses to early drafts of each chapter, as well as good advice on the organization of the whole study. Others who read portions of the book in its early stages include Elisabeth Young-Bruehl, Nannerl Keohane, Thomas Haskell, Nicholas Phillipson, Richard Sher, and Thomas Laqueur. George A. Kelly, James Sheehan, and George Steiner provided invaluable moral support along the way, something most first-time authors badly need. Mildred Covert typed the early versions and the final draft of the entire manuscript. I am happily indebted to all of these.

Some of the arguments presented here made earlier and differently staged appearances, notably: "Rethinking *Das Adam Smith Problem*," *Journal of British Studies*, XX (1981); and my critical introduction to Adam Smith's *Wealth of Nations*, New York, Modern Library College Edition, Random House, 1985. I thank both editors and publishers for permission to reprint.

Fellowship support for early stages of research and writing was provided by a Grant-in-Aid from the ACLS. Summer grants from the Senate Committee on Research at Tulane University supported the last stages of my work.

The book is dedicated to Mary, who sustained me through the dismay and elation of making a book.

Abbreviations

I have used the facsimile editions prepared by Bernhard Fabian in the *Collected Works of Francis Hutcheson*, 7 vols., Hildesheim, 1971. What follows is my own system of abbreviation.

Inquiry   *An Inquiry into the Original of Our Ideas of Beauty and Virtue* (1725)

Essay   *An Essay on the Nature and Conduct of the Passions and Affections* (1728)

Short   *A Short Introduction to Moral Philosophy* (1747)

System   *A System of Moral Philosophy*, 2 vols. (1755)

References to the works and correspondence of David Hume again employ my own abbreviations:

Treatise   *A Treatise of Hume Nature* (1739–40), ed. L. A. Selby-Bigge, Oxford, 1888.

$Enquiry_1$ *An Enquiry Concerning Human Understanding* (1748)

$Enquiry_2$ and *An Enquiry Concerning the Principles of Morals* (1751)
from *Enquiries concerning Human Understanding and concerning the Principles of Morals*, ed. L. A. Selby-Bigge, 3rd ed., rev. P. H. Nidditch, Oxford, 1975.

Essays   *Essays, Moral, Political and Literary*, 2 vols., in *David Hume: The Philosophical Works*, vols. 3 and 4, ed. T. H. Green and T. H. Grose, London, 1886.

Letters   *The Letters of David Hume*, 2 vols., ed. J. Y. T. Greig, Oxford, 1932.

x Abbreviations

> For the works and correspondence of Adam Smith, I have used the volumes in the Glasgow bicentennial edition and follow the system of abbreviations suggested by the editors of that edition.

Corr.   *The Correspondence of Adam Smith*, ed. E. C. Mossner and I. S. Ross, Oxford, 1977.

TMS   *The Theory of Moral Sentiments* (1759), ed. D. D. Raphael and A. L. Macfie, Oxford, 1976.

LJ(A)   *Lectures on Jurisprudence:* Notes dated 1762–63

LJ(B)   and *Lectures on Jurisprudence:* Notes dated 1766 from *Lectures . . .* , ed. R. L. Meek, D. D. Raphael, and P. G. Stein, Oxford, 1978.

WN   *An Inquiry into the Nature and Causes of the Wealth of Nations* (1776), ed. R. H. Campbell and A. S. Skinner, Oxford, 1978.

> *LJ(A)* references are given to the volume and page number of the original manuscript; *LJ(B)* is followed by a page number referring to the Edwin Cannan edition of these lectures in *Lectures on Justice, Police, Revenue, and Arms* (Oxford, 1896).
>
> I have modernized spelling and grammar except in instances where eighteenth-century usage seems to make an argument or observation clearer.

Preface: The Problem of Adam Smith

On March 9, 1776, one of the most remarkable books in the history of thought appeared in London. The book was *An Inquiry into the Nature and Causes of the Wealth of Nations*, a massive and forceful argument calling for an end to political supervision of economic activity. The author of the book, Adam Smith, "Formerly Professor of Moral Philosophy in the University of Glasgow" as he described himself on the title page of the first edition, was to have an enormous impact on subsequent European and American history. Only six weeks after the *Wealth of Nations* was published, a contemporary wrote to Smith, "You are surely to reign alone on these subjects, to form the opinions, and I hope to govern at least the coming generations."[1] By the end of the eighteenth century, six editions of his economic treatise had been printed in England; by 1786, four editions of two different translations had been published in Germany; by 1801, six editions of three separate translations had appeared in France. The exact circulation of the *Wealth of Nations* is not known. From the year of its publication to the present day, however, it has been taken as one of the most important books ever written. The *Wealth of Nations* both systematized ideas that had been widely circulated in Western societies during the eighteenth century and provided economic doctrines considered indispensable in the nineteenth and twentieth centuries.

Yet, while almost universal agreement exists about the importance of the *Wealth of Nations*, it remains a puzzling work that has affected its readers in different ways. Some have been struck by the enormous scale and complexity of the book. A text of almost half a million words composed over the course of twenty-five years, the *Wealth of Nations* treated issues that ranged from the causes of economic growth to the history of Western moral philosophy and education. William Strahan, Smith's publisher, once observed that the sales of the book had been far greater "than I could have expected from a work that requires much thought and reflection (qualities that do not abound among modern readers) to peruse to any purpose."[2] But most "modern readers" in fact would come to see the *Wealth of Nations* as a giant machine assembled to drive home one very easily understood point—namely, the view that self-interested pursuit of gain, unregulated by legislation or popular prejudice, ensured the greatest benefit to society. A century after its publication, Walter Bagehot observed that the doctrine of "free trade" had become in the popular mind almost as much Smith's subject "as the war of Troy was Homer's: only curious inquirers think of teachers before the one any more than of poets before the other."[3]

Until recently, most scholars have failed to distinguish or explain the difference between the complicated intentions of the *Wealth of Nations* and its actual historical impact.[4] The problem of the *Wealth of Nations*, however, is only one facet of the larger problem of Adam Smith. His reputation as one of the profound thinkers of his age had been firmly established sixteen years earlier with the widespread acclaim that greeted his first book, *The Theory of Moral Sentiments* (1759). Edmund Burke wrote in his review for the *Annual Register* that Smith's work

> is in all its essential parts just, and founded on truth and nature. The author seeks for the foundation of the just, the fit, the proper, the decent, in our most common and most allowed passions; and making approbation and disapprobation the tests of virtue and vice, and showing that those are founded on sympathy, he raises from this simple truth, one of the most beautiful fabrics of moral theory that perhaps has ever appeared.[5]

Smith's argument for the primacy of "sympathy" in moral life struck deep chords in many educated Europeans. Indeed, during the eighteenth century, the popularity of the *Theory* rivalled that of the *Wealth of Nations*. By 1801, nine editions had appeared in

Britain; three separate translations had been published in France; two in Germany.

The *Theory* and the *Wealth of Nations* were the only books Smith published before his death in 1790. Many brilliant and influential Smith commentators have been puzzled by sharp differences in the tone and the message of each work. In the late nineteenth century, German scholars coined the phrase "*das Adam Smith Problem*" to suggest there might even have been a fundamental change in Smith's thinking during the period between their publication.[6] Some of these scholars went so far as to argue that there was a dual personality in Adam Smith. How could a writer who had ascribed human conduct to the workings of "sympathy" later reverse himself and coldly ascribe all human action to calculated self-interest?

Much of the history of Adam Smith scholarship is a story of many different efforts made to answer this last question. But in fact the problem of Smith has even broader dimensions, most of which his students have begun to explore only in this century. The earliest solutions to *das Adam Smith Problem* were presented prior to 1896, that important year when Edwin Cannan published a newly found set of student notes on Smith's lectures on law and government given while he was Professor of Moral Philosophy at Glasgow from 1752 to 1764. These would later be supplemented by yet another set of student notes, discovered in 1958, on the very same topics. Taken together, the Glasgow *Lectures* showed that most of the central principles of Smith's economic theory—including an early version of his troubling chilly endorsement of "self-love" in book 1 of the *Wealth of Nations*—had been put forward at the same time as his theory of moral sentiments.[7] So it was evident that any supposed inconsistency in Smith could not be explained as the result of a later change in opinion or subject matter. Equally important, however, the *Lectures* also provided the basis for a partial reconstruction of an ambitious project Smith had described at the conclusion of the sixth and final edition of the *Theory of Moral Sentiments* (1790). In the year of his death, Smith stated explicitly that his grand intellectual design was to have fashioned a moral philosophy with three overlapping systems: the *Theory* at one end, the political economy of the *Wealth of Nations* at the other, and an account of law and government that would pull both ends into one coherent system of thought.

Today it seems clear that the study of Adam Smith should begin with his understanding of himself as a moral philosopher. But that task too is unenviably complicated, and not only because of the scantiness of his private correspondence and the fact that the most detailed statements of his views on law and government come sometimes awkwardly to us by way of his university students' notes. To explore Smith's thought exhaustively requires a knowledge of the history of Western ethical and political theory as well as familiarity with early-modern science, theology, and economic writing. Smith's economic doctrines can be traced to seventeenth-century natural law jurisprudence as well as to the contemporary writings of French Physiocrats. In short, even while we now see clearly what Smith's intentions were, the intellectual traditions and contexts relevant to understanding them are multiple. Thus, the questions central to grasping his thought do not lend themselves to study within the confines of conventional intellectual biographies or histories of particular ideas or intellectual traditions.

It is hardly surprising, then, that while Smith has been the subject of serious reflection for more than two hundred years, many questions about his intellectual career have yet to be resolved. Above all, Smith's understanding of himself as a "moral philosopher" has not been grasped in its full complexity, nor has it been clearly located within the history of European thought. Some writers have explored important individual strands of Smith's thought—naturalistic ethics, natural law jurisprudence, the attack on mercantilism—but we have yet to see how the various strands were integrated into a coherent moral philosophy of which, for Smith at least, they were components.[8] Uncertainty still shrouds the ambitious project Smith described at the conclusion of the sixth edition of the *Theory of Moral Sentiments*. The philosophical connections between Smith's theory of "moral sentiments" and his views of justice have not been fully explained, and much work remains to be done in showing how the *Wealth of Nations* was grounded in Smith's understanding of law and government.[9]

These are some of the issues addressed in this study, a book which is intended to be both less and more than another study of Adam Smith. Less, because I will focus here largely on Smith's debts to only two major influences on his thought: Francis Hutcheson and David Hume, the two other outstanding eighteenth-century Scottish moral philosophers. More, because this book also attempts to see Smith's liberal economic doctrines against the background of certain broader developments in the history of early-modern European thought. And many of those developments can be fully explored even while restricting the focus to Smith's career in Scotland. The general reader may feel, perhaps, that the question of capitalism too often disappears from view. But a fuller appreciation of Adam Smith as well as of the complex intellectual history of capitalism requires a thorough explanation of the major intellectual traditions that shaped Smith's understanding of himself as a moral philosopher.

This book, then, is partly a group of linked intellectual biographies, partly a study in how thinkers can be said to influence one another. It also develops a particular analytic argument concerning the historical emergence of certain key elements of capitalism as a view of the human condition. That argument has to be put very schematically for the moment. This study will show how Adam Smith's espousal of free trade, as a philosophical position, developed out of a complex vision of morality, law, and government that he took over from Francis Hutcheson and David Hume. I seek to grasp that vision by carefully exploring what these thinkers had in mind when they discussed the terms "virtue," "rights," "justice," and "commerce." The novelty of this book as a study in sources of Adam Smith's thought is my attempt to develop this analysis in some detail and then to show how it adds to an historical understanding of the *Wealth of Nations*.

The first chapter sets out the major themes of the study, emphasizing views that to me seem arresting and important for grasping the origins of arguments for free trade in Scottish moral philosophy. The separate chapters on Hutcheson, Hume, and Smith try to show how each thinker's argument for economic freedom can be understood in relation to his major innovations as a moral philosopher. The conclusion considers briefly how arguments for and against laissez-faire capitalism in the nineteenth century might be reconsidered against the background of issues explored in the previous chapters.

At the outset, I expected to connect my account of the moral philosophy Smith learned and taught in Scotland to social and economic changes in his native country. Eighteenth-century Scottish history is fascinating and complicated. Its central political event, the Treaty of Union of 1707, still appears to be an historically unique constitutional settlement. Neither a conquest, nor a federation, nor a surrender, the Treaty brought together the parliaments of two separate nations—England and Scotland—in a new political entity under a monarch they had shared since 1603. Through the rest of the eighteenth century, however, Scotland enjoyed what Alex Murdoch has called "a state of semi-independence." Real power rested with English ministers; but apart from suppressing the Highland rebellions in 1715 and 1745, they had no desire or occasion to use it. There was as yet no "British" politics. Thus, Scottish affairs were largely separate and distinct, revolving around problems of reforming the Kirk and improving the economy.[10]

There is no question that Adam Smith was very much aware of Scotland and that Scotland was aware of Adam Smith. A recurring minor theme in the *Wealth of Nations* was his sharp contrasting of Scotland's economic backwardness with England's enlightened practices. Smith made his first public arguments for free trade before Glasgow students and merchants. The earliest admirers, as well as the earliest critics, of the *Wealth of Nations* were Scotsmen.[11] But it would be too much to conclude that a concern to improve Scotland somehow infected Smith with the boldness and energy that made the *Wealth of Nations* possible in the first place. I say this mostly because Scotland in fact did not enter into a dramatically new economic era after 1707. The most significant economic change in eighteenth-century Scotland was a steady growth in tobacco trading that occurred in Glasgow during several decades after the Treaty of Union opened the American colonial market to Scottish merchants. Yet the benefits of that trade were limited largely to a small guild of tobacco merchants, and these so-called Glasgow "tobacco lords" were beneficiaries of a state-supervised economy that Smith rejected. Indeed, in his view the old mercantile system remained the order of the day in Scotland as late as 1784, when he found it necessary to add a concluding attack on that system in book IV as well as a long appendix condemning the herring bounty. At the earliest, it is only in the last decade of the eighteenth century that traditional forms of society and economy in lowland Scotland started to break up under the impact of industrial capitalism. Yet by that time, Smith was dead and his basic economic arguments—assembled in the 1750s and early 1760s—were at least three decades old.

Scottish economic and social history, then, simply did not take me deeply enough into the question of *why* and *how* Smith thought as he did. Moreover, in trying to explain how a moral philosopher came to formulate arguments of the kind we find in the *Wealth of Nations*, I could not escape two findings: (i) Smith worked from the outset of his career as a teacher of moral philosophy with a particular set of values and assumptions that he borrowed from Hutcheson and Hume, and (ii) his often critical reformulations of those same values and assumptions brought him to much of his most interesting and original work. The question that remained was, what inspired Smith's critical reformulations? Why was Smith, for example, more aware than the other two that, if fully put into practice, their economic doctrines promised drastic change and thus would meet substantial resistance? Here is where a biographical approach seemed appropriate. It by no means provides all the answers to this last question, but the fact remains that ideas and philosophical arguments are not produced by eras or by specific historical events. They are generated by individuals whose work can be understood as the product of a complex interaction of mind, various intellectual influences, and professional vocation. A biographical approach to the study of intellectuals, particularly in Smith's case, allows us to uncover a thinker's deepest assumptions and then to pursue the equally important question of how those assumptions are reformulated or questioned.[12] The specific issue of how Hutcheson and Hume served as sources of Adam Smith's thought is of course not the only context in which we can study Smith. But this is rich and still largely unexplored territory that deserves a full-scale study.[18]

Two final points concerning my treatment of Adam Smith deserve mention. This book began several years ago with a puzzle: how did the *Wealth of Nations* grow out of the work of a thinker who was a systematic teacher and writer of moral philosophy? That puzzle carried me back to the writings of Hutcheson and Hume, also eighteenth-century Scottish moral philosophers who explored many of the same economic questions that interested Smith. It involved me too in a rich and varied secondary literature, most of it recently published, that has allowed me to reconstruct the arguments of these three figures in terms of particular traditions of thought or language systems that were alive to them during the age in which they wrote. Seen in this context, this study may be taken as an attempt to synthesize the best of this recent scholarship in a comprehensive re-examination of the grand intellectual designs of Adam Smith. For while that new secondary literature has explored many of the discrete pieces of evidence on which my analysis relies, none of it has put toegther Smith's "moral philosophy"—i.e., his ethics, jurisprudence, and political economy—in quite the systematically historical fashion I've attempted here. Moreover, while my interest in the puzzle of how the *Wealth of Nations* grew out of Smith's moral philosophy is hardly new, my resolution of the puzzle is meant to suggest that work of earlier and more well-known scholars who attended to this same puzzle was often anachronistic and now needs replacement.

Finally, this book was planned and written to appeal to a nonspecialist audience, as well as experts in my field. It will introduce some readers to important new work in early-modern western intellectual history. To those already familiar with this literature or with other material presented here, I would say that surely we have enough scholarly books written only for specialists who might read or review them.

New Orleans, July 1985

I   Introduction: 'Free Trade' and Moral Philosophy

As all other arts have in view some good to be obtained, as their proper end, Moral Philosophy, which is the art of regulating the whole of life, must have in view the noblest end; since it undertakes, as far as human reason can go, to lead us into that course of life which is most according to the intention of nature, and most happy, to which end whatever we can obtain by other arts should be subservient. Moral Philosophy therefore must be one of these commanding arts which directs how far the other arts are to be pursued.
—A Short Introduction to Moral Philosophy, p. 1

i   Between 1660 and 1792, after the wars of religion had ended and before the wars of revolution had begun, many European thinkers felt that greater freedom in the pursuit of commerce and profit would provide a secure foundation for the prosperity, stability, and peace of mankind. The debate between "mercantilists" and proponents of "free trade" and "laissez-faire" during this period centered on the question of how great this economic freedom should be. In their struggle to influence the policies of statesmen and legislators, both groups of thinkers emphasized that growth in the wealth of society promised to augment the power and prestige of a polity. They stressed, too, that this link between economic prosperity and political power suggested an underlying harmony of private and public interests in the economic realm. But the mercantilists went on to underline a need their rivals saw no reason to emphasize. Mercantilism was in part a theory of state-building, arguing that political authority alone could ensure that individual economic pursuits would benefit society at large.[1] The mercantilists allowed that an individual pursuing profit need not feel himself restrained by the moral directives of Christian theology. But they also instructed him to see himself as part of his nation rather than as a creature of the politically indifferent market place.

Proponents of "free trade" and laissez-faire saw no reason to subordinate the interests of a merchant to his supposed responsibilities as a patriotic subject.[2] In letter x of the *Lettres philosophiques* (1734), an optimistic précis of the more liberal position, Voltaire went so far as to say that the achievements of free English merchants were comparable to those of classical Roman citizens. In Voltaire's view, the eighteenth-century English merchant was a uniquely praise-worthy figure who at once "enriches his country, sends orders from his office to Surat and to Cairo, and contributes to the well-being of the world."[3] Not all defenders of the ideal of free trade were so extravagant in their claims on behalf of commerce. But the view that there was a special consonance of public and private interests in a free economic market place became commonplace in advanced intellectual circles before the French Revolution threw matters into confusion again.

There are many ways to tell the story of the intellectual origins of this last view. Perhaps the most well-known version of the story tells of the rise of 'laissez-faire capitalism' as an attack on traditional systems of ideas and socio-economic relationships. The Marxian and Weberian analyses to be sure differed in their accounts of the nature of this attack. Marx insisted that capitalism as an ideology was a transient historical development rooted in a new configuration of exploitative class relationships. Weber contended that capitalism did not require a new dominant class so much as a new personal ethic that sustained a radical reordering of human personality. Both Marx and Weber, however, shared the still widely accepted assumption that the intellectual history of capitalism is a matter of fundamental ideological innovations that shattered preexisting ideas and practices in the economic realm.[4]

Contemporary scholars are still adding chapters to this story of capitalism as the rise of an independently conceived, insurgent ideology.[5] But recently a number of historians of thought have laid the groundwork for strikingly different approaches. One group, led by J. G. A. Pocock, retains the view of capitalism as a novel ideology, but argues that in the late seventeenth and eighteenth centuries the growth of capitalism was not the story of a steady, uniformly successful encroachment at the expense of traditional, medieval values.[6] "Commerce" was in fact frequently attacked, but in the name of values that were neo-classical rather than Christian. In Britain, where capitalism had its earliest successes, a tradition of political thought that historians call civic humanism or classical republicanism was surprisingly long-lived. It stressed the ideal of a society made up of citizens in arms, of individuals who saw property not as the basis of wealth-producing activity, but as a guarantee of political independence and self-sufficiency, of men who saw property in land as a condition that allowed them to realize their greatest virtue, citizenship. Against the background of this tradition of thought, many critics in Britain condemned the development of capitalism as a transformation of classical priorities. And we also find that, in response to this criticism, defenders of capitalism were obliged more to show how the rise of commercial society had superseded that earlier stage of society enshrined by civic humanists than to confront Christian suspicions about love of gain.[7]

Another group of historians, however, has provided evidence showing that the supposedly parvenu ideology of capitalism arose out of old ideas to a greater extent than has generally been appreciated. Certain characteristic elements of the ideological change we call capitalism, these historians argue, can be understood in terms of an endogenous process in post-Renaissance thought as a whole. We know, for example, that as early as the first half of the fifteenth century, Renaissance humanists such as Leonardo Bruni and Poggio Bracciolini had argued that if each individual pursued his own business affairs with industriousness and intelligence, then the pursuit of self-interest in commerce would benefit the community as a whole.[8] For seventeenth-century thinkers of the same convictions, the pursuit of economic self-interest appeared morally innocuous when contrasted to the wilder and more destructive passions of religious zealots and glory-seeking noblemen. Economic motives at least displayed consistency and predictability in their operation. And given freer reign, they might be counted on to countervail other unruly passions and thereby lead to peace and stability.[9]

One of the main purposes of this essay is to add another chapter to this last perspective on the story of the intellectual origins of capitalism. My concern will be to show how three moral philosophers came to identify the practical concerns of human life with the pursuit of economic self-interest, and how they came to argue that state and society must give the greatest possible freedom to that pursuit. Two of the three figures I treat here, Francis Hutcheson and David Hume, are well-known as moral philosophers; the third, Adam Smith, is not. Many students of Smith have found an exclusively economic argument for capitalism in the *Wealth of Nations*, in fact one of the most powerful cases for releasing economics from the traditional constraints of moral philosophy. The economic argument may well be the legacy of Smith's classic study. But we cannot allow ourselves to assume that this may have been his main intention as well. The architecture of Smith's thinking was that of "moral philosophy" in the broad classical sense. In practice, Smith presented his views on ethics, economics, and politics as separate systems. But his goal was that of a moral philosopher: to coordinate these systems in a unified philosophy. The analysis of economic matters was not disjunct from moral philosophy in Smith's thought; indeed, he identified it as an integral component of his moral philosophy.[10]

ii But is it legitimate to speak of "laissez-faire" and "capitalism" in the thinking of these three great eighteenth-century Scottish moral philosophers? Any reader who searches for the phrase "laissez-faire" in their writings will be disappointed. It is possible that Hutcheson never knew the term. During the lifetimes of Hume and Smith, *"laissez-faire, laissez-passer"* was a slogan associated with François Quesnay, a French physician at the court of Louis XV and founder of a sect known as the Physiocrats. Both Hume and Smith were familiar with the doctrines of the French "economists." But while they agreed with the Physiocrats in defending free internal and foreign trade, Hume and

Smith firmly rejected their contention that agriculture was either the sole or principal source of a nation's wealth. Moreover, Adam Smith chose the "system of natural liberty" and the "liberal system of free importation and free exportation"—not "laissez-faire"—as short-hand descriptions for his economic doctrines.

Even so, there is substantial linguistic justification for retaining the Physiocrats' famous if slippery term in studying Hutcheson, Hume, and Smith. First of all, "laissez-faire" appropriately describes that distinctive outlook on the role of government which supported all arguments for free trade, not just those of the Physiocrats. In the seventeenth and eighteenth centuries, defenders of free trade rejected the mercantilist position primarily because they doubted that state intervention could facilitate economic activity more readily than an alternative policy of allowing individuals the freedom to define and pursue their own economic interests. Because this study spends much effort in exploring the view of politics which served as a philosophical foundation for the doctrine of free trade, use of the term "laissez-faire" serves to focus attention on one of its main projects.

The term "laissez-faire" also provides a means of understanding an important aspect of the complex and detailed account of the commercialization of Western society that we find in the *Wealth of Nations*. A careful reading of this book shows that Smith never portrayed free trade as an unmixed blessing. It shows, too, that Smith thought the ideal of a completely free commercial market was something of a utopian dream. More profoundly than the Physiocrats, also more deeply than his friend Hume, Smith was especially aware that calling for government to end regulation of economic activity was not the same thing as calling for government to abdicate all its power in the economic realm. In chapter IV of this study, I will try to show how all these views found their reflection in Smith's pervasive awareness that for statesmen and legislators free trade and laissez-faire would always prove audacious and difficult guides for policy-making.

Finally, in this connection, it should be noted that including Hutcheson in a discussion of the intellectual history of free trade and laissez-faire raises some additional separate problems that will be treated in the next chapter. Here I would stress only that, while he was not an explicit supporter of the principles of free trade and laissez-faire, he did make certain philosophical arguments that Hume and Smith later developed in defense of those principles.

And what of "capitalism"? Use of this term would seem anachronistic if we view capitalism strictly as the economic logic of late eighteenth- and nineteenth-century industrialization, where the buying of human labor to power the operation of machines became the essential characteristic of Western economies. Hutcheson and Hume lived in a preindustrial age. Smith approached the heart of the industrial revolution with his discussions of the division of labor, specialization and exchange, and the extent of the market. But those discussions, as one economic historian has argued, were largely related to what is now called "proto-industrialization"—i.e., specialization by merchants, weavers, spinners, nailers, and pinmakers—rather than the requirements of industrialization for large factories.[11] One could also argue that when seen in this setting Smith's much disputed view of labor as *both* the cause and the measure of value makes some sense.[12]

Commerce in the eighteenth century, as in the three preceding it, was a matter of producing goods to provision the wide-ranging military and naval efforts of rival European nations and of furnishing commodities to overseas suppliers in exchange for goods to be sold as commodities at home. These activities created the global commercial network, celebrated by Voltaire and many other eighteenth-century observers, that supplied raw materials for Western factories in the nineteenth century. But few merchants in fact brought laborers directly into owner-supervised establishments, choosing instead to reap the profits of commodity circulation while leaving the risks of production to local domestic producers.

Yet many of the ideas used to explain and defend commercial society were carried over into the age of industrial capitalism. Two views of human nature that Adam Smith powerfully presented would become conventional wisdom in the thinking of that new class of men who purchased machines and bought human energy to power their new factories. First of all, there was the view of man as a laborer and improver. The primary means by which he betters his condition is the increase of his private wealth. Specialization is the rational form of labor; profit is the aim of those who direct labor and the unqualified expression of the successful improvement of our condition. Second, there was the argument that man by nature is an acquisitive creature. He is a trader and seeks before anything else his own personal gain; he also is most capable of rational action when in single-minded pursuit of that end.[13] But it would be misleading to suggest that these views help us to understand the historical origins of capitalism as a particular mode of production. The fact remains that the world of early modern commerce was not one in which a specific type of wage labor is the main clue to the nature of economic activity.

There can be no question, however, that capitalist relations would never have come to dominate industrial production without a set of related, antecedent changes in the world of commerce. Some of the crucial changes that served to guarantee the new order were unforeseen or overlooked by the subjects of this study—inventions in the textile industry, for example. But the transition to industrial capitalism also entailed a transformation of legal and political supports for economic enterprise. In helping us to understand this transformation, the views of commerce in Hutcheson, Hume, and Smith can be said to form an important part of the intellectual history of capitalism.

To the end of the eighteenth century, the global network of European commerce remained largely within politically defined channels, limited by privileges and prerogatives guaranteed by the state. Before capitalist relations could come to dominate industrial production, the political supervision of economic activity had to be eliminated in some areas, curtailed in others. Monopolies of all kinds, created by rulers who sought to increase their own treasuries at the expense of their rivals, had to be abolished because they hampered the reproductive capacity of capital. Statesmen and legislators also needed to understand that the demands of capital accumulation required the state to surrender its control over the movement of raw materials and human labor. Not all of the new demands made upon the state by the champions of capitalist relations required a diminishment of its power. Defenders of free trade recognized that state assistance sometimes would be necessary to open up new foreign markets or to protect nascent industries against external competition. At the same time, they called for state investment to create an infrastructure of education, transportation, and communications that would benefit a capitalist economy without demanding major outlays from it. But even here, the various political messages of capitalism were of one piece. Law and government must be the servants of economic activity; they also must give the greatest possible freedom to men who engage in trade and manufacturing.[14]

There are many ways of tracing the ascendancy of this view of politics, a view summarized—accurately, even if with sometimes misleading convenience—in the phrase "laissez-faire." One is through the impact of events themselves, which is the traditional province of political and economic historians. Another way is to keep events on the margin and reconstruct particular conceptions of human purpose that inspired or interpreted those events. Here the distinction between eighteenth-century "commerce" and nineteenth-century "capitalism" begins to blur. For while thinkers such as Hutcheson, Hume, and Smith knew little or nothing of factories and wage-earning laborers, they did address the deep and persistent problem of the proper relation between economic and political affairs. And it is precisely because these three thinkers help us to grasp the intellectual origins of political ideas crucial to capitalism, even if we view it strictly as a particular mode of production, that we can connect their views to its intellectual history.

My use of the word "capitalism" in this book, then, is fairly restrictive, but not historically inappropriate. As a description of the human condition, capitalism includes those views of human nature we touched on earlier. But the view of man as a trader who seeks before anything else his own personal gain is not the central historical novelty of capitalism. There remains the question of what conceptions of state and society follow from accepting or affirming that man is a self-interested creature. In response to that question, laissez-faire capitalism puts forward three new arguments. First, a society made up of self-interested men measures its well-being primarily in quantitative terms. Social prosperity from one year to the next, from one generation to the next, is dependent on the increase in the marketable value of economic goods men labor to produce and to trade. Second, society as a whole is a self-regulating mechanism. If one believes that in a free market competitive trade among individuals serves to prevent selfish passions from becoming destructive, it follows that man's common social destination will take care of itself. Thus, the health of a capitalist society is not the result of a comprehensive rational design. It is found in the extent of that society's ability to facilitate its members' desires to satisfy their own separate material needs. Finally, politics has no positive moral value or purpose in a capitalist society. Statesmen and legislators understand that their subjects do not pursue trade and profit for the conscious purpose of increasing the wealth and prestige of the state. But since the public good is founded on economic prosperity and growth, and not the proper activity of citizens, men with political power see that their primary responsibilities are legislative and administrative improvements that facilitate further increases in trade and profit.

From its inception, this view of the human condition has been criticized and defended in equally powerful terms. Critics lamented the displacement of traditional ideals of humanity and citizenship by narrow, even if practicable, goals of economic growth and improvement. Under capitalism, the ideal of an all-encompassing human excellence or "virtue" must be abandoned. Man lives a life where morals and economic activity have become different and opposite yardsticks. The human condition becomes one in which men live estranged from their better selves.[15]

Where critics of a free commercial society have found estrangement, many of its most able defenders have found unblinking honesty about human nature. It is said that the argument for laissez-faire capitalism follows from the recognition that men are in fact incapable of realizing human excellence or virtue. Capitalism can be seen as the realistic alternative to authoritative, but also chimerical, moral codes. A free commercial society in fact is not founded in any particular moral vision. It rather assumes that commercial activity allows men to enter into relationships where instinctive self-interest is channelled into the service of society at large.[16]

This essay is not concerned either to demolish or to defend capitalism as an economic theory or a philosophical position, but to trace its conception of politics back to certain developments in the history of early-modern Western thought. My interest here, most especially, is in philosophical assumptions—rather than historical events—that allowed for the development of laissez-faire economic philosophy. There is already an abundance of scholarship, much of it excellent, that deals with Hutcheson, Hume, and Adam Smith, or with their particular views of moral philosophy, ethical motivation, justice, citizenship, and commerce. I have conceived of a different inquiry here. My guiding assumption is that their ideas about law and government can be studied as a point of convergence in their moral philosophies for certain basic alterations in traditional humanistic conceptions of the nature of ethical, economic, and political activity. These three thinkers, first of all, shared what they took to be a novel view of personal ethics as a concern necessarily springing from our individual sentiments and passions. As a result, they no longer looked upon human virtue in terms of a person's conscious pursuit of a larger public good. Virtue was now the result of the proper orchestration of private passions. This view, in turn, served to support their understanding that the essentially commercial logic of human life required abandoning the view that politics is that realm in which man's deepest practical and moral concerns find resolution or fulfillment. They considered politics largely as a matter of administering laws and formulating government policies for further increasing wealth and facilitating commercial activity.

I believe this approach is an appropriate way of focussing attention on the fact that arguments for free trade and laissez-faire formed a complex and important episode in the history of Western moral philosophy, not one of its dead ends. The ascendancy of free economic activity in the thinking of Hutcheson, Hume, and Smith entailed a clear and carefully argued limitation of the moral weight traditional humanistic moral philosophy had given to politics. Or to put it another way, my argument is that we more fully grasp their economic doctrines if we understand how they were founded in a de-politicized view of individual morality and de-moralized view of politics.

The three great Scottish Enlightenment thinkers studied here were not the representative figures of their age. The Scottish Enlightenment is a term that can be used to designate two distinct and sometimes opposed schools of thought.[17] The first was the naturalistic, and at times skeptical, moral philosophy of Francis Hutcheson, David Hume, and Adam Smith. The second was the "Common Sense" school—Thomas Reid, James Beattie, and James Oswald—which ultimately came to control the teaching of moral philosophy in Scottish universities. This division is useful and accurate enough if one is concerned only with the history of high-level theorizing in eighteenth-century Scotland. But in some respects it is also arbitrary and misleading. The Common Sense critique of Hume, for example, did not lead to practical conclusions significantly different from those he put forward. Important figures such as William Robertson, Hugh Blair, Lord Kames, John Millar, Adam Ferguson, and Dugald Stewart cannot be easily placed in this binary scheme. Robertson and Blair were practicing Presbyterian ministers who headed the influential Moderate Reform movement within the Scottish Kirk. Scottish "Moderates" were the voices of liberal, enlightened Protestantism, analogous to the Latitudinarians in the Church of England. They borrowed in interesting ways from the moral teachings of Francis Hutcheson and Adam Smith. But given careers in the Kirk, their concerns often involved matters that did not interest the great Scottish moral philosophers.[18]

Whatever its internal differences, however, eighteenth-century Scottish thought above all else was an extraordinarily rich period for speculation on the meanings of the commercialization of Western society. Why then limit an analysis to my three figures? Why not include contemporaries such as Adam Ferguson and Lord Kames? Why not discuss the influence of Montesquieu as well? The obvious answer is that the figures chosen were the most profound thinkers of the great age of Scottish thinkers. Their arguments were richer in range of implication and their concerns were broader in scope than any of their Scottish contemporaries. And these three figures surely have given us doctrines that transcended their own time and place. The same of course is true of Montesquieu. Yet his seminal study of *The Spirit of the Laws* (1748) appeared two years after Hutcheson's death. And while this work was held in high esteem by both Hume and Smith, its influence on their thinking was "diffuse rather than specific." By contrast, their various intellectual debts to Hutcheson are easier to trace and often specifically acknowledged. Hutcheson, Hume, and Smith were, moreover, arguably the three most important thinkers within the Scottish Enlightenment itself. They served both as foils and as inspirations for their contemporaries. Scholars have noted that Ferguson's *Essay on Civil Society* (1767) and Kames's *Sketches of the History of Man* (1774) raised many of the same questions about commerce that Hume and Smith explored in their work. But these works appeared well after Hume and Smith had established the philosophical foundations of their economic doctrines.[19]

Finally, and most importantly, these three figures, as complete philosophers, illustrate certain basic alterations within the history of Western humanist thought that served to erode long-standing reservations about the self-interested pursuit of trade and profit and at the same time instated a view of human life that encouraged the free search for private economic gain.

iii   I will explore the basic alterations in Western humanist thought illustrated by Hutcheson, Hume, and Smith by pursuing three concerns. The first will be the main architectural elements in the thinking of Hutcheson, Hume, and Smith. These three figures thought of themselves as philosophers whose main branches of inquiry, while distinct, also explained each other and could not be lifted from a comprehensive structure of thought. In the history of Western thought, the moral philosophy of Hutcheson, Hume, and Smith represents first a contribution to an ancient and venerable project. Their shared conception of the all-embracing purpose of moral philosophy resembled that of classical Greek and Roman humanists. Hutcheson emphasized that his "moral sense" theory was to be understood as only one element in a system of thought that provided regulation for the whole of life. While Hume in the *Treatise* pursued a novel "experimental method of reasoning" in discussing "moral subjects," his broad notion of "moral subjects" included all of man's interconnected affairs.[20] The major concerns of moral philosophy that Hutcheson tried to bring together in a single work—ethics, economics, and politics—his one-time pupil Adam Smith first treated as separate systems. The goal, however, was ultimately the same: to draw the systems together in a unified philosophy.

The issue of the broad scope of the moral philosophies of Hutcheson, Hume, and Smith accounts for the particular way in which I tell my part of the story of the intellectual genesis of capitalism. I will explore the issue of the ascendancy of a free economic realm in terms of the broader interrelationship of ideas about ethics, politics, and economics, and that is undoubtedly a perspective my figures consciously sought to clarify. It also accounts for the conclusion of my story. An all-encompassing moral philosophy that aimed at regulating the whole of life became in practice a philosophy that set separate standards for governing different aspects of human life. I want to show why these separate standards worked so distinctly to the advantage of laissez-faire economic doctrines.

My second main concern is the meaning of "virtue," a slippery but nonetheless crucial term in the thinking of my figures. I will consider it, as they did, both in its private and in its public or political meanings. Hutcheson, Hume, and Smith felt that they put forward a more accurate and thereby a novel account of moral personality. This account is best described as a naturalistic theory of morals. It emphatically affirmed the role of human passions in moral conduct. Not all passions are commendable, to be sure. But if we seek to explain the principles of morality in terms of human nature seen in all its complexity, we must find the ways in which particular passions impel us to make moral judgments. A man's private virtue consists of the proper exercise and interplay of his appetites, instincts, sentiments, and affections. Since man has a variety of affections and appetites, however, it follows that virtue cannot be reduced to a single or primary ideal such as self-knowledge, prudence, or benevolence. Virtue did not center in any one affection, Adam Smith wrote, but in "the proper government and direction of all our affections."[21] The great Scottish thinkers knew they were not the first to argue that virtue and passions were intertwined. But they did view themselves as the first to give this argument a rigorously philosophical foundation. Thus, they saw themselves to have secured a new position in the history of Western moral speculation.

Before Hutcheson, the debate about the role of passions in moral life had been resolved in three ways.[22] The first was the view of classical Greek and Roman moralists: the achievement of virtue depends upon the discipline of the passions by reason. There were disagreements about the meaning of reason and the discipline reason entailed. But there was among the classical humanists a fundamental agreement on the place of passions in moral conduct. The good man was the wise man, hence moral activity would be determined by rational judgment. Affections, desires, and instincts are necessary to human activity, but passions left alone lead to false judgments that threaten the virtue of the ordered individual soul.

A second view of the passions contended that the idealistic view of moral judgment in classical humanism effectively put virtue beyond the reach of ordinary men. A practicable account of virtue would have to see passions as phenomena that could not be reduced simply to false or misguided judgments. Christian morality, as we find it in Augustine and his medieval scholastic followers, was a matter of the types of love that ruled one's will, not a question of reason. It was here that the discussion of morals was shifted from a purely ethical to a psychological framework.

This shift was later exploited by a series of sixteenth- and seventeenth-century moralists to argue a third view of the passions. Particularly in the works of seventeenth-century French moralists, the great Scottish thinkers found the theory that a moral judgment was in essence a matter of a willing choice between two different types of love, rather than (as Augustine believed) a choice based on faith.[23] They conceived love of self in terms of various kinds of "interests," and the proper exercise of one's will in choosing among one's interests as the central task in realizing "virtue." Hutcheson, Hume, and Smith borrowed from this view but also challenged it on significant points.

The Scots found a richer psychology of morals in the view that "virtue" was a matter of informed self-love. But they could never accept the paradoxical lesson that lay beneath it—namely, that virtue could be realized in spite of the fact that passions per se remained suspect. Virtue here remained in the end a matter of controlling passions. The work of control was now done not by reason or God, but by human institutions. Our suspect passions can be manipulated or harnessed in service to virtue. Within particular sorts of social, political, and economic frameworks, avarice, pride, ambition, and vanity can be channelled into conduct that creates public wealth or public glory. In short, passions can be manipulated in service of the "virtue" that is the public good. But the individual's exercise of his passions cannot in itself be called virtuous.

The Scots accepted the view that virtue was not the object of reason or of divine intervention. But they could not bring themselves to accept the view that "virtue" was homage unknowingly paid by the vices of our self-love. "What a malignant philosophy it must be," Hume wrote, "that will not allow to humanity and friendship the same privileges which are undisputably granted to the darker passions of enmity and resentment."[24] Granting unparadoxical moral privileges to the passions was central to the thinking of Hutcheson, Hume, and Smith. Indeed, it was the main concern of their naturalistic ethics, and it describes what they took to be their novel position on the role of passions in moral life. I will examine the details of this project in the chapters that follow. Here I would note only that this project in places gave rise to a novel and perhaps peculiar language. Hutcheson posited a special "moral sense" in man, a view for which neither classical nor Christian thought allows. Hume talked of virtue resulting from the "excitement" of our passions, the operation of "calm desires" and "appetites" for good. Smith defined virtue as a sense of "propriety" produced by the workings of an internal "impartial spectator" of our passions and affections. For modern readers, no doubt, these terms are peculiar. But they will become less so if we try to understand such terms as parts of the Scots' fundamental innovation in the debate about the nature of personal virtue, an innovation that opened the way for more familiar views of human purpose—especially the laissez-faire position—that perhaps we do not always see in their full complexity.

My third concern is the doctrine of free trade itself, and here I want to focus on one of the most significant ramifications of the Scots' moral philosophy. My argument on this point will of necessity be intricate.[25] Hutcheson, Hume, and Smith each understood that in "modern" European societies in the eighteenth century, notions of public good and commercial prosperity had become interchangeable. They also sought to affirm this development. And yet here they were obliged to address certain long-standing moral and political reservations about the free pursuit of trade and profit. In the view of some early-modern thinkers, the trader was not quite thief, but not quite citizen either. His exclusively economic concerns forced him to view all codes of conduct and authority in only instrumental terms. "We see that in countries where people move only by the spirit of commerce," Montesquieu observed in *The Spirit of the Laws*, "they make a traffic of all the humane, all the moral virtues; the most trifling things, those humanity would demand, are there done, or there given, only for money."[26]

In the writings of Hutcheson, Hume, and Smith, there are at least three different ways in which the philosophical problems of a free commercial society were resolved. One was to say that the moral difficulties it posed had been greatly exaggerated. Hutcheson's view that man was governed by an inherent "moral sense" was after all meant to dispel the notion that man ever could be governed wholly by self-interest. Hutcheson also marshalled his recognition of the primacy of instincts and passions in man to defend the morality of commerce. He distinguished between a "calm desire for wealth" and "the passion of avarice." An interest in money-making could be made to yield to considerations of long-term rationality. The individual trader could find his virtue in frugality.[27]

Hume and Smith found no merit in this argument. For them, money-making, even as a calm passion, was at best an amoral activity. The main motive for trade, Hume said in one of his essays, was "avarice."[28] And when in the *Wealth of Nations* Smith used the word "prudence" to describe the merchant's conduct, the term no longer carried the moral weight of a cardinal virtue. In other passages, Hutcheson himself would retreat from a moral defense of commerce. If one thought that moral judgments sprang from "gratuitous and disinterested" passions, Hutcheson conceded, it was plain that personal virtue could have nothing to do with profit. The alternative here was to defend commerce because of its ability to meet consistently a variety of our social needs. Hutcheson spoke of man's "right of commerce."[29] By this he meant that man was possessed of what Smith later described as a native "propensity to truck, barter, and exchange," because his individual labor could not provide him with all that he needed for life. Commerce, then, allows men to enter into relationships that channel self-interest into the material benefit of society at large.

Hutcheson, Hume, and Smith also emphasized that commerce satisfied social passions as well as social needs. Profits that lead to luxury or comfort represent hollow satisfactions unless accompanied by social recognition. Money-making may not be virtuous activity strictly speaking, but it surely involves some "communicating of pleasures to others," in Hutcheson's phrase.[30] This explained why wealthy men, quite rightly, felt no shame about their economic success. More important, it also explained the cosmopolitan nature of commercial civilization. Free pursuit of profit required commercial men to cross all political and cultural boundaries. With the advance of commerce, local interconnectedness brought about by economic activity extended to the whole world. Commerce may have been divorced from virtue, but it was wedded to peace.

Hutcheson, Hume, and Smith frequently stressed the "politeness" and cosmopolitanism of commercial society. It is a significant sub-theme in their thinking worth an essay in its own right. But this stress was not the central ground of their defenses of economic freedom. The recognition of a fundamental connection between trade and sociability demonstrated that the problem of commerce could not be reduced to a simple conflict between self-love and virtue. A vexing problem, however, remained: what do we make of the radically different aspects of human sociability entailed by money-making? Hutcheson never dealt adequately with this question, but Hume and Smith took it very seriously.[31] Our desire for social recognition could as readily represent a concern to manipulate the opinions of others as to provide for their moral or material welfare. The sociability of commercial men may constrain their avarice, but it nurtures their vanity.

In the last analysis, the Scots thought that the benefits of a free commercial society could be understood most unambiguously in political terms. And it is this argument, and its philosophical underpinnings, that will command much of my attention. Here I want to trace a summary of main points the following chapters are meant to establish and clarify.

The heart of the argument is that the advocacy of commercial freedom in the thinking of the great Scottish moral philosophers developed in the context of a sharply and consciously circumscribed view of the place of politics in human life. Stated so simply, this argument is familiar enough: thinkers such as Rousseau and Adam Ferguson saw (and denounced) it in the middle of the eighteenth century.[32] What is not so familiar is how that view was systematically underpinned by a complete philosophy of human life. It is difficult to decide which view had priority in Scottish thinking: the demotion of political activity as the primary vehicle for the attainment of human values or the ascendancy of the economic realm as the main avenue of human endeavor. But assigning priority here may be less significant than understanding the nature of the philosophical connection between the two.

My point can be illustrated in a preliminary way by returning to the observations with which this chapter began. The explicit criticisms of mercantilism by Hume and Smith clustered around two broad issues, one a matter of policy, the other a philosophical view of man. First, they rejected the mercantilist contention that government should remain as a shelter and protection of industry. Second, they challenged the mercantilist assumption that all human beings, whatever their particular concerns, in the end must see themselves to be politically defined entities.

The ways in which Hume and Smith challenged the technical arguments of mercantilist policy regarding money, balance of trade, and taxation are well-known and need not be rehearsed here. It should be noted again, however, that goals of mercantilist and free trade theorists were not opposite in every respect. Indeed, in formulating policies designed to increase wealth, mercantilists in the seventeenth century had first advocated many of the major reforms later called for by proponents of free trade: rationalization of the tax system, explicit policies to encourage productivity and inventiveness, and elimination of archaic customs and trade barriers.[33] In short, Hume and Smith were by no means the first voices raised in defense of economic improvement, reason, and liberty.

But there were of course major disagreements about how such ideals might be achieved. And, perhaps more important still, beneath these disagreements were irreconcilable differences about the ultimate ends of human conduct. The philosophical issue that divided free trade theorists such as Hume and Smith from mercantilists was not so much the technical logic of economic affairs as the political import of those affairs. Mercantilists saw government as a protector of domestic industry and as a promoter of economic improvements and internal trade. They emphasized the need for political intervention to guarantee the consonance of public and private interests. The economy was, in effect, the perennial charge of the polity, a "political" economy in the strictest sense. For the individual actors who inhabited the economy, this view of things required that the concerns of trade and profit-seeking, whenever appropriate, yield to the highest wisdom of public policy. The merchant's ultimate guide, then, was not the politically impartial logic of the market place but rather his identification with the power and prestige of his nation. In short, the individual subject's desires as tradesman must remain subordinate to his common responsibilities as patriotic citizen.[34]

Like the mercantilists, Hume and Smith were deeply interested in reading the political implications of economic activity. But they saw no reason to compel patriotism in the merchant, just as they saw no reason to assign personal virtue to him. Both argued forcefully against the belief that the primary obligations of "modern" political sovereigns were to create citizens and to nurture patriotism or symbolic cohesion in distinct societies. "Sovereigns must take mankind as they find them," Hume insisted.[35] In a commercial society, this means they understand that all economic goods are purchased by individual labor and, even more important, that a man's private passions are the primary cause of his labor. Full freedom can be given to these passions because economic freedom promises the greatest increase in goods and labor.

Such a view does not render the tasks of politics trivial. The point is rather that in commercial polities we have no reason to look upon political life as a realm of primary moral or social values. The central task of government is the defense of civil society, a task that promises to be less urgent as commercial enterprise successfully crosses all political borders. What remains would be largely administrative work, the making of laws and policies instrumental to further increases in wealth and trade. If there is any distinctively political virtue in a capitalist polity, it was the "negative" virtue of law-abidingness. Hume and Smith knew that respect for the law would not bring the same sorts of benefits to every subject.

iv This view of politics is not sui generis in all its elements. It rejects the central tenets of a civic humanism, a view of man as *zōon politikon*. Yet it draws in important ways from the second central tradition in classical humanist political speculation, natural law jurisprudence. My discussion of this debt will form a major part of this study.

In politics, as in ethics, Hutcheson proved to be a crucially important mentor of Hume and Smith. Yet as a political theorist, he had no clear or obvious intentions of becoming an innovator. The chief sources of his thinking were two seventeenth-century figures who, until very recently, have not figured prominently in the history of eighteenth-century English-speaking thinkers: Hugo Grotius (1583–1645), the Dutch jurist and statesman, and Samuel Pufendorf (1632–94), a German jurist who worked in the courts of Sweden and Prussia. We will see in the chapters that follow how, both in language and in structure, the discussions of law and government in Hutcheson and Smith reflect a great debt to these highly revered natural law jurists. Hume employed a new vocabulary to present his views, but in his *Enquiry Concerning the Prin-*

ciples of Morals (1751) he too acknowledged that his theories concerning property and justice in the main were consistent with Grotius's views in *De Iure Belli ac Pacis* (1625). The particulars of these debts are of less significance here, however, than certain broader conceptions of politics the great Scottish thinkers adopted from that natural law tradition of which Grotius and Pufendorf were seen to be the great "modern" exponents. The philosophical substructure of natural law politics corresponded to that of the naturalistic moral philosophy of the Scots on at least three points. First, like all natural law theorists going back to Cicero (the thinker Hume said had been "in my eye in all my reasonings" as he composed Book III of the *Treatise*),[37] the Scots by and large assumed human nature was fixed and universal. Understanding man's nature was a matter of deducing a single set of principles of conduct which were universally true. Second, natural law thinkers proclaimed a commitment to empirical inquiry along lines the Scots could recognize as their own. The aim of philosophy was to find laws *in* nature, not *for* it. Once gathered together, the observed "facts" of human experience could be reduced to certain basic universal rules or "natural laws." Finally, a central contention about man in natural law thinking was a point Hutcheson and his disciples had also arrived at in their examinations of human passions and sentiments: man by nature was a creature who could not live without society.

The natural law view of politics was founded primarily on this last point. If man could not live without society, he also could not live without law. In observing our inherently social condition, our reason tells us that the only acceptable form of life in society will be tied to a common agreement among rational men that they must live according to a system of law. In natural law politics, man is a legal or juristic person rather than the citizen-warrior of the civil humanist tradition. Moreover, he is a creature with "rights" that must be defined and protected in public law. His primary concern is not the art of ruling so much as the rational pursuit of his private concerns and interests.

For Hutcheson, Hume, and Smith, Grotius was the key figure in the "modern" natural law tradition, and he will play an occasional yet very important role in the argument of this study. One of the most formidable hurdles facing any student who wishes to explain the "politics" of the three great Scottish philosophers is their understanding of the terms "rights," "justice," and "property." Grotius is an invaluable guide to a firm knowledge of what they tried to convey with those terms, so we need to be very clear about his particular intentions and achievements.

In the history of Western thought, Grotius marked the beginning of the second of two great periods of natural rights theorizing.[38] His first important innovation was a radical departure from the Aristotelian assumptions that had governed earlier discussions of rights in a natural law context in the work of scholastic theorists of the Counter-Reformation. Their central task had been to re-establish Aquinas's concept of natural law by incorporating within it the language of subjective rights, a language first developed without any of the constraints of natural law by Jean Gerson (1363–1429). This project entailed rejoining the discussion of "right" in a broad and objective sense—i.e., the concept of "what is right"—and "right" in a more narrow and subjective sense—i.e., a "right" that each individual per se is said to possess.

The work of scholastic rights theorists had two results important for understanding Grotius and his later influence on Hutcheson, Hume, and Smith. First, the scholastics defined "right" as the two-fold object of the two kinds of justice defined by Aristotle, distributive and commutative. In this context, subjective rights were given both a primary and a strict definition. "Right" (*ius*) had the same meaning as "that which is just" (*iustum*) and "that which is equitable" (*aequum*). These rights, in turn, were described as the two objects due to any individual as a matter of justice. Justice in its strict sense was special among the cardinal virtues in seeking to render to each man that which is his private due. In its generic meaning, however, justice also stood for all virtues, since all moral virtues aim at achieving equity. A just man pursues justice in all his actions, as well as in specific individual relationships. He is "good" in an active and positive sense, as well as law-abiding.

This re-description of the two-sided Aristotelian notion of justice in terms of subjective rights provided the scholastics with a theory of rights limited by natural law, a clear standard of right in the objective sense. And if there were two senses of right, it followed that there should also be two senses of the notion of property. Property might express a right in a thing (*ius in re*), i.e., it designates that which is rightfully one's own. Yet it can also express a right to a thing (*ius ad rem*), i.e., it designates that which is rightfully each man's due. Each was a matter of justice according to Aristotle. Safeguarding the right to that which rightfully belongs to an individual and which in fact he does possess is "commutative" justice. Rendering that which is due to an individual as a matter of justice, but which he does not yet possess, is "distributive" justice.

This two-sided account of property—what James Tully has called property both as an "exclusive" and an "inclusive" right—rested on a particular conception of how one comes to have a thing. The main premise was that in nature there once had been a common ownership of all things. Individual or exclusive possession (*proprietas*), therefore, was carefully distinguished from a world held in common by all men (*dominium*). In scholastic thought, there were various criteria that accounted for the particular private distribution of property within society. But there also remained a natural law precept that made it clear that no one should be prevented from exercising an inclusive right to use common property. The important upshot of this restraint, Tully has argued, was the view that private and common property were "interdependent rather than mutually exclusive concepts." Private property in this context was justified only as a necessary means "to individuate and so distribute common property."[39]

In *De Iure Belli*, Grotius directly attacked the neo-Thomist views of justice and property. Many of the elements in this attack on scholasticism formed the basis of an alternative view of social order which—although in somewhat different ways—Hutcheson, Hume, and Adam Smith firmly embraced. In the history of Western thought, *De Iure Belli* has remained famous as Grotius's expression of a passionate desire for peace and notorious for its *Prolegomena* in which he ventured the untheistic assertion that things were good or bad from their own nature, and thereby logically prior to God commanding or forbidding them. The seminal significance of the book in natural law theorizing, however, lay elsewhere. Grotius was a profoundly anti-Aristotelian thinker, whose theory of rights produced radically delimited notions of justice and property. His attack on the Aristotelian view of justice was aimed squarely at the concept of distributive justice. Grotius recognized the distinction between two senses of "right": "what is right" in the wide sense and "what is our own" in the narrow sense. But he rejected the scholastics' attempt to limit the purchase of a person's subjective rights by grounding them in the restraints of natural law. According to Grotius, there was in fact no such category as distributive rights. Rights were entirely *self-referential*; they defined relations that existed between a rational man and whatever was appropriate to him in light of his personal merits or of his property. From this it followed that the law of nature could not include a two-sided Aristotelian theory of justice. Justice instead was a matter of preserving a peaceful community by means of respecting the rights of others. Distributive justice here was assimilated to commutative justice, and an objectively "good" society was seen by Grotius more simply as one in which "every one should quietly enjoy his own, with the help, and by the united force of the whole community."[40]

Grotius's simplification of justice to an injunction to respect the rights of others led to a view of human sociability and property altogether different from those of the scholastics. In his view, natural sociability was characterized narrowly by a negative duty to respect what belongs to others. If right is that "moral quality annexed to the person, enabling him to have, or do, something justly,"[41] property cannot be rendered as an inclusive right but solely as an exclusive right to use those things that one happens to possess. Again breaking with the neo-Thomist position, Grotius pursued a narrow notion of property as an additional support for his conflation of distributive and commutative justice. The definition of property in *De Iure Belli*, the same that later appeared in Hutcheson's *System* and Smith's Glasgow *Lectures*, was based on a conflation of the concepts of *dominium* and *proprietas*. The world was originally held in common, but in a manner different from that imagined by the scholastics. The state of nature is a "negative community," a world that belonged to no one and yet was open to all. Common ownership, as Tully puts it, now meant that "each owner has a right over his share."⁴² In such a world exercising one's rights was acting to make things one's own. In conflating *dominium* and *proprietas*, Grotius also dissolved the concept of a right to one's due. Property came only from individual taking or "occupation," and here it is impossible to speak of community as a form of property. This one-dimensional concept of right refers to what is "common" only to signify that which belongs to no one and remains open to the appropriation of particular persons. In short, property expresses an individual man's exclusive right to dominate the world, to use it for his private purposes alone. It is possible that property might be held by several individuals, each with his particular portions, but it can never be held in common. Even here the exclusion of others from one's portion is the basis of property. As Pufendorf would later write in a paraphrase of Grotius's view, "Property or Dominion, is a Right, by which the very Substance, as it were, of a Thing, so belongs to one Person, that it doth not in whole belong, after the same manner, to any other."⁴³

Emphasis on legal protection of exclusive rights was the first of two main ideological messages in Grotius. He announced that the law of nature was that each man was the free master of his own property and actions. In civil society, laws represent a code of injunctions showing us the proper ways to respect the rights of others. Men by nature are sociable creatures, but their sociability is rooted in rational self-interest: "it consists of leaving others in quiet possession of what is already their own, or doing for them what in strictness they may demand."⁴⁴ Respect for another's rights, in short, was less a matter of the active exercise of personal liberty than the common self-restraint that was the essence of political order.

For Grotius, the only possible guarantee of such self-restraint was the absolute power of one ruler. His passionate desire for peace was based on the view that the cause of war was usually a dispute over rights. And it was this view that prompted his transformation of an initially radically individualistic view of civil society into an absolutist theory of sovereignty. Supreme power, Grotius argued, could not be a function of popular consent. Because civil society was instituted for the peaceful preservation of rights, it followed that there also arose "a superior right in the state over us and ours, so far as it is necessary for that end." A rational political order represents a legal transfer of each member's rights to one ruler. And for such a transfer to take effect, it must be complete and irrevocable.[45]

In the next chapter, I will say something about the fate of Grotius's two key arguments during the century that separated *De Iure Belli* and Hutcheson's earliest arguments for natural rights in the *Inquiry into the Original of our Ideas of Beauty & Virtue* (1725). But some important points regarding Grotius's influence should be noted here. First, the essentially legalistic view of politics in the great Scottish thinkers clearly owed much to Grotius and his later followers. Second, there can be no question that in Grotius we find the original source of notions of rights, justice, and property that were central elements in the Scots' justification of an emerging capitalist civilization. The account of rights in Grotian natural law thinking, for example, spoke to a view of freedom that did not find its practical expression in politics. "Rights" instead were those rational private interests we pursue in an economic market place. Third, the Scots' refusal to take up Grotius's absolutism should be understood largely as a quarrel over means rather than ends. They thought the "rights" and property of subjects in a polity were best protected by laws that secured them against the avarice or caprice of their rulers, not by the absolute power of those rulers.

On one crucial point, however, there was a radical discrepancy in perspectives here, and this discrepancy explains why I will not consider Hutcheson, Hume, and Smith exclusively in the natural law tradition. In natural law philosophy, men are urged to see themselves as parts of a community where differences are resolved by an appeal to a just system of rules or laws. We observe the ethical and legal codes of our society because we are obliged to do so by our reason. This is one of the "facts" of our nature. Now it is the view of society and politics specifically as the creations of human reason that the great Scottish thinkers could not fit with consistency into their frame of reference. Their notion of a naturalistic ethics derived from their refusal to underwrite an account of human nature with the central premise of natural law thinking—namely, the primacy of reason. Indeed, that was one of the great "prejudices" of ancient moral philosophy Hume saw Hutcheson to have escaped in his earliest works. Thus, where natural law thinkers had seen human society and politics to be the products of a "natural" community of rational agents, Hutcheson and his disciples viewed them instead as the products of "natural" instincts that were essentially non-rational: family affections and sexual instinct, on the one hand, resentment, jealousy, and stinginess, on the other. Hutcheson ultimately wavered in this view, but Hume and Smith never doubted that man's sociability and his concern for justice had more to do with these feelings than with the so-called "dictates of right reason."

The appropriate starting point for understanding the Scots' view of politics, then, is a notion of human psychology and virtue fundamentally (and self-consciously) different from that of natural law thinking. In tracing that view, we will still arrive at a conception of politics that owed much to the earlier tradition. But what is of interest in this context is how certain assumptions in natural law thinking about politics were incorporated in a moral philosophy deeply accommodating to laissez-faire capitalism. One key move, it appears to me, was made by Hutcheson when he set out to prove that morality "flows from kind affections or passions."[46] If a person's virtue was not primarily a by-product of knowledge or external discipline, as humanistic moral philosophers before Hutcheson had assumed, it followed that politics, even if reduced to law-abidingness, was no longer a primary concern in the moral life of an individual man. Virtue was instead a matter of appropriately ordering the sentiments and instincts, or privately pursuing passions and interests that happen to benefit society at large, even if indirectly. Positive virtue, in short, was no longer a conscious concern in law or politics. The control of our darker passions and the ordered pursuit of private material interests were now the substance of a politics without positive moral connotations.

One might argue that these views represent the natural law view of politics in extremis. But that extreme position had its philosophical foundation in a view of human conduct the Scots took to be opposed to the natural law view and uniquely their own. It is this unique view on which I will focus much of my account of the moral and political ideas that were among the sources of Adam Smith's economic doctrines.

II Francis Hutcheson

I know not for what Reason some will not allow that to be Virtue which flows from Instincts, or Passions. . . . —Inquiry, *p. 175*

In our modern plans of laws, where little regard is had to the education and discipline of the subjects, their natural liberty is little confined in any sense; and a people is denominated free, when their important interests are well secured against any rapacious or capricious wills of those in power. The Greeks and Romans seem to have had another precise meaning to populus liber, *denoting by that term only* Democracies, *or such forms where the supreme power, or the chief parts of it at least, were in some popular assembly, so that the people in a body had the command, or had their turns in commanding and obeying.*
—A System of Moral Philosophy, II, *p. 282*

i   Because this essay explores in chronological order the two most important Scottish sources of Adam Smith's thought, the discussion begins with Francis Hutcheson (1694–1746). The more technical writings of seventeenth-century English market theorists or eighteenth-century French Physiocrats would be central if our attention were elsewhere.[1] This study, however, makes no pretense of a full survey of the many influences and contexts relevant to understanding Adam Smith. My concern is with the largely unexplored groundwork of the doctrine of free trade in the history of early-modern moral philosophy in Scotland. As Professor of Moral Philosophy at the University of Glasgow, Hutcheson first instructed Smith in the philosophical meanings of morality, politics, and economics. Smith's view that morality is a matter of the proper orchestration of our passions— a phenomenon he described as "propriety"—derived from Hutcheson's use of the notion of a "moral sense" to show that moral judgments were not primarily matters of reason or of self-love. The central elements of Smith's account of politics—his explanation of rights, his theory of property, and his notion of justice—also had their immediate source in Hutcheson's Glasgow lectures on natural law theories of government and jurisprudence. Later, when Smith himself was hired by Glasgow in 1751, his responsibilities included the very same courses in natural law theory Hutcheson had taught him in 1737-40.[2] In short, like Hutcheson, Smith at the outset of his career conceived himself as a moral philosopher, a practitioner of that "commanding art" that brought views on ethics, politics, and economics into one final and harmonious system.

A careful exploration of Hutcheson's moral philosophy taken in its entirety is a difficult task and cannot be fully met here.[3] He was not simply the founder of a school of Scottish philosophers of feeling or sentiment. Nor should he be characterized as a consistent or explicit supporter of the principles of free trade and laissez-faire. Hutcheson was a thinker with a variety of ideological messages. Those I will explore in this chapter are three that David Hume and Adam Smith repeated after him: morality was a matter of sentiment and instinct, politics a question of reason and law, and the economic market place the realm in which we inevitably pursue the vast portion of our practical affairs. The initial project in this chapter will be to understand how these views came together in a unified body of thought, as Hutcheson clearly intended them to do.[4]

At first glance, they seem to form a moral philosophy with ambiguous implications. Regardless of his intelligence or his economic and political station, a person makes ethical judgments because his natural sentiments prompt him to do so. Each man born into the world might be regarded in this respect as equal to any other. But reason and experience tell us life is more complex: men have not created their polities to enforce moral equality, but to secure their separate and often disparate interests. A polity is a law-governed society, and as such is not primarily concerned to promote virtue and excellence. It aims to secure a variety of human "rights" against the rapacity or caprice of those with power. There is, moreover, no exalted moral status to be found in ruling over or with one's fellows. Man's interests in the realm of politics, according to Hutcheson, derive from his material situation, from his activity as a laborer and from his intuitive sense that he should be given a free title to the fruits of his labor. In his public affairs, then, man is less a creature of sentiments, more a "doing, demanding, possessing" creature. He pursues self-interest, rather than virtue, and "nine-tenths, at least, of the things which are useful to mankind are owing to their labour and industry." A just and rational polity, then, must have laws that encourage and protect commercial activity among its subjects, as well as protect their rights.[5]

Hutcheson's specific reflections on "commerce" have interested historians of economic thought who see his work here as perhaps the chief immediate inspiration for Adam Smith's involvement in economic discourse. W. R. Scott showed, for example, that Hutcheson's discussions of the importance of the division of labor to society and of a number of other technical subjects in book II of his *System of Moral Philosophy* had been used in his university lectures as early as 1737, the year that Smith enrolled at Glasgow as a student. Scott also established that the order of treatment of economic matters both in Smith's own later Glasgow lectures on law and government and in Book I of the *Wealth of Nations* corresponded to that of Hutcheson's *System*.[6] Other scholars have drawn deeper parallels. John Rae, Smith's biographer, suggested that the "strong love of all reasonable liberty which characterized [Smith] must have been, if not first kindled, at any rate quickened by contact with Hutcheson." More recently, W. L. Taylor has seen Hutcheson's discussion of "natural liberty" in book I of the *System* as coming "very near to being an outline of Smith's central thesis of laissez-faire" in the *Wealth of Nations*.[7]

Historians of economic thought have not failed to emphasize that Hutcheson's technical economic discussions were very fragmented. (His longest sustained discussion—on the "Values of Goods and Commerce, and the Nature of Coin" in book II—was only slightly more than eleven pages.) Scott cautioned that the parallels between Hutcheson and Smith in this area "may be nothing more than a coincidence."[8] It is also generally accepted now that Hutcheson's account of the scope of economic liberty was far more limited than Smith's. In fact, his explicit prescriptions for economic policy included "agrarian laws" to prevent immoderate economic acquisition. He also defended the "common rights" of a community to have access to "such things as are inexhaustible and answer the purpose of all."[9] Even with these qualifications kept in mind, however, it would be misleading to suppose that an internal history of the development of economic discourse can help us in grasping what is arguably a more important issue in understanding how Hutcheson's thinking served as a source of Smith's economic doctrines. That issue is what Hutcheson himself conceived as the overall objective of his 'moral philosophy.'

It perhaps is not surprising that economic historians concerned with tracing Hutcheson's influence on Smith have paid so little attention to this matter. Hutcheson spoke explicitly of everyman's "right" to engage in commerce. But ultimately he was not deeply concerned—as Smith would be in the *Wealth of Nations*—with exploring the special changes and challenges wrought by the historical phenomenon of an ever-expanding commercial market.[10] A further problem has been created by the fact that Hutcheson's work cannot be understood fully unless we trace the historical origins and significance of certain traditions of thought that guided his thinking on such key topics as virtue, justice, rights, and commerce. David Hume seized on the linking of "virtue" with passions and sentiments as the crucial innovation of the moral sense argument. Yet Hutcheson himself thought the innovation far less significant than his related discovery that this argument provided additional support for his defense of certain already well-established views regarding the purpose of human life. These he combed from the writings of classical and Renaissance humanists and of certain figures who identified themselves with the tradition of "modern" natural law and natural rights thinking begun by Hugo Grotius.

In fact, most of the arguments developed by Hutcheson, including his technical economic discussions, had been explored by earlier Western natural law thinkers. A close reading of Hutcheson's texts on moral philosophy suggests that one of his chief purposes was to trace the general outlines of modern natural law and natural rights theorizing as it had developed over the course of the previous century. Even if we focus primarily on the natural law context, however, we will need to ask at least two additional questions to determine the purpose of Hutcheson's moral philosophy. First of all, how did Hutcheson portray the development of the Grotian natural law tradition? Second, what did he see as his own distinctive contributions to that tradition? Here, too, are questions that need to be given much greater prominence in any full account of the relationship between Hutcheson and Adam Smith.

My analysis of Hutcheson's answers proceeds along two related paths that Hume and Smith travelled down as well. The first explores the main arguments and the ideological implications of the moral sense theory. Hume was correct in his account of the historical innovation in this argument. Hutcheson's view that virtue flowed directly from instincts and sentiments reversed the traditional humanist assumption that denial, restraint, or enlightenment of our passions was the first step to virtue. Here too, as we shall see, was the philosophical groundwork for a novel, although ultimately unpersuasive, attempt to link virtue and commerce.

My second concern will be to explore what Hutcheson himself saw as one of the most important innovations of his moral philosophy: joining an ethics based on a moral sense with a politics based on his liberal interpretation of Grotian natural law and natural rights theory. In Hutcheson's view, his work here was novel for at least two reasons. First, the philosophical assumptions of the moral sense argument provided a new support for one of the key arguments in most previous natural law writing: man by nature is a sociable creature. The presence of a moral sense demonstrated conclusively that, because of certain "natural feelings in our hearts," all men are obliged to serve one another.[11] Second, like other natural law theorists before him, Hutcheson also thought it necessary to distinguish between moral and political duties, between the public and private senses of what we mean when we talk of what is "right." In his view, the moral sense argument served to sharpen and clarify that distinction. It also was primarily out of this often very elaborate distinction that Hutcheson developed his positive views of commerce.

Seen from another angle, however, there was ultimately a fundamental problem in all of Hutcheson's work here. For the argument for a moral sense was based on his clear refusal to underwrite an account of human nature with a central premise of natural law thinking—namely, the primacy of reason in human conduct. There were, in other words, two opposite assumptions about human nature informing Hutcheson's ethics and his Grotian natural law politics. It seems that Hutcheson himself was sometimes aware of this contradiction, but he never resolved it. Both Hume and Smith saw this same contradiction very clearly and then attempted to resolve it by carrying the novel assumptions of Hutcheson's naturalistic ethics into the realm of political theory as well. In doing so, they retained Hutcheson's Grotian views of law and government, but then explained those views in terms of instincts and sentiments rather than "right reason." In chapters III and IV, we will explore the relevance of this project for understanding the philosophical foundations of their economic doctrines.

ii   Francis Hutcheson was born in 1694 into a Scots-Irish family in Armagh, Ireland.[12] His paternal grandfather, a Presbyterian minister, had migrated from Ayr in lowland Scotland early in the seventeenth century. His father, also a Presbyterian minister, brought up his children to respect the severe traditional Calvinist tenets of Presbyterianism. Although they were loyal supporters of the Glorious Revolution, the Hutcheson family's Presbyterianism by law excluded Francis from attending Trinity College or Cambridge and Oxford. So after attending a dissenting academy in Killyleagh, he enrolled at Glasgow University in the fall of 1711. He studied for six years at Glasgow before returning to Ireland, and during this time his traditional Calvinist views underwent fundamental change. The immediate sources of that change were two of his teachers: John Simson (1668?–1740) and Gershom Carmichael (1672–1729), both of whom promoted tempered views of Christianity that would have shocked Hutcheson's forbears. Simson was Professor of Divinity, and his open-minded moderation on theological issues brought him into frequent conflict with the orthodox Presbyterian community in Glasgow. In 1715, in the middle of Hutcheson's years as a student, he was brought to trial before the local Kirk Assembly and forced to admit his mistakes. Charges of heresy were brought against Simson again in 1726, and three years later he would be suspended from his teaching duties at the University. Carmichael held the Chair of Moral Philosophy, and while he too preached of a benevolent God that orthodox Calvinists refused to recognize, his more important role in our story was to introduce young Francis Hutcheson to Grotian natural law and natural rights philosophy. The most vital period of this tradition had passed when Hutcheson encountered it as a Glasgow student. But that tradition nonetheless deeply shaped his views, and we will return to a careful exploration of the place of natural law and natural rights thinking in Hutcheson's work at the conclusion of this chapter.

Despite his heretical Glasgow teachers, Hutcheson was licensed to preach and was invited in 1720 to become pastor of a Scots-Irish Presbyterian congregation in Magherally. But he chose instead to accept an invitation of friends in Dublin to set up a dissenting academy of his own. Hutcheson lived in Dublin for the next decade, until he moved back to Glasgow to succeed Carmichael as Professor of Moral Philosophy in 1730. During his years in Dublin he published his first two works, *An Inquiry into the Original of our Ideas of Beauty and Virtue* (1725) and *An Essay on the Nature and Conduct of the Passions and Affections* (1728). And it was the success of those books that made Hutcheson's very considerable intellectual reputation in the eighteenth century. A great variety of Enlightenment thinkers found his argument for an inherent moral sense intriguing and attractive.[13] Five editions of the *Inquiry* were published during that century;

the book was translated into French in 1749, into German in 1762. Three editions of the *Essay* were printed during Hutcheson's lifetime; two more were published after his death.

The gist of the moral sense argument in Hutcheson was that moral judgments are products of a human faculty distinct from reason and analogous to the ordinary five senses. Men by nature are creatures moved by certain feelings that in turn prompt judgments of approval or disapproval. We never consciously decide to approve or disapprove; we are instinctively determined to do so.

In presenting this argument in his earliest books, Hutcheson set out, in the first place, to provide a more systematic generalization of an idea first suggested by Anthony Cooper, the Third Earl of Shaftesbury (1671–1713), in his *Characteristics of Men, Manners, Opinions, Times* (1711). There Shaftesbury had attempted to show that morality could not be reduced to a question of precepts that either reason or enlightened self-interest provides to guide our passions. His explicit and novel affirmation of the role of human passions in moral life was launched as an attack on a variety of seventeenth-century English moralists who had argued that moral distinctions were derived from reason, in the same way we derive mathematical distinctions. Shaftesbury responded to these rational moralists with the assertion that moral distinctions were made by a moral sense rather than by reason. We have an "inward eye," he wrote, that discerns "the fair and the shapely, the amiable and the admirable, apart from the deformed, the foul, the odious, and the despicable." A moral judgment, therefore, was not a matter of philosophical enlightenment, but the product of an intuitive response to a particular property in an observed action. It was essentially similar to our aesthetic judgment. Both express responses of feeling to properties in objects or persons, not rational inferences from something we know to be objectively "true."[14]

It followed from these views that virtue was not a matter of wisdom or enlightened self-love, but instead a function of our natural sociability. This point was the groundwork for the second main object of attack in the *Characteristics*, the moral and political views of John Locke.[15] Shaftesbury had once been Locke's pupil, but his criticism of his former teacher was pointed and harsh, and it found major flaws in both the *Two Treatises on Government* (1689) and *An Essay Concerning Human Understanding* (1690). In Shaftesbury's view, the *Two Treatises* had been based on the erroneous assumption that every person in a society was naturally independent and thus each was entitled to rely on his own private power to preserve himself when he deemed it necessary. Shaftesbury criticized Locke for neglecting the fact that familial affection, parental love, and sexual instinct were as fully "natural" as the desire for individual self-preservation. He thought, too, these feelings and instincts more easily explained our social condition than the abstract contractual bargaining posited by Locke in the *Second Treatise*.

In short, the moral sense led to the view that man was inherently sociable, not separate and self-dependent. For Shaftesbury the greatest merit of this view, however, was that it served as an appropriate replacement for the traditional rationalistic framework of Western moral theory that had been pulled down, without an adequate replacement, by Locke's critique of innate ideas in the *Essay*. If society and morality were guaranteed by the workings of an "inward eye" that instinctively discerned the need to harmonize one's passions with those of our fellows, there was nothing to fear in the view that reason does not serve as the first motive to human association. Moved primarily by a various array of sentiments and passions, man could be seen as a creature for whom self-interest and social good are interchangeable notions.

Shaftesbury's views were praised often and quoted at length in the *Inquiry* and the *Essay*. But Hutcheson was not simply a thinker who carefully repeated Shaftesbury's views. One of the main concerns in his first two books, in fact, was to defend those views in the face of a clever and incisive attack, and here Hutcheson covered his ground with sometimes ingenious skill. That attack had come from Bernard Mandeville, whose *Fable of the Bees* (second ed., 1723) had stripped, in Leslie Stephen's words, "the fine coating of varnish which Shaftesbury had bestowed upon human nature." Mandeville was a far more troubling figure than

Hobbes, the other great English critic of theories defending man's inherent goodness and sociability, primarily because unlike Hobbes he acknowledged that individual men enjoyed the company of their fellows. But not of course for the reasons Shaftesbury and his admirers had supposed: man's sociability was rooted in self-love, not natural benevolence. According to Mandeville, men live in society because of their vanity, because they seek the flattery and admiration of others, and because they believe others are possibly aids to satisfying their material desires. Indeed, the main source of social progress and interdependence was not benevolence but pride, what Mandeville liked to call "self-liking." By nature men are indolent, and they overcome their instinctive indolence only because they are also self-seeking. To preach virtue and benevolence in the face of these obvious facts, Mandeville argued, would be ruinous to society. Some individuals do come to find "virtue" as a result of extraordinary self-restraint or self-denial. But we must also see that virtue here is attained at the cost of other benefits, such as sociability or the common pursuit of wealth. Mandeville thought that the vast majority of men would not pay such a cost. Hence, we have no alternative but to accept that our "public benefits" are rooted in our "private vices." And a philosopher's concern to locate virtue in man's private passions is dangerous nonsense.[16]

Hutcheson's defense of Shaftesbury attempted to shore up the moral sense argument at Mandeville's two main points of attack: first the issue of "self-liking," or what Hutcheson preferred to designate "self-love"; and second the broader question of the connection between "virtue" and human passions and sentiments. Hutcheson observed that the moral sense argument did allow for the possibility of vicious forms of self-love: "Sometimes violent passions, while they last, will make us approve bad actions in a *moral sense*, or very pernicious ones to the agent, as advantageous." Neither case, however, proved Mandeville's point; each was instead an instance of "some more violent motive to action, than a sense of moral good," or of a passion that blinded a person to his own best interest. Strictly speaking, actions motivated by self-love could be called morally vicious only when they resulted in the injury of another. This left a reasonable man free to see that some actions flowing from self-love might have neither good nor ill effects. The pursuit of basic material needs, for example, was "perfectly indifferent" morally speaking, because "the preservation of the system requires, that every one should be *innocently solicitous* about himself." Self-love could also be seen in more positive forms in our spontaneous emotions such as friendship, parental love, gratitude, and honor.[17]

Mandeville, then, had a greatly oversimplified notion of the nature of self-love. According to Hutcheson, the main reason for this could be found in his equally over-simplified conception of the nature of virtue. Mandeville's understanding of virtue rested on the familiar, but entirely misleading, assumption that proper moral conduct resulted only when a person had extirpated all passions from his conduct. Virtue was founded on the ability to restrain passions. For Hutcheson, there were two mistakes in this view. The first was neglect of the fact that "virtue" could also be used as a term that described actions contributing directly to a larger social good. The second and more important error was a refusal to see that such actions in fact spring instinctively from our passions. For Mandeville, all human passions by definition were self-referential; hence all instinctive acts were, either in disguise or openly, matters of "self-liking." But this perspective, Hutcheson observed, leaves a central question entirely overlooked. If we follow Mandeville in assuming that by nature man can only be selfish, that we have no natural concern for the good of others, how could the concern for virtue ever have come to loom so significant in our affairs?

Hutcheson's strongest defense of the moral sense sprang from his attempt to answer this last question. And he began here by enlisting aid from a source that Shaftesbury had overlooked: the epistemology of Locke's *Essay on Human Understanding*. Hutcheson followed Locke in the view that knowledge of the external world must have its origins in the working of our five senses, and he saw the moral sense argument as a logical extension of that view. What was true of the natural world must also be true of the human world. Each of our external senses was a "determination of the mind to receive ideas from the presence of an object which occurs to us, independent of our will." A moral sense, in turn, was a "determination of our minds to receive amiable or disagreeable ideas of action when they occur to our observation." Locke had shown that our knowledge of the external world derived from the involuntary workings of our senses; Hutcheson demonstrated that judgments regarding good and evil must also derive from the working of a "sense" that instinctively comes into play when we observe the conduct of others.[18]

There were several similarities between man's five cognitive senses and the moral sense. The engagement of the moral sense results in pleasure or pain, as did the operation of an external sense. All our senses affect our conduct, whether we wish this to be so or not. For Hutcheson, the most important point in his analogy between the moral sense and man's external senses was that both must be seen as universal principles. However well or poorly the five senses happen to work, they surely were characteristic of man as such. Hutcheson recognized that one of the principal arguments against the universality of a "moral sense" was the great variety in moral perceptions in society at large. But he insisted that such variety was not telling evidence against his argument. The range of difference in what men happen to designate as "virtue" and "vice" provided no more reason to doubt the moral sense than variations in perceptions of the external senses give us cause to believe that those senses are not everywhere the same.

The moral sense, then, was not a guarantee of human goodness; it more specifically suggested that "men are naturally dispos'd to virtue." It also suggested that our moral judgments need not be explained in the abstract terms of reason or inference. Pure reasoning, Hutcheson argued—and here he made a point that would be etched indelibly in the thinking of Hume and Smith—was far too slow and self-scrutinizing to serve as the spring of our most important decisions. "The Author of Nature . . . has made virtue a lovely form to excite our pursuit of it." This was not to say that reason and the moral sense had nothing in common. When mistaken, our "immediate powers of perception internal or external" can be corrected by reason; there can be both a "right and wrong state of our moral sense, as there is in our other senses." But the role of reason here was circumscribed: it cannot insist that the moral sense or our external senses abide by its *a priori* rules of method. Reason was rather an *ex post facto* judge, the corrector not the master of our senses.[19]

Finally, Hutcheson argued that man's senses apprehend events in the natural and human worlds by means of perceptions that in some fashion come to be registered consciously in the mind. He acknowledged there was in reality no "moral" organ similar to those that register our responses to the natural world. He also saw that an adequate explanation of moral judgments entailed what Locke had called "concomitant ideas"—notions such as motivation, agency, obligation, and consequence—for these were the terms that serve to describe human conduct in objective detail. Hutcheson's main point here, however, was consistent with his earlier contentions. Once our observation of an action by another person prompts us to respond with feelings of approval or disapproval, we must say that these responses depend upon "certain sensible feelings or ideas" which can be explained only in terms of the workings of an instinctive moral sense.[20]

iii Two recurring assumptions in Hutcheson's argument are crucial for understanding the complex ideological implications of positing an inherent moral sense. The first was that human nature was primarily a matter of instincts, sentiments, and passions, many of which had positive roles to play in a person's moral life. The second was that all moral judgments must be accounted for in terms of the positive workings of passions and spontaneous affects, rather than as the results of their control and manipulation, as Mandeville and a great variety of perhaps less cynical moral theorists before him had thought.

A number of commentators, both past and present, have taken these views to represent the starting point of a new era in the history of moral philosophy. David Hume very likely was the first. In 1740, he observed privately in a letter to Hutcheson that both of them agreed that morality "is determin'd merely by sentiment, it regards only human nature & human life," and then added the comment that the consequences of such a view were "very momentous."[21] Hutcheson, too, at times underlined the novelty of his argument. There was a moment of extraordinary optimism toward the end of the *Inquiry* when he proclaimed that the discovery of a moral sense had given "virtue" the equivalent of Newtonian certainty. The moral sense, he wrote, showed that we have "practical dispositions to virtue" implanted in human nature itself, "a universal determination to benevolence in mankind." That universal benevolence, Hutcheson continued, "we may compare to the principle of Gravitation, which extends to all bodies in the universe." To uphold this view, he then offered an elaborate series of algebraic formulas that he thought might serve as a "universal canon to compute the morality of any actions."[22]

These formulas were cleverly parodied by Laurence Sterne: Hutcheson "plus's and minus's you to heaven or hell," he wrote, "by algebraic equations—so that none but an expert mathematician can ever be able to settle his accounts with S. Peter."[23] Later, more admiring commentators have seen his work here as part of his larger and more significant concern to explore the intricacies of what today we term the psychology of moral judgment.[24] Stressing the novelties of Hutcheson's thinking, however, in certain respects can be misleadingly one-sided. His defense of "virtue" in the face of Mandeville's attack certainly rested on a novel and nuanced view of the role of passions and instincts in moral conduct. But for Hutcheson, an adequate reply to Mandeville at the same time entailed an emphatic reassertion of a Renaissance humanist view of the moral philosopher as both advocate of an all-encompassing excellence and trainer of character.

Beginning with Petrarch in the fourteenth century, Renaissance humanists sought to revive the classical ideal of *virtus* in attacking a dark Augustinian strain of Christianity that had prevailed in much of Medieval thought and had been reasserted explosively by Martin Luther and subsequent Reformation theologians such as Calvin and Knox. Augustine and his later followers took the classical ideal of virtue, the pursuit of an all-encompassing human excellence, to be based on a mistaken view of what men could do for themselves. The possibility of the autonomous pursuit of human excellence had been foreclosed by original sin and man's innate corruption. When men did succeed in acting virtuously, it could only be as the result of divine intervention. Renaissance humanists refused to embrace this view; they claimed that man was in fact capable of obtaining such excellence, and they elaborated an ideology in which the main aim of a person's life should be the pursuit of virtue.[25]

When Renaissance humanists and their followers in the seventeenth and eighteenth centuries spoke of virtue they began by focussing on two broad points. First, a man of true virtue should display all the leading Christian virtues, and, second, he should also pursue those central cardinal virtues argued by classical moralists. Most humanists were determined to present their discussions of virtue in the framework of Christian belief (Hutcheson himself once remarked, "One has better reason to deny the inclination between the sexes to be natural, than a disposition in mankind to religion.").[26] Nonetheless, the novelty of humanism in early-modern and still Christian Europe in the last analysis was primarily a matter of restoring classical ideals. There were at least four of recurring significance, all of which would be advocated by Hutcheson after he became Professor of Moral Philosophy at Glasgow in 1730. First was prudence, a virtue he described as a "cautious habit of consideration and forethought, discovering what may be advantageous or hurtful in life." Second was temperance, for Hutcheson "that virtue which restrains and regulates the lower appetites toward sensual pleasures." The branches of temperance were modesty, abstinence, honesty, frugality, and moderation. Fortitude was the third cardinal virtue; it was the least complex of the group, but important nonetheless. Fortitude was to be seen in the conduct of heroes, those "public-spirited" men about whom Smith later wrote with uncharacteristic fervor in the *Theory of Moral Sentiments*. Finally, there was justice. For the ancients and their modern admirers, this was, as Hutcheson observed, "the sovereign virtue to which all the rest should be subservient." Justice could be discussed in its divine, natural, and civil manifestations. But in general it was considered the greatest good of all, the overarching virtue beneath which the others rested.[27]

A second element of continuity between Hutcheson and his

humanist predecessors lay in their common stress on the practical utility of moral philosophy. After his move to Glasgow, Hutcheson came to speak of his work as a contribution to the "art of regulating the whole of life," "one of these commanding arts which directs how far the other arts are to be pursued."²⁸ This emphasis on moral philosophy as our main source of practical wisdom and guidance had also been one of the characteristic themes of the Renaissance humanists. A recurring point in their denunciations of the scholastic tradition, for example, was the insistence that moral philosophers and educators show themselves to be of some practical usefulness. This project specifically entailed a recognition that thinkers and teachers ought to guide men to virtue, not simply describe or speculate upon its content. Hutcheson too stressed that one of the principal concerns of the moral philosopher must be to provide the "rules and maxims" that guide us to "universal good," hence his algebraic formulas for calculating virtue. But this concern for practical influence also required philosophy to be combined with eloquent rhetoric. Contemporaries thought that Hutcheson was more moving as a teacher than as a writer. But the purpose of his writings was essentially the same as that of his classes: stirring his students to pursue a life centered in virtue.

Even in his most optimistic moods, however, it seems clear that Hutcheson in the end could not have seen the virtue assured by a moral sense to be quite the same thing as that single standard of all-embracing excellence championed by Renaissance humanists. When he defined virtue in the *Short Introduction*, for example, as a term denoting "any power or quality which is subservient to the happiness of any sensitive being," he clearly conceived it not as a question of knowledge or wisdom, but rather as a matter of our internal dispositions, a "habit or disposition which perfects the power of the soul."²⁹ In the pursuit of virtue, an individual aimed at the perfection of his will and affections. Perfection here signified the achievement of an internal equilibrium, the preservation of a "mediocrity" between extremes of excess or defect in our passions; it was not the old humanist ideal of all-embracing excellence, but a new naturalistic assumption that virtue results primarily from an inherent ability to order one's passions and the good disposition toward others that must follow from this.[30]

The reasons for Hutcheson's change in perspective can be traced to a variety of developments in post-Renaissance thought. Many thinkers had continued to uphold the ideal of virtue in the seventeenth and eighteenth centuries in spite of the powerful challenges thrown up against Renaissance humanism by Hobbes's theory about the universal primacy of self-interest and by the ironic disbelief of those French moralists from whom Mandeville had derived so many of his views. But of course the ideal had not been upheld without significant alterations.[31] In searching for what Hutcheson was trying to convey with the term "virtue," we must note two alterations of particular significance. The first was a direct by-product of his moral sense argument: a break, although not always a conscious one in Hutcheson's case, with the classical psychological assumptions that had governed Western humanist thought since the Renaissance. The second was his adherence to the rights-based view of justice developed by Grotius within the natural law tradition. Each of these developments was doubly significant, because each also allowed Hutcheson to forge a vocabulary in which the traditional normative goals of early-modern humanist moral philosophy came to embrace commerce and money-making as worthy human endeavors. Those activities, as we shall see, were not everywhere condemned in traditional humanist writings. But at the same time they had not been, before the seventeenth and eighteenth centuries, central to any conception of life dedicated to the ideal of virtue. At most, a comparatively small number of Renaissance humanists had found it possible to view commerce and virtue in terms other than that of confrontation.[32] Hutcheson, however, sought to demonstrate that commercial activity had foundations both in virtue and in reason.

The first point to recall in explaining this complex pattern of intellectual change is that the recovery of confidence marked by the Renaissance had not been founded on an acceptance of human nature per se. Both classical and Renaissance humanists set out ideal patterns of how men *ought* to behave. In this context, the achievement of virtue required discipline of the passions. Followers of Plato, Aristotle, and Cicero of course disagreed among themselves about the meaning of reason, hence the often great differences in their accounts of what such discipline entailed. But about the role of passions in the good life there was general consensus: virtuous men are wise men; therefore, moral activity always ought to be determined by rational judgment. Prudence, temperance, and fortitude describe the paths that lead us to rational self-control and self-improvement. Classical and Renaissance humanists, in short, were confident that man had the ability to develop his mind to master himself, and this ability was the essence of man's dignity. But such views also were founded on an antithesis between reason and the passions—in effect, an original distrust of man taken as he is, a creature in the full sense, a nature guided by passions and instincts as well as by reason. In this context, virtue was seen as what we aspire to, not one of our inherent features. Spontaneous affections, desires, and feelings are necessary to human activity, but when left alone such passions inevitably lead to false judgments that imperil the virtue of a rationally ordered person.[33]

"I see no harm in supposing that men are *naturally* disposed to *virtue*," Hutcheson wrote in the *Inquiry*.[34] There was perhaps no "harm" in such a supposition, but it did in fact suggest a need for a major revision in the guiding assumptions in humanistic theory that informed Hutcheson's thinking in other areas. The first was a substantial tempering of the didactic ambitions of the moral philosopher. In moral sense theory, where reason was guide rather than master of passions, virtue logically could not be spoken of as an ideal to which moral philosophers urged men to aspire. If by nature "many are really virtuous who cannot explain what virtue is," a good life is not primarily a function of enlightenment. Indeed, it can be achieved without pursuit of self-cultivation or public service. Moreover, if virtue was not, as Hutcheson himself remarked at the outset of the *Short Introduction*, "directly taught, or produced by instruction," a moral philosopher could no longer argue that his knowledge will be directly instrumental to the achievement of a good life.[35]

Both of these were views David Hume would explore in much greater detail in the new "science of man" he tried to construct in his *Treatise of Human Nature*. As we shall see in the next chapter, Hutcheson's description of man as a creature of sentiments and his affirmation of man's inherent desire to attain virtue led to a significantly altered definition of moral philosophy in Hume's treatment. Moral sense theory had redefined the issue of virtue in terms of observing moral judgment as an internal process, abandoning the view that virtue was the goal of a series of rational decisions meant to shape man according to a predetermined ideal vision of what he ought to be. Or, as Hume later remarked, morality now was a matter "more properly felt than judg'd of."[36] It followed from this view that moral philosophy must be more a matter of accounting for feelings than of directing judgment.

But Hutcheson never came to surrender a view of himself as practitioner of the "commanding art." He remained determined to preach virtue even in the face of an argument that brought such a view of a moral philosophy into question. For him, the practical implications of his new view of human passions were more limited in scope. In his earliest books, perhaps the main intention of his argument, as we have seen, was to answer Mandeville. In later works, he also used his new account of passions to provide an explicitly moral affirmation of the increasingly commercial preoccupations of his age.

Those humanists before Hutcheson who had praised the initiatives of commercial men did so largely on utilitarian grounds. The enlightened self-interest of the merchant had been seen to serve the public good by supplying a country's material needs rather than adding to its virtue. Hutcheson's view of human passions, however, allowed him to find certain kinds of commercial activity virtuous as well as useful. There was, to be sure, desire for money that was no more than simple greed or avarice. But in modern law-governed societies, money-making usually will be guided by considerations such as a "good bargain" or "gainful employment." Here commerce demanded a passion for profit that was "calm" rather than "intense." In this distinction Hutcheson found the psychological ground of "frugality" and "liberality," those two specific aspects of commercial life he thought worthy of the humanist epithet "virtuous." Both were virtues crucial to the practical management of our "estates and worldly goods." Frugality was the particular wisdom of the profit-seeker, his way of rationally guiding his passion for wealth. Liberality was his code of honor; he was generous to others, because profit without social status was profit without inner satisfaction. Money-making was a passion that usually sought to gain the approval of others.[37]

This subtle attempt to link "virtue" and "commerce" was not, however, at the center of Hutcheson's argument for commerce and economic improvement. Considered in the context of Hutcheson's own views, it was also unpersuasive for at least two reasons, one of which Hutcheson himself recognized. First, we can grasp without much difficulty Hutcheson's distinction between passions for money-making that are "calm" and those that are "intense." But we cannot see why the calm passions should win when confronted by our violent passions.[38] Hutcheson's own definition of avarice suggested that the two types of economic passions were so closely interconnected that it may be impossible to distinguish between them. As for the "honor" of commercial men, this also might be explained very differently as a passion that is the opposite of virtuous "liberality." Acts of kindness can be seen as charity from one perspective; from another, they can be taken as disguised self-love. A wealthy man's exercise in "liberality" allowed him to disguise his greedy life as selfless. So public acclaim for his hypocritical philanthropy was only a further affirmation of his own high opinion of himself.

These last points were views notoriously associated with Hutcheson's original bête noire, Bernard Mandeville. Mandeville had argued that the moral problem of a commercial society was not selfishness so much as an amoral sociability. The conflict at the heart of commerce was between our concern for the welfare of others and our concern for their good opinion; and the passion that guided the pursuit of profit, Mandeville argued, was vanity rather than avarice. Hutcheson simply found no persuasive way to answer Mandeville's emphasis on the darker aspects of the sociability of commercial men.[39] His failure may also explain in part why Hume and Smith, who otherwise followed him on so many other issues, never found direct links between commerce and virtue. As we shall see, they took commerce largely as amoral activity, the benefits of which were to be measured in political and economic terms.

The problem Hutcheson did see in his effort to link virtue and commerce was internal to his new conception of virtue. The initial thrust of his moral sense theory had been to provide a philosophical buttress for Shaftesbury's ethics powerful enough to disprove Mandeville's notion that all human conduct was narrowly self-interested. Yet, given the view that moral judgments must spring from "gratuitous and disinterested" passions, Hutcheson came to recognize that he could not make a moral argument for commerce on the basis of his conception of morality. Virtue did not derive from conscious calculations and therefore could not be "approved under the notion of its being profitable to the agent." Nor could virtue be understood as something "profitable to those who approve it."[40]

iv The moral implications of an individual life devoted to trade and money-making were never fully resolved in Hutcheson's mind. The political implications, however, posed less of a philosophical problem, and to explain why this was so, we need to turn now to the philosophical distinction between ethics and politics that I have suggested is central to understanding Hutcheson's moral philosophy. One point, however, needs to be emphasized immediately as we shift our ground here. When Hutcheson grouped commerce with law and government as issues best determined by the "rules and dictates of right reason," the question of the particular virtue of commercial life lost much of its significance. That was because, first of all, reason and virtue, as we have seen, were not one and the same for Hutcheson. And then, although he had found it difficult to assign personal virtue (as he understood it) to money-making, in explaining the difference between "right" in personal morality and "rights" in politics, he in fact had a philosophical means of demonstrating that commerce, whatever its moral import, was among man's preeminently rational concerns.

The rest of this chapter will show how Hutcheson proceeded

with that demonstration and will then place it within the larger context of his last two published texts on moral philosophy. This will be an intricate operation, and our first step must be to comprehend the meaning of natural rights terminology in its relationship to the account of individual morality contained in moral sense theory. As early as the *Inquiry*, Hutcheson made it clear that he saw personal morality and politics as the two main topics treated in his moral philosophy. But at the same time he distinguished sharply between "right" in personal ethics and "rights" in public affairs. Because a person is born into society with an inherent moral faculty, he has instinctive notions of "right" and "wrong." Those are the concepts one employs both to characterize human actions and affections and to judge the result of an action and the intentions of those engaged in actions. Morality is thus a matter of praising actions that benefit society and condemning those that harm it, also of evaluating motives that govern actions with implications for others. But for Hutcheson, politics represented an altogether different activity. Where ethics concerns socially situated passions and feelings, law and government concern the ordering of the affairs of individual "rational agents." Here too Hutcheson made use of a notion of "right," but in this context the term describes an individual man's rational interests, not his spontaneous feelings as a social creature.[41]

In the *Inquiry*, Hutcheson began his first examination of natural rights with a broad definition that he repeated in later works:

> Wherever it appears to us, that a faculty of doing, demanding or possessing any thing, universally allowed in certain circumstances, would in the whole tend to the general good, we say that any person in such circumstances has a right to do, possess, or demand that thing. And according as this tendency to the public good is greater or less, the right is greater or less.[42]

He went on to say that rights of this sort are derived from our moral sense. But he meant this in a special sense that became clearer in his account of the five major types of natural rights: perfect, imperfect, external, alienable, and inalienable.

"Perfect" rights were defined as those whose violation would make life intolerable. Their observance leads to the public good "either directly, or by promoting the innocent advantage of a part." Hutcheson gave three examples of "innocent advantage": our rights to life, to the fruits of our labor, and to faithful performance of contracts. The predominantly economic character of these rights is an issue to which we will return. The point to note here is that while Hutcheson considered perfect rights to be rational precepts, what made them "perfect" was a peculiar kind of sanction he felt they received in our nature. He argued that since by definition violation of perfect rights made life intolerable, we can use violence to secure such rights when threatened. This prospect, in turn, must put fear in the heart of any person who would contemplate violating the perfect rights of others. Now although Hutcheson does not show exactly how perfect rights derive from the moral sense, "reason" and "sentiment" here at least seem to be at one for Hutcheson. The relationship is perhaps best described as supplementary or ancillary: our rights are not made known by our natural sentiments or feelings so much as they are confirmed by those feelings.[43]

"Imperfect" rights were distinguished from perfect rights, because their violation, while reprehensible, does not make life miserable or intolerable. Any failure to respect imperfect rights, in other words, represents for rational men something akin to disappointment. Their violation, unlike that of perfect rights, would not deprive us of any real "positive good." It follows that violence cannot be allowed in any attempt to secure imperfect rights.[44]

In trying to understand the connections among Hutcheson's views of ethics, politics, and economics, the particular instances of imperfect rights in the *Inquiry* are extremely important. His three examples of imperfect rights were: (i) "those which the poor have to the charity of the wealthy," (ii) those "which all men have to offices of no trouble or expence to the Performer," and (iii) those "which Benefactors have to returns of Gratitude and such like." All three represented personal relationships potentially governed by principles of benevolence. Indeed, imperfect rights, rather than the perfect ones, were those explicitly grounded on the supposition that men were governed by a "moral sense."

The important and curious point here, however, was the manner in which Hutcheson gave benevolence political meaning. Why should our expectations that others act on principles of benevolence be understood in the context of "imperfect" rights? Hutcheson's answer required a distinction between the "good" and the "political" in man which emerged from the following passage:

> the absence of *good* is more easily born than the presence of *misery*, so the power of our *good wishes* toward the *positive good* of others, is weaker than that of compassion toward their *misery*. He then who violates imperfect Rights, shows that his *self-love* overcomes only the desire of *positive Good* to others; but he who violates perfect Rights betrays such a *selfish* Desire of advancing his own *positive Good*, as overcomes all the power of *compassion* toward the *misery* of others.[45]

The argument here is that the highest principle of conduct governing political relationships must be distinguished sharply from that governing individual moral relationships. On the one hand, Hutcheson viewed politics as a realm of restraint, or rationally defined and circumscribed self-interest. On the other, he saw morality as a matter of instinctive compassion, of "good wishes" that cannot be set apart entirely from our political concerns, but nevertheless cannot carry the same intellectual weight in determining the practical affairs of a rational polity.

This view of politics as a realm governed by rules distinct from those of morality also guided Hutcheson's discussions of his three other types of rights. "External" rights were those which represent the legal settlement of apparent conflicts between perfect and imperfect rights. They arose in cases where a person's pursuit of his own advantage might violate the imperfect rights of others and where, at the same time, any attempt to deny an individual his right to pursue that advantage "would do more evil than all the evils to be feared" from that same pursuit. Hutcheson gave three examples of external rights: (i) "that of a wealthy miser to recall his loan from the most industrious poor tradesman"; (ii) "the right of a wealthy heir to refuse payment of any debts which were contracted by him under Age, without fraud to the Lender"; and (iii) "the right of taking advantage of a positive law, contrary to what was equity antecedent to that Law, as when a register'd deed takes place of one not register'd, although prior to it, and known to be so before the second contract." These examples tell us in part that, for Hutcheson, external rights resolved tensions that arise between a rational code of economic relationships and the benevolent impulses inevitably appearing in our social and personal affairs. Taken in their entirety, rights define a rational, hence internally consistent, political order. Yet external rights codified in law may be seen more precisely as the outcome of subordinating our imperfect rights to our perfect rights. Since by definition imperfect rights represent those which, when violated, we have no title to recover, however, the subordination is of course rationally consistent for Hutcheson. The "contriving and settling" of our rights was best exercised in defining rational ways in which we can pursue our "innocent" advantage. It did not involve us in creating a political order one might want to call "good" in the moral sense. For Hutcheson, such a project would involve dangerous "mischief."[46]

After external rights came the "alienable" and the "inalienable." The distinction between these two required an understanding of what rights may be called alienable. Two points were involved. First, a right was said to be alienable if the alienation of that right represented a free and conscious action on our part. Alienation here has its original meaning: an act that transfers the ownership of anything to another. Second, the alienation of a right must serve some valuable purpose. In practical terms, the first point meant that our "right of private judgment," our "inward sentiments," and our "affections" were inalienable. "We cannot command ourselves to think what either we ourselves, or any other person pleases," Hutcheson argued. Our personal morals are determined neither by private concerns nor by external authority. The second point suggested that our lives and limbs were not subject to "alienation." We are free to hazard our lives in any good action, but absolute submission to another person can never serve a positive purpose.[47]

David Brion Davis and Duncan Rice have shown that this last point—i.e., that absolute bondage was incompatible with a rational social order—was seized on by anti-slavery writers during the eighteenth century.[48] But that was not the main concern of Hutcheson's argument. His discussion of "rights," as we have noted, was primarily concerned to define a political order inhabited by rational and compassionate men. And its ultimate overall result was a systematic, hierarchical ordering of the economic and moral concerns men bring to politics. That order, given the views we have considered so far, can best be described as a conceptualization of political life in which moral impulses are subordinated to rational economic self-interest.

Hutcheson was not the first thinker to present such a view of politics. An economic or commercial bias was characteristic of the natural rights tradition from its inception. Richard Tuck has suggested that writers who used the language of "rights" in defining a polity inevitably brought forward a concept of man as an "owner" of his liberty and other moral attributes. And given their deep concern with the nature of possession and property, rights theorists in the history of Western thought undoubtedly represent one of the philosophical starting points of what in modern times would become a distinctively "economic" form of discourse.[49] The point I want to emphasize, however, lies elsewhere—namely, in the ordering of human values that resulted from Hutcheson's joining of the moral sense argument and rights theory. Three points are of special significance, for each one of them would be argued again in somewhat different form by Hume and by Smith.

First, Hutcheson's conception of man's fundamental moral feature—his instinctive and unpremeditated compassion for his fellow creatures—found its way into politics strictly as an "imperfect" right. By nature we expect men in public affairs to observe principles of benevolence and humanity; but given other concerns we pursue, we cannot expect (nor should we want) political authority to compel us to act on such principles alone. The "political" man can be a "good" man, but only because he freely chooses to be so.

Second, the predominantly economic character of Hutcheson's discussion of rights followed from an instrumental view of political life. Government was not a realm of virtue or value in and of itself. It represented the rational accommodation of man's material and economic concerns:

> That we may see the foundation of some of the more important rights of mankind, let us observe, that probably nine tenths, at least, of the things which are useful to mankind, are owing to their labour and industry; and consequently all men are oblig'd to observe such a tenour of action as shall most effectually promote industry, and to abstain from all actions which would have the contrary effect.[50]

Hutcheson here was of course not using "industry" in the modern sense. The significant point to note is that his identification of man as laborer was an additional support, rather than the primary philosophical groundwork, for a view of politics that did not assign public life any primary or positive value in human affairs. For Hutcheson, politics mediated between our self-love and our compassion; it established order for a society of men concerned to secure their own material well-being.

Finally, like Hume and Smith, Hutcheson was careful to emphasize that he was not simply an advocate of the unfettered pursuit of self-love. He considered his project more complex: to explain in its entirety man's mode of conduct in "civil society." He acknowledged that a person's concern for his material well-being was not motivated by "general benevolence." But he also thought that this concern was shaped by other unselfish considerations—by one's family and friends, by one's desire to appear honorable in the eyes of others. As a result of these counterbalancing concerns, self-love must be seen to be "as necessary to the good of the whole as benevolence." There was no need, in other words, to follow Mandeville in looking upon self-love as a private vice that could lead inadvertently to public good. The "self" in Hutcheson's view clearly was a far more complex object of attention.[51]

Civil society for Hutcheson, then, was the product of the inability of individuals to serve their material self-interests by isolated labor. The work of each simply "cannot furnish him with all necessarys, tho' it may furnish him with a needless plenty of one sort." From this it followed that a just and rational society must sanction and encourage at least one right in addition to the five we have already discussed—what Hutcheson explicitly called "the right of commerce." In the *Inquiry*, he explained this sixth right briefly and simply: rational men living in society must be free to sell their goods and labor and should be assured that contracts and promises will be kept. Again the view of politics here was not self-interested in any narrow sense. But it was at the same time founded on the contention that man is a "possessing and demanding" creature who by reason expects that a central concern of his polity will be to accommodate this fundamental feature of his character.[52]

v   The account of natural rights we have just explored appeared in the final section of the first edition of the *Inquiry*. Most of it was later repeated both in the *Short Introduction to Moral Philosophy* (1747) and in the unfinished manuscript of the *System of Moral Philosophy* (1755). Hutcheson dropped the explicit affirmation of "commerce" as a distinct right in these last works, but he also espoused a theory of justice which supported the same view of law and government he first put forward at the end of the *Inquiry*. Again he suggested that a political order in which man is conceived of as a juristic person defined by his "rights" is one in which most men will be concerned to safeguard their commercial activity. Where justice is not maintained, Hutcheson wrote, "the commerce of a nation must sink, with all its attendant profits." The pursuit of justice in his view was partly a matter of maintaining a legal framework within which men engage in commerce and seek what material security and comfort might come with the successful pursuit of their trade.[53]

A careful reading of Hutcheson's texts shows the extent to which his affirmation of commerce was directly linked to particular philosophical conceptions of virtue, rights, and justice. In the last analysis, however, no amount of careful reading alone would enable us to understand all the issues that concerned Hutcheson in the formulation of his moral philosophy after he moved to Glasgow. Much of the problem we face here was described by

Hutcheson himself in a brief preface to the *Short Introduction*. He noted, first of all, that his work drew very heavily, and usually without acknowledgment, from "more eminent writers" in the past. His original intention had been to make references in his text to those writers. But on "considering that this could be of no use except to those who have the cited books at hand," he spared himself that "disagreeable and unnecessary labour." But Hutcheson then noted that the key "modern" influences on his thinking would be easily discerned by "learned" men: his moral doctrine had been shaped by Shaftesbury and Richard Cumberland, and his account of the law of nature and nations derived from "Grotius, Pufendorf, especially with Barbeyrac's copious notes, Harrington, Locke, or Bynkershoek, to mention no more." He then concluded that any reader who wanted a fuller understanding of his thinking in these areas "must have recourse to these authors."[54]

Enough has been said earlier in this chapter about Hutcheson's reformulations of Shaftesbury's ideas. The problem that remains is to explain how recourse to the other writers mentioned in the preface will help us to understand Hutcheson's main intentions in the rest of his moral philosophy. There is no question that, for Hutcheson, the greatest modern thinkers before him, apart from Shaftesbury, had been Grotius, Pufendorf, Cumberland, and Locke, all seventeenth-century exponents of natural law and natural rights. Grotius and Pufendorf, for example, were the first to explore the important distinction between perfect and imperfect rights.[55] It is also clear, however, that Hutcheson involved himself in a complicated project as he sought to provide his readers with an easier access to the views of all these thinkers. Both the *Short Introduction* and the *System of Moral Philosophy* reported his own understanding of issues that in fact had prompted a series of intensive debates involving a number of previous seventeenth and early eighteenth century thinkers who, like Hutcheson, followed in the footsteps of Grotius. To understand Hutcheson's work here, it is essential to begin by reconstructing certain parts of those debates in some detail. Here, too, is our best means of resolving what I already have suggested is the key to understanding how Hutcheson's moral philosophy later influenced Hume and Smith—namely, how he came to identify himself as yet another follower of Grotius.

We must begin by recalling the main points in the ambiguous message of Grotius's *De Iure Belli*. First of all, Grotius announced that, as a law of nature, each man was the free master of his own property and actions. In the state of nature, he argued, men live in a "negative community," a world that belonged to no one and yet was open to all. The exercise of one's natural rights in this setting is a matter of acting to make things one's own. Property expresses an individual's exclusive right to dominate the world, to use it for his private purpose. Justice, in turn, is strictly a matter of preserving a community where each person may enjoy the free use of his property with the approval and protection of the whole society.

Yet this sharp emphasis on legal protection of exclusive rights was only the first of two historically important messages in Grotius. His radically individualistic view of society must also be understood in terms of his passionate desire for peace in the face of the horrors of a century of religious and dynastic warfare.[56] This is what prompted Grotius's commitment to an absolutist theory of sovereignty. If civil society was instituted for the peaceful preservation of rights, he concluded, the only sure means of maintaining social peace was a complete and irrevocable transfer of each member's rights to one sovereign ruler.

During the century that separated the publication of *De Iure Belli* and Hutcheson's earliest thinking about natural law and natural rights, there were two different—although not unrelated—contexts within which subsequent natural law theorists explored Grotius's arguments.[57] The first involved efforts to clarify his political message. Grotius's rights theory, as Richard Tuck has remarked, potentially had both conservative and radical applications. Attempts to resolve this ambiguity formed a crucial part of English-speaking political thought throughout the seventeenth century. The most intense debates were sparked by the continuing conflict between King and Parliament during the middle decades of that turbulent century. At one end of the ideological spectrum, the Grotian argument that individuals must renounce their rights when they set up a sovereign power gave rise to the absolutism of John Selden (1584–1654) and Thomas Hobbes (1588–1679). At the other extreme, Grotius's radically individualistic account of rights—his defining them as relations that existed between a rational man and whatever was appropriate to him in light of his personal merits and his property—also provided various opponents of the established order with a philosophical groundwork for their theories of resistance. The Levellers, for example, argued that the right of self-preservation was inalienable and then insisted that under certain circumstances rational men must take up arms to recover their natural rights. Later, this same argument found its final and perhaps most important expression in John Locke's *Two Treatises of Government*, a work that Tuck has described as "the most faithfully Grotian political theory available from the presses of the late seventeenth century."[58]

Cutting across these political debates among English-speaking Grotians was a second dispute that began during the Civil War period but then lasted well into the eighteenth century. This dispute, which also prompted the writings of a new generation of Continental natural law theorists, involved a series of contrasting efforts to put Grotius's philosophical principles in a more logical order. But why were such efforts necessary in the first place? Grotius had broken with the traditional Aristotelianism of scholastic natural law thinkers in presenting a radically individualistic theory of rights. But at the same time he continued to share their view of man as by nature a sociable creature. In his mixed emphasis on both individuality and communality, Grotius ultimately failed to provide a clear answer to a question that preoccupied his disciples and admirers for over the next one hundred years. Why should rational men ever move from a world where they once possessed a full complement of natural rights to their present state of obedience to civil law?

This question required a rigorous reexamination of the overall relationship between the law of nature and natural rights. The first efforts here were again those of Selden and Hobbes, who argued that a Grotian natural rights theory in fact required a new, strongly individualistic psychology and ethical theory. Indeed, both attempted to understand all moral and political obligation in terms of the egotistical motivation of men who originally lived in a state of total freedom. According to Selden, the obligation to obey natural law was not a matter of innate rationality but of prudent self-interest—or more specifically, of fear that we may suffer at the hands of God in this life or the next if we fail to respect the laws of nature. Hobbes altered this position with his notorious declaration that the after-life was irrelevant to the prudential calculations of men. Thus, while he followed Selden in seeing the state of nature as a state of total freedom, Hobbes linked all natural rights to the principle of self-preservation, arguing that moral and political obligations are ultimately matters of self-interest, not commands of God.[59]

The resistance theorists of the Civil War pursued a rival strategy in explaining the relationship between the law of nature and natural rights. The fundamental philosophical view linking them together was an assertion of the primacy of innate, God-given rationality in human motivation. We must presume, they argued, that our predecessors could never have intended to leave us bereft of all rights. Two somewhat different political messages, however, followed from this argument. On the one hand, supporters of Parliament and constitutional monarchy, who attacked the king's authority, also sought to safeguard their own authority by stressing the rights of the commonwealth as a whole, rather than those of separate individuals. On the other, radical critics of both King and Parliament went further in defending the notion of the inalienable rights of all men.

After the restoration of the monarchy in 1660, neither of the two extreme political applications of Grotian natural rights theories had any strong appeal. But the question of the proper relationship between natural law and natural rights continued to attract widespread and careful study. In the final quarter of the seventeenth century, the most famous attempt to resolve this question was made by Samuel Pufendorf. His two most important books, *De Iure Naturae et Gentium* (1672) and its epitome *De Officio Hominis et Civis* (1673), displaced *De Iure Belli* as the most influential statements of natural law and natural rights philosophy; they also later became standard fare in eighteenth-century university curriculums.

It was Pufendorf who developed, far more elaborately than any previous natural law thinker, a theory of political obligation based on the notion of a social contract. He followed Grotius, Selden, and Hobbes in arguing that a sovereign ruler was the exclusive political representative of society. But he based his absolutism on substantially different notions of how individuals, who once possessed a full array of natural rights, came to accept the authority of their ruler. Pufendorf argued, first of all, that men consent over time to the establishment of a political association and a sovereign. They have done this by means of a linked set of contracts that not only serve to make a state, but also create a new awareness regarding the moral obligations men have to each other in society. An initial contract among the members of a particular community creates the rudiments of a state. But since this contract is among individuals with full freedom to exercise their rights, it is voluntary and limited in its purposes to the goal of individual self-preservation. Later there follows an explicit "decree," enacted by a choice of the majority, that determines the particular form of government to be introduced into the community. The final step that creates the state is a second contract by which the community confers political power on its ruler or rulers. This too is a voluntary subjection, but, once made, irrevocable. For it entails a pledge of obedience to sovereign authority that, by definition, must have full use of its subjects' power to provide for social peace and common defense.

This succession of arguments, as Leonard Krieger has suggested, was for Pufendorf a logical demonstration of how originally free and rational individuals must have gradually organized themselves into a single political order under one authority.[60] Yet that authority was founded only in part on the natural rights of its subjects. Pufendorf also stressed that the passage from liberty to authority had created a nexus of new obligations to others that must be correlated with natural rights. In his view, a "right" was not (as Hobbes had argued) simply a power of doing whatever was necessary for one's self-preservation. It also included "some moral effect, with regard to others, who are Partners with men in the same Nature."[61] In Hobbes's world, where originally each individual was free to obstruct another as each of them pursued private interests, there simply were no rights. Pufendorf argued that the equality of all men in the state of nature implies that a man is free to use a thing for his private purpose only when he has gained the consent of others. Put another way, any right entails a definite obligation to someone else.[62]

While Pufendorf was hailed by contemporaries as a loyal follower of Grotius, his argument here clearly undercut the radicalism of the Grotian view of rights as an expression of each individual's exclusive right to use the world for his private purposes. This point in fact was made explicitly in *De Iure Naturae* when Pufendorf denied the existence of private property rights of a Grotian kind in the state of nature. A "compact of men, whether tacit, or express," he wrote, was necessary for men to take exclusive possession of things.[63] Yet if seen from another perspective, we should not make too much of this divergence from Grotius. For his view of property also provided Pufendorf with additional support for an absolutist theory of sovereignty fully consistent with that of Grotius. He later concluded that if mutual agreements confer rights, such as property, those same rights later cannot under changed circumstances in the future be pleaded for in defense of action that might seek to reconstitute the original agreements.

After Pufendorf, there are four other natural law thinkers whose work came to figure in Hutcheson's moral philosophy. The first was Richard Cumberland (1631–1718). He joined an ongoing campaign to refute Hobbes by countering with two arguments the contention that the state of nature must be a state of unrestrained freedom where property rights have to be created by contract. First of all, Cumberland reasserted Grotius's view that property rights antedated such contracts. The law of nature, he wrote, does not prescribe self-preservation, but instead those acts necessary to sustain a sociable being. Respect for property must be understood as one means of fulfilling our natural obligations to preserve and benefit mankind as a whole. Secondly, Cumberland explained the motive for obeying the laws of nature in a fashion earlier pursued by John Selden, but with one important difference: where Selden had insisted that God issues natural law at a specific moment in history, Cumberland argued that we learn to obey the laws of nature as a result of our experience of the world as it has been created by a lawgiving God.[64]

In rehabilitating the Grotian theory of property, Cumberland ultimately had no radical political message in mind. His brief mention of men consenting to property, Tuck has pointed out, carried little weight. Yet Locke would raise ideas similar to Cumberland's in his *Two Treatises of Government*, and there they supported a forceful theory of resistance. Locke assumed, like previous Grotian natural law thinkers, the state of nature was an unoccupied world awaiting occupation. But he also argued a new point: the actual physical labor of men was the way in which they had come to occupy such a world. Unlike Pufendorf, then, Locke thus thought it unnecessary to await the agreement or consent of others before appropriating things for one's own use. He went on to argue that a Grotian theory of property supported more liberal political conclusions than Cumberland had recognized. In the *Second Treatise*, Locke tried to show that the natural rights that all men have over common property also provided the foundation for a right of resistance to absolute government. He began by arguing that labor provided the solution to the problem of how common property had become private property. But he then went on to argue that, although labor conferred a right not to have property taken without consent, it cannot confer an absolute right. A society of men can establish government to secure their property; they also can draw up explicit agreements about the distribution of property. But such actions can never, as Grotius and Pufendorf had argued, exclude that fundamental natural right every man has to preserve himself and his family.[65]

Locke's work marked the end of perhaps the most vital period of natural rights theorizing in the history of Western thought. With the gradual return of political stability and the continuing expansion of commerce, exponents of natural law and natural rights at the outset of the eighteenth century turned to the less contentious task of scholarly hermeneutics and academic popularization of classic texts in the tradition. This was largely the kind of work pursued by two figures who were the chief immediate sources of Hutcheson's understanding of the natural law tradition. Gershom Carmichael, his teacher and predecessor in the chair of moral philosophy at Glasgow, annotated a new Latin edition of Pufendorf's *De Officio Hominis et Civis* (1718) that became a standard text in eighteenth-century Scottish university curriculums. Equally important for Hutcheson was the work of Jean Barbeyrac (1674-1744), a French legal theorist and historian who in his day was the greatest continental European exponent of natural law and natural rights. He annotated and translated into French Pufendorf's *De Iure Naturae et Gentium* (1725) and later also annotated a new Latin edition of Grotius's seminal *De Iure Belli* (1735). In their annotations, both Carmichael and Barbeyrac continued to pursue discussions of the intellectual legacy of Grotius.[66] Both were deeply concerned to establish a line of his authentic heirs. They praised Pufendorf and Cumberland as the most important preservers of Grotius. They also commended chapter v of Locke's *Second Treatise* as a new and convincing justification for Grotius's conception of property. But for Barbeyrac, who took the dominant political attitude of the natural law tradition to be a conservative one, Pufendorf remained a figure second in importance only to Grotius himself. Thus, he never mentioned the English radicals, and he saw Locke's theory of resistance as a divergence from the main absolutist line of the Grotian tradition. Carmichael, on the other hand, saw the logical political attitude of the tradition as a liberal constitutionalist one. Hence, he insisted that the *Second Treatise* was a corrective to Pufendorf's absolutism as well as to his view of property. Despite these differences, however, both Barbeyrac and Carmichael stressed the cohesiveness of the tradition far more than its divisions. And, in the end, neither one made any effort to provide a critical overview of natural law and natural rights thinking as it had developed since Grotius's historic breakthrough.[67]

vi This is of course a truncated account of more than one hundred years of natural law and natural rights thinking. There are subtleties in each of the figures above that we have not recovered, also other important writers who discussed the issues we have just explored. But there is quite enough here to help us grasp much of what Hutcheson was about in the *Short Introduction* and the *System of Moral Philosophy*. The most plausible approach to both works is to read them, first of all, as Hutcheson's attempt to provide what was missing in the scholarly apparatus of Carmichael and Barbeyrac: a critical overview of the modern Grotian natural law tradition. This effort, in turn, prompted Hutcheson to address again the two large questions that had preoccupied other disciples of Grotius before him. First, what was the dominant political attitude of their tradition of thought? Second, what was the proper way to understand the relationship between the law of nature and natural rights?

As we begin to explore Hutcheson's answers to these long-standing questions, we should note the great extent to which he aligned himself with Grotius in discussing such key issues as rights, property, and justice. "Property or Dominion" is a right, he wrote, "which one man may have exclusive of his fellow men." It stems partly from the "general right" which men have to use animals and inanimate things to serve human purposes. Yet property also represents the just reward for an individual's effort to take or "occupy" such things as are fit for his immediate use. For the earth, and all it contains, originally was placed in a "negative community." It was a state "not yet in property, yet lying open to the occupation of any one." And finally: in established civil society, justice is an injunction to respect the exclusive rights of others. Hutcheson argued that magistrates must reject all plans of polity that aim at a "wisely proportioned distribution" of property "according to the indigence or merit of their subjects." No such plan would ever "satisfy men sufficiently as to the just treatment to be given themselves, and all who are peculiarly dear to them."[68]

Both the language and the substance of these statements identify Hutcheson as a follower of Grotius. But there can be no question that he was also a self-conscious critic of attempts to find a conservative political message in Grotian accounts of natural law and natural rights. Hutcheson accepted Gershom Carmichael's view that the logical political attitude of the tradition was a liberal constitutionalist one. He also mounted a careful and eloquent defense of Locke's account of the right of resistance. "What is alleged about some peculiarly divine right, and inviolable sanctity of governors, especially monarchs," Hutcheson insisted, "is a mere dream of court-flatterers." Even more pointedly, he later dismissed the charge that defending the right of resistance naturally tended to excite seditions and civil wars. "In all ages there has been too much patience in the body of the people, and too stupid a veneration for their princes or rulers," he wrote, "which for each one free kingdom or state has produced many monstrous herds of miserable abject slaves or beasts of burden, rather than civil polities of rational creatures."[69]

It is necessary, however, to exercise a degree of caution in making this point. It has been suggested that Hutcheson's view of rights ultimately "was even more conducive to egalitarianism than Locke's."[70] But this overestimates the radical implications of Hutcheson's arguments, as well as his distance from Locke on this issue. There is to be sure an egalitarianism implicit in moral sense theory. But it would be a mistake, for reasons we explored in the previous section of this chapter, to think of Hutcheson as an egalitarian in his social and political attitudes as well. Indeed, we have just seen that Hutcheson followed Grotius in rejecting any effort to found a polity on the ideal of distributive justice. Moreover, he also treated the right of resistance, like Locke, as an indispensable guarantee of the "common rights of the community"—a means of preserving a community of sociable men, not the inalienable rights of separate and self-interested individuals. Thus, the general rule for each good subject was "to bear patiently many injuries done only to himself." In fact, "the rights of the governor, as they are more important than those of any one private man, may be deemed more sacred than his private rights." Hutcheson also made it clear that only when an attempt to trample upon the rights of one individual is made a "precedent against all the rest" is a ruler "plainly perfidious to his trust."[71]

There is no doubt, however, that Hutcheson placed an exceptionally strong emphasis on the view that government is strictly a servant of society. Indeed, he insisted that "the people" will always have a better claim to adjudicate disputes between state and society, "since they at first entrusted their governors with such powers, and the powers were designed for the management of the people's interests."[72] Why Hutcheson argued in just this way will become clearer if we now move on to explore his account of the relationship between the law of nature and natural rights. In his chapter "Of the Law of Nature" in the *Short Introduction,* he began by laying it down as an axiom that men are innately rational and sociable creatures. He then proceeded to comb from the writings of Pufendorf, Cumberland, and Locke passages explaining the relationship between natural law and natural rights. He reiterated, first of all, Cumberland's account of the obligatory force of natural law. "God our Creator" has implanted in us a sense of right and the powers of reason. Both serve as our guides to experience by allowing us to "discover what conduct tends either to the common prosperity of all, or that of individuals, and what has the contrary tendency." Both also show that "all sorts of kind offices generally tend to the happiness of the person who discharges them, and the contrary offices to his detriment." Hutcheson concluded that all practical directives developed by "right reason" must also be seen as "so many laws, inacted, ratified by penalties, and promulgated by God in the very constitution of nature."[73]

Hutcheson had one main point in mind here: the familiar view that the law of nature required acts necessary to sustain a community of rational men. That point is worth emphasizing because this is also the specific intellectual context within which his remarks on the division of labor and "natural liberty" can be best understood. His main emphasis in discussing both of these issues was to "show the necessity of living in society." First of all, Hutcheson stressed that the division of labor is a clear logical expression of the need for cooperation among all men. "The friendly aids of our fellows" not only provide for "external things"; they also banish our solitude and allow for the exercise of "the natural powers and instincts of our species," such as "love, or social joys, or communication of pleasure, or esteem, or mirth." A similar argument figured prominently in Hutcheson's denial of Hobbes's view that a state of nature was a state of total freedom. The account of "the state of natural liberty" in Hobbes was based on the assumption that each man pursued his self-interest when left to his own devices in the state of nature. Yet it is, Hutcheson countered, "a foolish abuse of words" to describe a state of such absolute solitude as our "natural" state, for in this condition "neither could any of mankind come into being, or continue in it a few days without a miraculous interposition." He then concluded that while law and government remain absent from the state of natural liberty, the law of nature—as arranged and enforced by our Creator—must still obtain.[74]

Having emphasized man's inherent sociability prior to law and government, Hutcheson then went on to develop a theory of rights based on exactly the same assumption. Much of his argument here, as we have noted before, was taken from the writings of Pufendorf. Yet it also included a defense of a right of resistance that Pufendorf had specifically excluded. Hutcheson began—sometimes using direct quotations from Barbeyrac's edition of *De Officio Hominis et Civis*—by insisting that all rights must be divided "according as they are more or less necessary to the preservation of social life." This principle then informed his restatement of the five major types of natural rights he had first put forward in the *Inquiry*. Later, Hutcheson carried the argument further in defending the view that society itself may be the subject of rights. Thus, while he followed Grotius in describing the general rule regarding property as leaving "each one the free administration of his own," he also noted "singular exigencies" when this rule must yield to the "common rights of mankind." For if there are common laws binding all men, there also must be common rights, "not specially regarding the utility of any one, or a few, but that of all in general." And because such rights also obtain in the state of natural liberty, they should ultimately be considered previous to those of civil societies.[75]

The upshot of this last discussion was that doctrine of the right of resistance we examined earlier. Here we should note, finally, that Hutcheson was aware that he had used many of Pufendorf's arguments in arguing that the dominant political attitude of the Grotian natural law tradition was not a conservative or absolutist one. The "burdens of civil subjection," he concluded, had been exaggerated by Pufendorf as well as by Hobbes. Pufendorf's great achievement was to have shown how rational men consented to a just constitution of political power. But he then lost sight of the fact that the main goal of that project—"the common good of the whole body"—remained a clear, indisputable standard by which men must always judge the strength of their civil obligations.[76]

So far we have considered the extent to which Hutcheson's moral philosophy might be treated as a contribution to the mainstream of Grotian natural law and natural rights theory. It remains to analyze what new elements he sought to introduce into that tradition. The most significant change introduced by Hutcheson can be found in his account of the relationship between natural law and natural rights. As we have seen, he rejected the argument that a Grotian natural rights theory required a strongly individualistic psychology of the sort that both conservative and radical rights theorists had put forward in the middle decades of the seventeenth century. We also have seen that he derived from Cumberland, Pufendorf, and Locke the counter-argument that rights must be understood in terms of man's innate sociability. If we turn, however, to the entire range of arguments Hutcheson used to defend this last view, we find that he incorporated one very significant new emphasis in his account.

The innovation was worked out most elaborately in Hutcheson's effort to rehabilitate the original Grotian view of property as an exclusive right. He began by following Carmichael and Barbeyrac in preferring Locke's labor theory of property over that of Grotius and Pufendorf. His preference was based partly on the view that Locke's demonstration that men acquire property by labor made it unnecessary to "have recourse to any old conventions with Grotius and Pufendorf, in explaining the original of property." Hutcheson agreed with Locke that reason tells us that we are entitled to property in the product of our labor partly because this is what serves to "excite men to industry." And yet, as James Moore has shown, Hutcheson did not embrace all of Locke's argument on this point.[77] In fact, he explicitly rejected Locke's notion that the activity of mixing one's actual labor in things makes them one's own exclusive property. This notion, he remarked, arose "from some confused imagination that property is some physical quality or relation produced by some action." Hutcheson then insisted by contrast that Locke overlooked the extent to which certain "strong feelings" in our heart prompt us to discover the right of property. For it is familial affection, as well as self-love, that causes men to labor. And our moral sense tells us that "it must be inhuman and ill-natured" to take from another person what he has acquired or improved by his own labor.[78]

It should be evident by now that the new emphasis in Hutcheson's restatement of Grotius's theory of property was the naturalistic psychology of his moral sense theory. That same emphasis occurred, although in less developed arguments, at two other key points in his account of natural law. The first was his description of "the state of natural liberty" in the *System*. Here he began by referring his readers to the discussion of the moral sense in book 1. He then insisted that it provided conclusive proof that the state of nature "is so far from being that of war and enimity, that it is a state where we are all obliged by the natural feelings of our hearts, and by many tender affections, to innocence and beneficence toward all." Hutcheson also discussed natural rights in the same terms. The natural right of self-preservation is intimated by an "immediate sense of moral evil in all cruelty occasioning unnecessary pain, or abatement of happiness to any of our fellows." He also spoke of our understanding of "natural liberty" in terms of a strong "sense" nature has implanted in each man. This prompts "many tender affections toward others in some nearer relations of life," but also a powerful impulse to exercise those affections according to one's "own judgment and inclination." Hutcheson concluded by repeating that our right of "natural liberty" was suggested not only by the logic of self-interest, but also by "many generous affections, and by our *moral sense*, which represents our own voluntary actions as the grand dignity and perfection of our nature."[79]

vii The overall effect of this line of argument is to suggest that a more careful analysis of the role of sentiments, passions, and feelings in human conduct would provide new guidance in resolving the central concerns of thinkers who endorsed values and concepts articulated in the natural rights theory of Hugo Grotius. In the following two chapters, we will see that it is precisely this shift in priorities that both David Hume and Adam Smith found in Hutcheson's writing and teaching. We also will see that their somewhat different attempts to refound Grotian views of justice and property on a thoroughly naturalized theory of human nature provided key philosophical supports for their liberal economic doctrines.

Hutcheson's ultimate intentions here, however, are obscure. One difficulty is that he apparently never decided exactly how much weight he wished to assign to his new stress on the role of sentiments and feelings. Sometimes Hutcheson seems to be pointing to questions that never occurred to earlier natural law thinkers. As Moore points out, the issue of what sentiments or affections prompt men to engage in labor never troubled Locke.[80] In the *Second Treatise*, he explained the necessary motivation to labor in terms of the duty men have to their Creator to preserve themselves and others. The effect of Hutcheson's argument was to direct attention away from this well-established view that our rational understanding of the law of nature obliges us to respect the right of property that men have in the products of their labor. Elsewhere, however, it seems clear that Hutcheson had no such philosophical innovation in mind. In his discussion of the state of natural liberty, for example, he seems to be proposing that, although the role of sentiments ought to be stressed, rational understanding remains our primary guide in moral and political conduct. He also continued to describe the laws of nature as the practical dictates of an innate "right reason." And he insisted that all rights, while made known by the "natural feelings" of our hearts, must ultimately be understood in terms of their particular benefits for society as a whole.[81] At the end, the implication seems to be that certain sentiments and feelings (at most) give an initial instinctive confirmation of views that later careful rational analysis tells us must be true.

We need to mention briefly a final difficulty concerning Hutcheson's intentions. Despite the uncertainty surrounding his ambitions as a natural law philosopher, the line of thinking we uncovered in the previous section clearly did not force Hutcheson to abandon the general framework of Grotian natural law philosophy. Yet, as I noted at the outset of this chapter, Hutcheson was a thinker with a variety of ideological messages. He ought not to be seen exclusively as a natural law theorist and advocate of greater commercial freedom. He was both, and more besides. For example, in some previous histories of eighteenth-century British thought, Hutcheson has been portrayed primarily as a follower of James Harrington (1611–77). In his preface to the *Short Introduction to Moral Philosophy*, Hutcheson himself grouped Harrington with the natural law thinkers we have examined above as one of the key sources of his political thought. But there is no question that the tradition of thought to which Harrington belonged offered a significantly different view of politics. A civic rather than legal humanist, Harrington was a forceful and influential early-modern champion of the Aristotelian view that man was *zōon politikon*, above all a political animal. Direct participation in politics, he argued again, was the means by which one realized one's full worth and value. Thus, unlike the juristic person of the natural law tradition, a virtuous citizen was actively engaged in a community of political equals where all men share in the art of ruling themselves. What private concerns he happens to retain are not important ends in themselves, but means for him to nurture the "virtue" of life centered in politics.[82]

One of the chief difficulties in understanding Hutcheson's moral philosophy, taken in its entirety, is explaining why he saw fit to endorse values associated with both of the two great traditions of classical political speculation. A plausible strategy here would be to view Hutcheson as a highly syncretic thinker who refused to regard civic humanism and natural law jurisprudence as distinct and opposing ideologies. As we saw earlier, Hutcheson emphasized that the accumulation of goods in society benefited mankind by encouraging commerce and a further division of labor. But this emphasis, as Moore has shown, was later qualified by an insistence that no indivdual or society should accumulate or occupy so much property that the independence of other individuals or societies was threatened. It was here that Hutcheson echoed Harrington in praising the practice in free republican governments of limiting appropriation to safeguard the liberty or autonomy of its citizens. The limits he imposed on appropriation also followed Harrington with his denunciation of "luxury," his contempt for standing armies, and his concern to enlist citizens in a rotation of military and civilian obligations.[83]

Hutcheson's mixing of the rhetoric of natural law jurisprudence and civic humanism might also be understood as one of the results of his effort to continue the work of his former Glasgow professors in revamping orthodox Scottish Protestantism. Like John Simson and Gershom Carmichael before him, Hutcheson provided his students a liberal vision of Christianity radically at odds with Calvinist doctrines of predestination and election. In this attempt to put "a new face upon theology in Scotland," he clearly drew support from both the legal and the civic humanist traditions. As we have seen, he echoed Cumberland, Simson, and Carmichael in arguing that God is a law-giver who provides all men with senses of right and reason. He also refashioned civic humanist rhetoric in urging the Scottish gentry to involve themselves more deeply in the affairs of the Church of Scotland. In 1735, Hutcheson published a short pamphlet entitled "Considerations on Patronages" that supported a new parliamentary bill aimed at breaking a near-monopolization of Church patronage in Scotland by the English ministry. This arrangement, Hutcheson argued, violated the terms of the Treaty of Union between England and Scotland in 1707. He urged the "gentlemen of Scotland" to support the new bill and to prepare themselves to resume their "natural power" of determining appointments of ministers in the Church of Scotland.[84]

At first glance, the message in Hutcheson's account of property and in his "Considerations on Patronages" seems clear enough: safeguard and enlarge the powers of the landed citizen according to the classical republican ideal that Harrington and his other followers had championed. It is arguable, however, that Hutcheson's ultimate intentions here remain obscure. In other places, Hutcheson himself acknowledged that civic humanist ideals differed sharply from those of the natural law and natural rights tradition. He acknowledged, too, that natural law jurisprudence provided a clearer guide to the practical realities of modern political life.[85] Finally, it seems clear that Hutcheson's liberal Protestantism was not very deeply embedded in the civic humanist tradition. Patronage in the end was not revamped citizenship. It was a means by which men of property might "have some power to serve their friends, or the men they esteem and love," especially their sons. It was, too, a means of assuring Scottish gentlemen that they would have ministers "capable of entertaining them agreeably in public with rational and edifying discourses."[86]

The practical message of such discourses would also have much in common with that preached by the Latitudinarians of the Church of England. Faith was no longer consolation, but a spur to improvement. For Hutcheson, as for the liberal English Protestants, the emphasis had shifted from man's inherent weakness and depravity to work or "labor" as roads to happiness and prosperity. And if Christians could live more fully in this world, so too could the Church. Like the English Latitudinarians, Hutcheson urged Protestant believers to accept that the business of the world at times might supersede the formal requirements of religious worship. Thus, while Hutcheson still saw religion as the cement of his society, he ultimately sought to broaden contemporary conceptions of Protestantism in ways that respected not only the traditional privileges of the gentry but also the new practical concerns of men involved in commerce and foreign trade.[87]

A fuller examination of the grand designs of Hutcheson's moral philosophy must await another study. It should be said that they pose a problem that it will not be easy to solve.[88] Yet the problem finally is one by which David Hume and Adam Smith were not greatly perplexed. In the chapters that follow we will find that they came to view Hutcheson's thinking largely as a contribution to Grotian natural law and natural rights philosophy. It is, therefore, the particular character of that contribution which we must keep in mind as we now move on to explore his influence on Hume and Smith.

III David Hume

Nothing is more vigilant and inventive than our passions. . . .
—Treatise, III.II.vi, *p. 526*

Sovereigns must take mankind as they find them, and cannot pretend to produce any violent change in their principles and ways of thinking.
—"Of Commerce," Essays, I, *p. 292*

i Unlike Hutcheson, David Hume (1711–76) long has been taken seriously as an original thinker. He was by intention an innovator. He saw his new "science of man" as the first empirically verifiable theory of human nature that explained why men act, think, and feel in all the various ways they do. But while taken seriously, Hume has met a curious fate: he is a theorist whose political and economic views have satisfied almost no one. Contemporaries found his stress on the "artificial" origins of justice eccentric and worrisome, because it suggested justice was an "unnatural" ideal.[1] Most of his students in the nineteenth and twentieth century have found him important as "an eliminator of the obscure, the inadequate, and the otiose" rather than a framer of new ideas and hypotheses. His thinking should be remembered, John Stuart Mill once remarked, as the work of "the profoundest negative thinker on record."[2]

Hume's projected "science of man" developed positive perspectives in only one area: his economic writings, often recognized by historians of economic thought as major contributions to the development of classical liberal economic ideology, show that Hume was something more than an arch-skeptic. Yet here too Hume's views have been faulted. The moral and political assumptions behind his enthusiastic endorsement of free commerce at times seem perfunctory for a thinker of Hume's gifts.

Duncan Forbes, one of the most able of contemporary students of Hume's thought, has observed that for Hume it was "an unquestioned assumption" that "the good life is dependent on economic progress."[3] Iconoclast and *provocateur* in politics, Hume seems to have changed hats in the market place to become a celebrant and publicist for an emerging commercial civilization.

Hume himself was partly responsible for his image as an eccentric or purely negative philosopher. His theory of justice, for example, was in some respects an ironic exercise. Hume knew there was nothing novel in the substantive conclusion of that theory. His definition of justice was fundamentally Grotian: a just polity is concerned to assure that "every one knows what he may safely possess"; it establishes and maintains rules that protect the exclusive property rights of its members.[4] What was new in Hume's account was the way he arrived at this familiar view. He broke with the traditional natural law view of man as a rational agent and instead treated politics as a matter of passions, as a question of psychological activity. His description of justice as an "artificial" virtue also distinguished it from the "natural" virtue embodied in individual moral judgments.

Hume himself thought that the implications of this argument were neither dangerous nor disturbing. Because he traced both justice and morality to the workings of our passions, he felt the distinction was purely descriptive, rather than normative, in its intent. Or, as he wrote in reply to Francis Hutcheson, one of the first critics of his theory of justice, "I have never call'd Justice unnatural, but only artificial."[5] Any full-scale consideration of Hume's social theory would require us to recognize Hume's frequent irony and to specify what Hume's politics signified for established traditions of moral and political discourse in eighteenth-century Britain. Much of this work has been accomplished skillfully in the recent studies of James Conniff, Duncan Forbes, and James Moore.[6] But Hume's social views must also be understood in the context of a problem that has been largely overlooked in recent scholarship. Perhaps the central puzzle of interpreting Hume, as Norman Kemp Smith once observed, is "not so much in regard to his arguments taken singly . . . but in regard to their bearing on one another, and upon the central positions they are intended to support."⁷ This chapter will try to describe Hume's place in the intellectual history of capitalism primarily in the context of this issue. The issue is one where a careful exploration of Hume's intellectual relationship with Hutcheson is extraordinarily illuminating.

It is important to be clear at the outset about what kinds of questions we will explore here. In the first place, it should be said again that Hume (like Hutcheson) lived in a pre-industrial age, so he knew nothing of factories and wage-earning laborers, of capitalism as a new mode of production. Yet there can be no question that he called for certain changes in thinking about eighteenth-century commerce that later provided philosophical and political supports for that new order of production. In his *Political Discourses* (1752), Hume pointedly argued against the mercantilists that the wealth created by commerce was not money per se, but an ever-increasing stock of productive labor and marketable resources. He also stressed that government ought to be deeply concerned with augmenting the stock of labor and goods of its society. And in essays that explained how this could best be achieved, Hume formulated most of the same recommendations for a policy of free trade that we now usually associate with Adam Smith's *Wealth of Nations*.

For students of Hume, the vexing point here, and our starting point as well, is to see how his conception of the proper relationship between polity and economy stands in relation to the main announced intention of his philosophy—formulating a "science of man," a positive general theory of human nature explaining why men act, think and feel in all the various ways they do. Those scholars who stress that Hume was more than a purely negative thinker attempt to show that he in fact fulfilled his goal. They argue that his denigration of reason was always prelude to a corresponding "elevation of feeling and sentiment" that he generalized into a total theory of man. There is an interplay of skeptical and naturalistic phases in Hume's thought, but it is naturalism that carries the day. Two modern commentators go so far as to speak of this victory as the groundwork of Hume's "modern paganism" and "radicalism." According to Peter Gay, Hume makes plain that "man is his own master: he must live in a disenchanted world, submit everything to criticism, and make his own way." Shirley Letwin, too, sees Hume as a thinker who "meant to cut the ties between man and God, and restore to man a purely human nature, such as pagans found sufficient before Chritianity removed men into a higher and more spiritual sphere." In short, Hume is best seen as a philosopher of "man's wholeness."[8]

These readings prevent us from accepting the familiar but misleading picture of Hume as "the profoundest negative thinker on record." Yet this sort of approach can also give rise to an oversimplified explanation of the ideological implications of Hume's "science of man." Letwin, for example, finds the guiding intention in Hume's philosophical enterprise in the following famous passage in book II of the *Treatise:*

> Nothing is more usual in philosophy, and even in common life, than to talk of the combat of passion and reason. . . . Every rational creature, 'tis said, is oblig'd to regulate his actions by reason; and if any other motive or principle challenge the direction of his conduct, he ought to oppose it, 'till it be entirely subdu'd, or at least brought to a conformity with that superior principle . . . nor is there an ampler field, as well for metaphysical arguments, as popular declamations, than this suppos'd preeminence of reason above passion. The eternity, invariableness, and divine origin of the former have been display'd to best advantage: The blindness, unconstancy, and deceitfulness of the latter have been as strongly insisted upon. In order to shew the fallacy of all this philosophy, I shall endeavour to prove *first,* that reason alone can never be a motive to any action of the will; and *secondly,* that it can never oppose passion in the direction of the will.[9]

There are loud and distinct echoes of Hutcheson's ethical theory here, and the passage surely does describe some of Hume's main concerns as a philosopher. But the emphasis on "paganism" in Hume is arguable. Classical "pagan" psychology, as Hume himself learned early in his life, was based on a sharp antithesis between reason and passion. References to Hume's "radicalism" also oversimplify his message. The extent of Hume's stress on the force of sentiment and passion in human action was novel, but it is not clear that Hume wished this stress to lead to the "radical" view that man become his own master. Hume was a thoroughly secular thinker, but he was by no means a rebel or a reformer. The ideal moral character for him was that person who could "suit his temper to any circumstances." And for the subjects of a polity, "No maxim is more conformable, both to prudence and morals, than to submit quietly to the government, which we find establish'd in the country where we happen to live, without enquiring too curiously into its origin and first establishment." Hume's message here seems little more than a maxim of conventional wisdom: make the best of what is at hand.[10]

In the last analysis, labels such as "radical" and "conservative" are not consistently useful in taking the measure of Hume's social theory.[11] If a genuine conservatism argues that the present division of wealth and power corresponds to some deeper reality of human life, then Hume might be called a conservative. But his defense of the place of habit and custom in society had nothing of the sense of crisis or immanent loss so characteristic of modern conservatism. Sheldon Wolin has called Hume's a conservatism without the "benefit of mystery."[12] But even this useful qualification leaves major problems unsolved. Hume once told Lord Kames, for example, that his argument for free trade in the *Political Discourses* was "levelled against the narrow malignity and envy of nations, which can never bear to see their neighbours thriving, but continually repine at any new efforts towards industry made by any other nation. . . . This narrow spirit of nations, as well as individuals, ought carefully to be repressed."[13] To advocate greater economic freedom as forcefully as Hume did in his economic essays was to reject any view of politics that took the wisdom and power of existing political systems to be the only means by which the consonance of public and private interests could be maintained. The established practice of the age that Hume so often endorsed as a rule of government was not everywhere a reliable guide.

In sum, Hume seems Janus-faced as a social theorist. He spoke the language of both political submission and economic liberty. The puzzle takes on additional complexity when we recall that the relationship between Hume's political and economic views and his central philosophical concern to underscore the influence of passions, sentiments, and feelings still needs systematic study. In this chapter I want to show that some of the major problems involved in characterizing Hume as a social theorist can be resolved by examining the ways in which he made use of a naturalistic view of man he encountered in the writings of Francis Hutcheson. My ultimate concern will be to locate Hume in the intellectual history of capitalism, but that concern necessarily involves understanding the larger outlines of his moral philosophy.

ii David Hume was born in Edinburgh on April 26, 1711, the second son of Joseph Hume.[14] His gentry family was moderately prosperous, Hume's father being both advocate and landowner. As a young man, Hume appears to have been precociously bookish and hyperserious. In the fall of 1723, he was sent to the University of Edinburgh to begin studies for a career in law. But his legal studies left him "nauseous," so he turned instead to scholarship and philosophy. The results here at first were even more disabling. Study of classical humanist moral philosophy revealed to the young Hume a tradition of thought "entirely hypothetical & depending more upon invention than experience. Everyone consulted his own fancy in erecting schemes of virtue & happiness, without regarding human nature, upon which every moral conclusion must depend." At the age of eighteen, he imagined himself on the verge of formulating an alternative "new scene of thought." But that scene quickly receded from view. Unable to follow out any train of thought, Hume would suffer through a period of agitated depression until the age of twenty-three.[15]

By the spring of 1734, his condition had become unbearable. He then left Scotland to experiment with a new career as a clerk in a firm of Bristol sugar-merchants. Hume would later praise merchants as "one of the most useful race of men in the whole society." But by temperament he was not made for what he called their "more active scene of life."[16] He soon quarreled with his employer about matters of grammar and style in business correspondence and retired in annoyance after four months in the world of commerce. Yet the experiment helped Hume to overcome his depression and his writing block; and he was now ready to return to his philosophical studies. He left for France in the summer of 1734, and there composed books I and II of the *Treatise*, which were published in London in January 1739. Hume also returned to Edinburgh in 1739, and there spent most of the year working on book III.

Between April of 1739, and March 1740, shortly before book III went to press, Hume and Francis Hutcheson exchanged several letters concerning an early draft of this book. In the Introduction to the *Treatise*, Hume remarked that his new "science of man" had been most influenced by five British philosophers: Locke, Shaftesbury, Mandeville, Hutcheson, and Dr. Joseph Butler. But his correspondence during the year he completed book III shows very clearly Hutcheson's influence had been the preeminent one. In the last letter Hume sent to Hutcheson before mailing the manuscript of book III to his publisher, he spoke of the book's greatest achievement as giving greater rigor and clarity to ideas he first had found in Hutcheson's work. Indeed, he told Hutcheson in March, 1740, that "morality, according to your opinion as well as mine is determin'd merely by sentiment, it regards only human nature & human life. This has been often urg'd against you, & the consequences are very momentous."[17]

For Hume, Hutcheson's "momentous" achievement was not the "moral sense" argument per se. In his writings, Hume would only once refer to the concept of a "moral sense," in the title of the second of two sections on "vice and virtue in general" in book III, part I of the *Treatise*. The text itself, however, was concerned with moral "feeling" and "sentiment." According to Hume, a person gets a pleasing sentiment of approval upon encountering qualities in others that are directly agreeable to him. Yet the same sentiment also will appear when we encounter qualities that tend to promote the well-being of particular individuals or of society at large. The spark of moral judgment,

Hume argued, was not reason, for clearly the well-being of society does not necessarily lead to one's own well-being. It was instead a fundamental property, an "internal habit of mind," called "sympathy." Hume used this term both to explain how we come to know what others feel and to account for how we have a moral reaction to their situation.

The notion of a particular "moral sense" was not a subject of open dispute between Hume and Hutcheson, so we have to speculate about why Hume dropped the term from his arguments. But there is little mystery here. Given Hume's announced interest in describing various non-rational "habits of mind" that guide thought and action, it is likely he feared using the term "moral sense" might suggest, unintentionally and misleadingly, a simple analogy with external senses. Hence, he dispensed with Hutcheson's famous phrase. For Hume, "sympathy" was essentially a disposition we have to feel what others are feeling. But it was not, as Barry Stroud has observed, a particular moral feeling or sense in itself.[18]

Yet for Hume all these clearly were minor matters in measuring Hutcheson's importance as a thinker. He took Hutcheson's central message to be a fundamental redefinition of the relationship between reason and passions in the conduct of human affairs. The "momentous" move here was not positing a moral sense, but demonstrating that virtue, as Hutcheson had written in the *Inquiry*, flows from "affections or passions." Hutcheson showed that knowledge and virtue could no longer be thought of as one and the same, which was the view of those classical humanists who had left the young Hume so dissatisfied. He also proved that morality was nothing "in the abstract nature of things," and here broke the spell of Descartes and his many rationalist followers in the eighteenth century. They had confounded "the faculty by which we discern truth and falsehood, and that by which we perceive vice and virtue." A moral judgment in reality was a matter of "the sentiment or mental taste of each particular being." It sprang from psychological activity distinct from those mental operations that lead to knowledge and truth. In brief, for Hume the fundamental significance of Hutcheson's thought was not what some supposed to be his argument for an inherent goodness or benevolence in man. It was rather his careful demonstration that when men happen to pursue virtue and goodness, they do so because of the prompting of instinctive predispositions.[19]

Hutcheson himself found much of Hume's account of the dramatic consequences of his work difficult to accept. He even sent Hume a polite but clear warning about what he took to be a major defect in book III. The manuscript, he observed, "wants a certain warmth in the cause of virtue." Hume shot back, however, that by design his book had the careful, clinical tone he would seek to establish as a trademark of the new eighteenth-century "science of man." Hume wrote to Hutcheson: "There are different ways of examining the mind as well as the body. One may consider it either as an anatomist or as a painter; either to discover its most secret springs & principles or to describe the grace & beauty of its actions." Hutcheson wanted both roles played at once, but Hume said bluntly he had not come to trumpet the old humanist cause of "virtue." The aim of the *Treatise* was to delve into the ordinary feelings and sentiments that inevitably lie behind even our "noblest attitudes & most vigorous actions."[20]

As we have seen already, Hutcheson remained too much the traditional humanist to surrender his belief that the pursuit of virtue was itself one of men's passions. The only surviving letter from Hutcheson to Hume in September, 1739, however, suggests that when first confronted with a draft of book III Hutcheson for a moment wavered in this conviction.[21] And that perhaps explains why Hume carried on with the strictly "anatomical" inquiry of book III in the face of the substantial criticism Hutcheson had made in later correspondence. In the same letter that Hume spoke of their shared "momentous" discovery of the primary role of sentiment in human conduct, he in fact pressed on Hutcheson what he took to be one of the central controversial points of book III:

> When you pronounce any action or character to be vicious, you mean nothing but that from the particular constitution of your nature you have a feeling or sentiment of blame

from the contemplation of it. Vice & Virtue, therefore, may be compar'd to sounds, colours, heat & cold, which, according to modern philosophy, are not qualitys in objects but perceptions in the mind. . . .

For Hume, the question at this point may have been largely rhetorical, but he then asked Hutcheson if he thought this was not "laid a little too strong?"[22]

We do not have Hutcheson's actual reply. But there can be no doubt that he thought it "laid" much too strong. Four years after the publication of the *Treatise*, Hutcheson was among those who stood strongly opposed to Hume's application for the chair of moral philosophy at the University of Edinburgh. Hume at the time heard a rumor that Hutcheson felt he was a "very unfit person for such an office." He wrote to his friend William Mure of Caldwell (1718–76): "What can be the meaning of this conduct in that celebrated & benevolent moralist, I cannot imagine. I shall be glad to find, for the honour of philosophy, that I am mistaken."[23] But Hume was not mistaken. On April 3, 1745, the Edinburgh Town Council voted to appoint Hutcheson himself to the chair. Hutcheson declined the offer because of illness and instead sent a list of his own recommended candidates. Hume's disappointment surely would have been even greater had he known the identities of the mediocre candidates Hutcheson found acceptable.

In tracing the course of Hume's intellectual career, the story of his dealings with Hutcheson is important, first of all, because it prevents us from accepting Hume's well-known but also misleading picture of the *Treatise* as a work that "fell *dead-born from the press;* without reaching such distinction as even to excite a murmur among the zealots."[24] The "zealots" at first did ignore Hume; their crusade against the "barbarous infidel" of Edinburgh would be mounted in the 1750s. But it is clear that for the liberal Scottish Protestants, who in the 1730s had fought to secure a new and liberal theology in the universities in Glasgow and Edinburgh, the *Treatise* brought a cloud of scandal over Hume he would never be able to escape. After Hutcheson's death in 1745, his protégé William Leechman, then Professor of Divinity and later Principal of Glasgow University, would continue to warn Scottish students away from Hume's scandalous speculations.[25]

Secondly, the story of Hume's relationship with Hutcheson is fascinating on its own terms, because it represents one of those rare cases in the history of thought where we find an amply documented instance of the tangled ways in which an intellectual relationship based on "influence" happens to work.[26] On the one hand, while Hutcheson saw that Hume's arguments were much like his, he also saw they were by no means exactly alike; and the differences troubled him greatly. On the other hand, while Hume deeply admired Hutcheson, and looked upon him as an original thinker, he did not simply paraphrase his arguments. In the *Treatise*, Hume sought to show that all of human conduct, not simply our concern with virtue, was grounded in certain nonrational "natural propensities." Man for Hume was fully a creature of his passions. Not just moral judgment, but all human conduct is primarily a matter of the exercise of our various appetites, instincts, sentiments, and affections. Hume made it clear that not all passions were commendable. But since by definition each of our passions is an "original existence," an animating principle in us more powerful than reason, an adequate account of human affairs must show how and which particular passions move us to act as we do.[27]

There are at least two reasons that explain why Hutcheson objected so strongly to this fully naturalistic view of life, and it may be useful to explore them in some detail because both reveal a great deal about the perceived ideological message of the *Treatise* in the Scottish intellectual world. The first undoubtedly was the question of Hume's religious views. In revising book III, Hume tried to meet part of Hutcheson's criticism that his work lacked "a certain warmth in the cause of virtue." He offered explicit apologies for appearing to doubt the soundness of traditional religious doctrines and even added an appendix in which he attempted to portray himself as a deist. The potentially most controversial section of the *Treatise*, "Reasonings concerning miracles," was removed from the final manuscript Hume sent to his publisher. Here criticism of religion had gone beyond doubting the truths of revealed religion to raising questions about deistic "natural" religion as well. None of these concessions, however, masked the completely secular character of Hume's view of human nature. Through the rest of his career, Hume in fact would never bring himself to accept Hutcheson's view that religion and reason shared an intellectual meeting ground.

A second and equally important difference concerned the question of how moral philosophy ought to be presented. As we have seen in the previous chapter, the model for Hutcheson had been that of Renaissance humanism: moral philosophy must be both analysis and rhetoric; it explained human needs and passions, but it also stirred the soul to pursue the ideal of a life bent on the achievement of excellence and all-encompassing virtue. Hume in some moods wanted to believe his anatomical speculations about human nature would be of service to a didactic humanistic moralist such as Hutcheson, "the painter" of virtue as Hume referred to him. But he also insisted that here were two models of moral philosophizing that ought to be pursued separately. Hutcheson recognized the need to ground virtue in a careful analysis of human nature, but he then begged the obvious and very important question that followed from this recognition. What was the connection between the new view of man as a creature of passions and instincts and the humanist view of man as an aspirer to virtue? Hume told Hutcheson that he simply took this connection for granted. Hutcheson thought that the moral sense argument showed that the pursuit of virtue was natural to man. But in fact he had raised serious doubts about his point. Hume observed that if man was primarily a creature of instincts and passions, then moral standards and social rules must be seen as devices that meet particular human needs and desires. Hutcheson was right in stressing that it was natural for men to live in society, but that stress represented no more than emphasis of an empirical fact, not clear evidence of inherent virtue. A scientific philosopher must explain institutions such as the rules of justice and property by showing that behind actions that led to their creation lie some "motive or impelling passions distinct from virtue." Hume concluded that virtue as an ideal could "never be the sole motive of any action."[28]

In Hutcheson's understanding of moral philosophy, these

views surely were more ominous than "momentous" in their implications. For Hume's "science of man" was in part based on the premise that issues at the center of Hutcheson's work (and at the center of a tradition of Renaissance rhetorical moral speculation with which Hutcheson clearly identified himself) should be put aside as "uncertain and unphilosophical." The great questions in Western humanistic thought were important, but also unanswerable by the "science of man." As Hume wrote to Hutcheson, "For pray, what is the end of man? Is he created for happiness or for virtue? For this life or the next? For himself or for his maker?" Attempts to solve these questions, Hume observed, "are endless & quite wide of my purpose."[29] Hume's hope was that his reflections on the habits and infirmities of human nature would inspire his readers "with more modesty and reserve, and diminish their fond opinion of themselves, and their prejudice against antagonists." But this was not moral philosophy as Hutcheson understood it. The contention that there were no final answers to the great questions of life clearly signified an abandonment of the idealistic, teleological tradition of humanistic thought Hutcheson had fought to establish in Scotland. This abandonment, as much as Hume's thoroughgoing secularism, explains why Hutcheson thought his brilliant young admirer unfit to teach moral philosophy.[30]

Thirdly, the tangled story of the Hutcheson–Hume relationship can also serve as a means for clarifying some of the broader problems in interpreting Hume's social theory. These are the problems I sketched out at the beginning of this chapter, and they will be my main concerns in the following discussion. Hutcheson began the tradition of reading Hume in negative terms. But their correspondence and a careful reading of Hume's text show that the question of the intentions informing the *Treatise* is a very complex one. In the face of Hutcheson's criticism, Hume protested privately that his new "science of man" did have positive goals. Indeed, he claimed to provide for philosophers a new set of questions and a new analytical vocabulary for responding to these questions, both of which had first been inspired by his reading of Hutcheson. Norman Kemp Smith in his classic study and Barry Stroud in a more recent work have provided the most careful and persuasive accounts of Hume as a naturalistic philosopher, and they have shown how Hume's epistemology and ethics find their origins in Hutcheson's moral sense theory.[31] There is no need here to repeat their analyses. My main concerns will be to show, first, how a naturalistic idiom also informed Hume's theory of justice in the *Treatise;* and second, how that same new idiom continued to serve as the philosophical groundwork for many of Hume's later political and economic essays—especially for those in the *Political Discourses,* where he made his most forceful arguments for a policy of free trade.

In book III of the *Treatise,* Hume began his account of justice with a question Hutcheson had resolved with his notion of "external rights." If an individual has borrowed money and the agreed day of repayment arrives, what motive will that person have to return the money? Hutcheson's answer had been offered in the context of an account of ways in which rational individuals must go about pursuing their advantage without damaging the interests of others. "External rights" arose in cases where an individual's pursuit of his own interest seems to violate the rights of others and yet where, at the same time, any attempt to block such a pursuit would do more evil than to allow for it. A wealthy miser, for example, has an external right to recall his loan from a poor man because reason tells us the promise of order in economic transactions is more important to the well-being of society than individual acts of benevolence.[32]

Hume agreed that justice requires repayment as originally promised, but he could not accept the argument that reason had a primary role to play in determining this view. Because men were primarily creatures of feelings and passions, he argued, we cannot conceive that justice, any more than morality, was first discovered by "deductions of our reason." Men must be "sensible" of the advantages of life in a law-governed society, and such a sensibility was not a phenomenon to be explained as a matter of the "rights" of rational men. Of course there might be particular instances where rational self-interest moves us to repay debts. A failure to repay in some circumstances might damage one's reputation and thus make any future attempt to borrow more difficult. But, Hume emphasized, there was not a universally true principle of "right reason" at work here. We can readily think of instances where one's reputation would not suffer from an individual act of injustice. Hence, the argument that our primary motive in acting justly is rational self-interest is not always true. An alternative view, also common in natural law theories of justice, that repayment is necessary because it contributes to the well-being of a community of rational men, leaves itself open to the same objection. How will a community benefit if the individual to whom repayment is due is my personal enemy or a vicious man whom rational men know deserves scorn? Indeed, Hume asked, what if this individual turns out to be the very "miser" Hutcheson spoke of in the *Inquiry* and can "make no use of what I would deprive him of?" In short, the traditional natural law accounts of justice seem to require acts that at times will damage rather than benefit particular individuals and society at large.[33]

Hume's ultimate concern, as we shall see in a moment, was not to challenge the view that repayment of loans is just or that justice itself is a virtue. He in fact had no quarrel with the ideological message of Hutcheson's natural law theory of justice. When he said that a just society is one in which "every one knows what he may safely possess," he was in full agreement with Hutcheson. What Hume sought to demonstrate was that while rules of justice were designed to help men retain exclusive control over their property, the motives for this design had little to do with reason. Put another way, Hume wanted to show that rules of justice were in one essential respect similar to those of personal morality. Both were matters of the excitement and restraint of passions; both were approved of and obeyed without "the intervention of thought or reflection."[34]

Hume's theory of justice, therefore, can be accurately, if not fully, understood as an expansion of Hutcheson's account of the non-rational psychology of moral judgment into a broader theory of social and political relationships among men. Reason can tell us what ends the rules of justice must serve. But it is not, as natural law theorists assumed, our central motive for observing those rules. Ignoring this crucial fact was also the recurrent flaw in contractual or consensual theories of the origins of justice and civil society. In this respect, both the absolutist and the liberal constitutionalist schools of natural law philosophy had misconceived the problem of social order in the same way. "To form a society," Hume wrote, " 'tis requisite not only that it be advantageous, but also that men be sensible of these advantages; and 'tis impossible . . . that by study and reflection alone, they should ever be able to attain this knowledge." Our passions must be the original source of this sensibility. Because while the rules guarding property are essential to the order and well-being of society, the effective operation of those rules depends upon the support of our passions.[35]

Hume took the original achievement of his theory of justice in book III to be a demonstration of how this process must occur. The heart of his argument was that rules of justice, like those of personal morality, flow out of particular passions. Like Hutcheson, Hume saw rules guarding private property and assuring orderly economic transactions as essential to the well-being of society. But for him the central philosophical issue to be understood in accounting for those rules lay elsewhere:

> Whatever restraint they may impose on the passions of men, they are the real offspring of those passions, and are only a more artful and more refin'd way of satisfying them. Nothing is more vigilant and inventive than our passions; and nothing is more obvious, than the convention for the observance of these rules. Nature has, therefore, trusted this affair entirely to the conduct of men, and has not plac'd in the mind any peculiar original principles, to determine us to a set of actions, into which the other principles of our frame and constitution were sufficient to lead us.[36]

Hume was careful not to say that our "vigilant and inventive" passions spontaneously dictate what the content of the rules of justice will be. He acknowledged that "understanding" must first give rise to social rules. At its inception, justice was in fact a means of ordering "the heedless and impetuous movement" as well as the "limited generosity" of human passions. This is precisely why we must speak of it as an "artificial" virtue. But Hume also went on to make the same point Hutcheson had raised in discussing private morality. Like our code of ethics, rules of justice could have had no lasting influence of human conduct if they had been seen to stand opposed to the exercise of passions. Any account of justice that failed to explain how justice had positive support in human passions was void of content.

Rules of justice, Hume argued, were not abstract rational propositions, not those natural law dictates of "right reason" that specified various "rights" of "rational agents" in society. Rather, these rules resolved a dilemma brought about by a specific "opposition of passions, and a consequent opposition of actions." Since man was primarily a creature of instincts and passions, it followed that sexual attraction and familial affection were the original principles of human relationships. But these were not to be understood as the basis of a broader attachment to society in the abstract. While generosity to family and relations "must be acknowledg'd to the honour of human nature," it was at the same time a kind of "selfishness," a "limited generosity," that "intead of fitting [men] for large societies is almost contrary to them." The inherent "contrariety of passions" here was heightened by three difficulties in the "outward circumstances" of family life. In isolation, the total labor of an individual family often threatened to fall short of its needs. A family that would try to meet all its needs would fail to perfect any special economic skills. Finally, and most important of all, in this world of deep economic insecurity, men were inherently suspicious of one another because there was not a sufficient quantity of goods to supply everyone's desires and necessities.[37]

The remedy for this "contrariety of passions" cannot be the embrace of a mere idea of justice. The innate partiality of our affections was too strong to yield to an abstraction. The remedy emerged as men gradually came to share a common recognition of the fact that the main cause for insecurity among them was instability in the relationship between them and their external goods. That insecurity was removed "by a convention enter'd into by all members of the society to bestow stability on the possession of those external goods." Thus, society was founded neither on reason nor on spontaneous natural affections. It was the result of each person's desire to know "what he may safely possess."³⁸

The view of society in book III mirrored a notion of society previously put forward by Grotius and his followers. But Hume was careful to emphasize the novel ground on which he explained that notion. Rules protecting property sought to restrain passions, he noted, but only in "their partial and contradictory notions." Observing these rules was not merely an instance of men allowing their self-interested passions to conform to impartial dictates of right reason. For if such restraint were contrary to these passions, "it could never be enter'd into nor maintain'd." That "convention" into which men enter to establish society, then, was not an explicit promise, since a promise itself can be understood only in terms of already established social conventions. The situation here more closely resembled what James Moore has called a gradual "convergence of judgments in the form of conventional behavior." Put another way, it was only over time that men came to develop "a shared sense of interest in the perpetuation of a working relationship." And it was only when this "common sense of interest" produced a corresponding resolution in actual behavior that we have what can properly be called a "convention or agreement" among men. Subsequent occasional experience of the inconveniences that follow from ignoring that convention served to drive home the original lesson that self-interested passions were best served when restrained by the common interests of society. In sum, Hume understood justice as a specific "habit of mind" that controled self-interested passion by "an alteration of its direction" rather than by an injunction to observe the dictates of right reason.³⁹

iii   After the first two books of Hume's massive philosophical tract appeared in 1739 and in the midst of final revisions of the manuscript of book III, Hume wrote a brief anonymous pamphlet in which he sought to draw attention to the originality of his enterprise. The *Treatise*, he wrote, had "such an air of singularity, and novelty as claim'd the attention of the public." If accepted, his new philosophy would "alter from the foundation the greatest part of the sciences," "shake off the yoke of authority," and "accustom men to think for themselves. . . ."[40] In this century, Hume has found some readers who take him at his word.[41] But the matter of his originality, particularly his central stress on the force of sentiment and passion, is more complex than he makes it sound. And it bears directly on our ultimate concern in this chapter, explaining Hume's role in the genesis of laissez-faire capitalism as a philosophically grounded doctrine.

Although he prided himself in the break, Hume was by no means the first Western thinker to abandon the rational ideals of humanism for the sake of a more naturalistic view of man. What we need to understand here, however, is how Hume's shift made him so receptive to a view of the human condition that emphasized the free pursuit of economic gain. The context in which Hume's naturalism emerged has been studied in a number of recent works concerned with the intellectual history of capitalism.[42] Perhaps the most remarkable has been Albert O. Hirschman's *The Passions and the Interests*, an essay in which both Hutcheson and Hume play key roles. Hirschman emphasizes the often ignored fact that many defenders of economic improvement in the early-modern period sought to explain trade and profit-making in terms of the variety of different motivations that lead men to engage in moral or socially useful behavior. They built their arguments for commerce not on the simple abstraction *homo œconomicus*, but on the naturalistic assumption that man was a creature driven by a complex array of passions, some of which could be put—either consciously or unconsciously—to good uses. It was in this context, for example, that "frugality" attained its moral status as the paradigmatic virtue of the profit-seeking trader. The great importance of frugality in commercial life showed that the motives involved in money-making could not be reduced to prodigality or mere avarice. Profits followed from self-restraint, and so "love of gain," guided by the logic of investment, here found a moral dignity.

Hirschman shows that in the history of Western thought this view of economic life emerged from a complex philosophical reassessment of the place of passions that began in Renaissance philosophy. The desire to discriminate among passions developed first from the recognition that "moralizing philosophy and religious precept could no longer be trusted with restraining the destructive passions." Earlier classical and Christian ideas that called for repressing passions or preventing them from finding outlets were replaced by two views. The first, dominant during the seventeenth century, called for "harnessing" the passions. The assumption here—central to mercantalism, as we shall see—was that in certain artificially arranged circumstances passions could be channeled to good purposes. Passions per se remained suspect; they could not be expected to harness themselves. But it was thought that within particular kinds of political and economic frameworks even our darker passions—pride, ambition, avarice, and vanity—might be channeled into conduct that created public glory or public wealth.[43]

According to Hirschman, the "harnessing" solution proved to be unsuccessful for two reasons. The first was political: no explanation could show convincingly how those charged with imposing political and economic structures on other men would harness their own passions to some larger social good. Second, greater refinement in the analysis of passions—a key concern in that general project Hume spoke of as the new "science of man"—raised the possibility of utilizing "one set of comparatively innocuous passions to countervail another." This last point also turned out to be the solution of the political problem.

In the second strategy for controlling the passions, which emerged during the eighteenth century, particular sorts of passions, rather than institutions or enlightened individuals, were assigned the role of taming truly "wild" passions that required control. The most common formulation of this role, according to Hirschman, took the form of opposing the "interests" of men to their "passions." Although initially the term "interest" was confined to discourse about states, "interest" in the eighteenth century centered on economic advantage as its central meaning. "Interest" thereby came to inhabit a middle ground between reason and passion. It spoke of the pursuit of selfish goals to be sure, but it also referred to concrete objectives obtained by means of calculation, discipline, and prudence. "Interest" partook of the better nature of both reason and passion. It was "the passion of self-love upgraded and contained by reason" and "reason given direction and force by that passion." Self-interested men were not virtuous so much as predictable in their actions. They knew where their "true interests lay, and were open to argument and direction in seeking them out."[44]

Hirschman's main thesis is that this wedging of "interest" between the two traditional categories of human motivation, reason and passion, accounted for the high level of optimism about commerce in eighteenth-century thought. It seemed the basis for a new social and economic order in at least two respects. First, the eighteenth-century conception of "interest" was used to fault the mercantilist view that frequent political intervention was needed to guarantee the consonance of public and private interests. The by-product of actions of "interested" men appeared to be a web of interdependent relationships. Domestic trade created more cohesive nations, while foreign trade helped to avoid wars among them. Second, there were also new benefits for society resulting from the characters of free commercial men. The most recurrently emphasized was predictability. The traditional fear of the inconstancy of our passions was overcome by the argument that men in pursuit of their "interests" were single-minded and methodical, rationally one-dimensional. Thus, the insatiability of the desire for economic gain here became acceptable because of its unique quality as a passion, the very constancy of the desire.

Hirschman argues that in the course of explaining how moral judgments spring from non-rational sentiments, Hutcheson was among the first to distinguish between benevolent and selfish passions on the one hand and calm and violent "motions of the will" on the other. In the *System*, he illustrated this last contrast by distinguishing economic activity motivated by a "calm desire for wealth" from that moved by the simple "passion of avarice." The calm desire is said to act with calculation and rationality, and is therefore roughly synonymous with the eighteenth-century notion of "interest." Yet, as we saw in the previous chapter, there was a conceptual difficulty in Hutcheson's argument that rendered it unpersuasive. His definition of avarice—"an excess of frugality and defect of liberality"—not only shows that his two broad types of economic passions were closely interconnected; it also leaves open to question which of those passions would in practice countervail the other. Hume resolved this problem in the *Treatise*, Hirschman observes, by means of a more elaborate account of the passions. He distinguished "betwixt a calm and a weak passion; betwixt a violent and a strong one"; and this allowed Hume to speak of the acquisitive drive, in effect, as a passion with a double identity. It is at the same time Hutcheson's "calm desire" and a passion "strong" enough to triumph over "violent" but also "weak" passions.[45]

Hirschman provides a necessary corrective to the traditional but misleading picture of Hume as a perfunctory analyst of economic psychology. Hume's affirmative claims on behalf of the "love of gain" can now be seen as the culmination of a fundamental reassessment of the place of passions in human conduct. Hume apparently celebrated the growth of commerce specifically because it had activated benign human passions at the expense of malignant ones. His view—arguable, but in no way perfunctory—was that if our predictable "love of gain" could prevail over our turbulent "love of pleasure," we would find ourselves in a world where destructive and dangerous passions are firmly held in check.[46]

This accurate general perspective on Hume begins to become somewhat misleading, however, when Hirschman asks us to see the "interests-versus-passions" thesis as a central unspoken paradigm in eighteenth-century thought. Hirschman concedes that his main argument is an unfamiliar one, and that it was in fact not always at the center of arguments explicitly made by the early-modern defenders of free commerce. He first tries to explain the unfamiliarity of the "interests-versus-passions" thesis by suggesting it must be understood as a "tacit dimension" of eighteenth-century thought. The thesis is built (by Hirschman) on "bits and pieces of evidence" and in the end must be taken as one of the "propositions and opinions shared by a group and so obvious to it that they were never fully or systematically articulated." With regard to Hume this explanation is implausible for at least two reasons. First, the central project of his new "science of man" was what he himself once described as a systematic "adjustment in the boundaries of the passions." The very explicitness of this formulation of intentions seems to belie Hirschman's attempt to save his argument by speaking of it as a "nonarticulated basic theory." But the "interests-versus-passions" thesis is more seriously weakened by a second consideration, a consideration thus far central to this entire essay. Although Hume saw himself to be driving a wedge between two traditional categories of human motivation, he did not frame his original project quite as Hirschman has described it. Inspired by Hutcheson, one of Hume's prime concerns was to show that moral judgments could not be reduced either to self-love or reason. The wedge he then drove between these familiar views was a more sweeping contention that moral choices in reality stem from the workings of certain instinctive sentiments distinct from both self-love and reason. Indeed, the central thrust of the *Treatise* had been to show that all variety of thought and action could be seen as rooted in our feelings and passions.[47]

At first glance, this appears to be a more daring proposition than the "interests-versus-passions" thesis Hirschman brings forward. But it remains to show what Hume saw as the historical novelty of this demonstration and then to explain how it happened to produce the particular economic biases of his thought. Hume's positive reassessment of the place of passions in human affairs provided for a more complicated, but also somewhat less original, argument than the Hirschman thesis allows. I want to show in what follows that Hume's later advocacy of free trade in the *Political Discourses* was rooted philosophically in his original understanding of law and government rather than in claims for the benign character of the love of gain. This approach to Hume is based largely on the premise that we can trace a deep level of philosophical continuity in his view of politics. And this requires that we not only explain why Hume initially saw the *Treatise* as a potential landmark in Western thought, but also account for his later apparent disavowal of that judgment and for the fate of certain arguments about politics that Hume made in book III.

At least two points seem to lie behind Hume's perception of the originality of the *Treatise*. In the first place, his "science of man" purported to be a comprehensive account of human nature free of the declamatory rhetoric and the normative concerns in both rationalist and theologically based moral philosophy. Hume thought it possible to understand man without lingering in traditional speculation about "ultimate principles." His study of man focussed on instincts and passions that are the sources of all thought and action, and the issue of man's "wickedness or goodness" was simply irrelevant to this kind of inquiry. Because he saw justice as a matter of self-interested passions, Hume argued that the appropriate philosophical question to pursue is whether a person acts wisely or foolishly in tying his self-interest to a society that establishes and enforces rules to guide his conduct. "For whether the passion of self-interest be esteemed vicious or virtuous, 'tis all a case; since itself alone restrains it: So that if it be virtuous, men become social by their virtue; if vicious, their vice has the same effect."[48]

This was the kind of clinical speculation that greatly disturbed Scottish contemporaries such as Hutcheson and Thomas Reid. But in Hume's mind his argument was much more than a challenge to the traditional humanist view of justice as the "sovereign" or over-arching virtue which embraced all other virtues. The account of justice in book III of the *Treatise* also had to be understood in light of the second chief objective of Hume's philosophy: fashioning a new philosophical idiom which would describe fully and coherently the ways in which our various passions and intincts move us to think or act as we do. This new language produced difficult and sometimes slightly cryptic passages, and that surely explains why Hume extended and reformulated certain arguments a number of times during the course of the *Treatise*. He also made it clear, however, that his intention was not simply to affirm man as a creature of passions per se. His goal as a philosopher was to discriminate among the passions and show that many of them were, in Hume's words, "vigilant and inventive." In the last analysis, this was the central creative purpose of a fully naturalistic theory of human nature Hume celebrated as his new "science of man" and "total alteration" of philosophy.

Yet Hume's "total alteration" of philosophy, at least in the realm of political thought, turned out to be a great deal less sweeping in its character than he announced. In its exploration of the "artificial" nature of justice, book III opposed the natural law view that there are certain eternal and immutable rules of justice demonstrable from the very nature of things. But in its conclusions, Hume's new naturalistic theory of justice was remarkably similar to that first argued in Grotius's *De Iure Belli ac Pacis* and later taken up by a number of eighteenth-century Western thinkers, including Scottish philosophers such as Francis Hutcheson and Thomas Reid. Hume, of course, never spoke of men in society as creatures with "rights," yet his theory of justice was founded on the familiar natural law proposition that in society men relate to one another as owners of property. Even though his argument used the language of passions, Hume still affirmed one of the central messages of Grotius and his followers. Politics was primarily an economic problem, because rules of justice aim to secure the material interests of family households that make up a community. Whether we say that men in society are attempting to serve particular passions or to secure natural rights, they still have law and government for purely instrumental purposes, not to realize a higher form of self. A law-governed society, Hume argued, afforded them security in obtaining the material goods they need. Justice was not a matter of guaranteeing equity or achieving a substantive equality of goods that might speak for a positive sociability inherent in man. It was a procedural or strictly legal equality of treatment.[49]

All of these were views characteristic of the Grotian natural law tradition we have touched on repeatedly in the previous two chapters. If we see book III against the background of that tradition, it should be evident by now that Hume did not so much shake the authority of Grotius as argue for his authority in a new way. His specific quarrel with the Grotian view of justice focussed on the following question: Why and how do men continue to observe the rules of justice when their interest in doing so is not immediately apparent? Hume had learned from Hutcheson to doubt that reason alone could supply the motive needed here. Out of this doubt came his novel concern with explaining why the rules of an essentially Grotian view of justice could never succeed in restraining men unless they were founded in the non-rational sentiments. Hume's explanation of those foundations, however, involved him at the same time in a re-examination of that categorical distinction between private and public virtue that had allowed for the Grotian simplification of justice. Thus, Hume's account of the "artificial" nature of justice also reformulated in a new language the long-standing Grotian distinction between private and public senses of "what is right." In the process of elaborating his new account, Hume would come to describe man's condition in society using essentially the same distinctions Grotius had made and Francis Hutcheson had repeated after him.

In book III of the *Treatise*, Hume explored at least four separate points in his account of the different demands that moral and political codes make on human nature. First, following Hutcheson, Hume said that motives compelling men to perform good actions were based on inherent feelings we have for each other. He stressed, however, that our desire for justice was more specific. It derived from a concern to acquire and secure external goods in a world of scarcity. While moral acts were good in and of themselves, respect for the rules that govern property represented, as Hume would later observe in the *Enquiry Concerning the Principles of Morals*, a "cautious, jealous virtue."[50] To be just was in large part to respect laws that facilitate the pursuit and enjoyment of private property.

Second, it followed from this view of justice that once rules regarding property were established, men must come to distinguish between those acts toward others which are motivated by their feelings and those acts motivated by a desire for external goods. Rules of justice ask that men treat each other as legal equals in the pursuit and enjoyment of property. But those rules also require us to treat each other with an emotional indifference that plays no part in our ethical relationships. Hence, even the "miser" must be repaid. By nature, men are sociable; but in their public affairs, their separate interests make for a world where the "peace and interest of society" require that "men's possessions should be separated."[51]

Third, the desire for justice was neither "spontaneous" nor instinctive. This was partly what Hume meant in speaking of justice as an "artificial" virtue. "Families, friendships, and humanity are relationships which arise directly from normal human feelings," while laws and government are matters of particular judgments that aim to restrain spontaneous conduct. It was not that the necessity for institutions such as property, contract, and government is unintelligible to untutored men. Hume's point was that because such institutions aim to remedy particular inconveniences in social life, their introduction required some kind of explicit justification beforehand.[52]

Finally, it followed from all of the points above that respecting rules of justice would be a way of acting that became consistent only over the course of time. By nature, man is neither a political nor a law-abiding creature; force and habit bring him to obey the law. Stressing the historical and conventional origins of justice, however, was not tantamount to saying justice was an unnatural principle. Hume emphasized at the end of book III that, although he thought justice an "artificial" virtue, he took "the sense of its morality" to be natural: " 'Tis the combination of men, in a system of conduct, which renders any act of justice beneficial to society. But when once it has that tendency, we *naturally* approve of it. . . ." If we did not do so, Hume concluded, it would have been impossible for "any combination or convention" ever to produce such a sentiment.[53]

iv So far, in considering book III, we have discovered how Hume's naturalistic view of human nature embodied values and preoccupations characteristic of a variety of Grotian natural law theorists before him. One result of adopting this perspective is that we can explain an important part of what Hume had in mind when he described the *Treatise* as a "total alteration" of Western thought. It is clear that Hume saw himself as a self-conscious critic of a key philosophical premise in the existing literature of natural law philosophy. His specific "alteration" here was to show that respect for ethical and legal codes must be explained in terms of the elementary passions and instincts of man's nature, not as obligations dictated by "right reason." But that appears to be the full extent of Hume's innovation. In the realms of moral and political thought, we have found that Hume's "total alteration" was not a repudiation, but a reformulation, of natural law doctrines.

Secondly, and more directly important to the broader concerns of this study, adopting this perspective on the *Treatise* also leads us to the conclusion that the philosophical origins of Hume's economic views were in his essentially Grotian views of law and government, rather than in his general reassessment of the passions. This point is centrally important to any examination of Hume's place in the intellectual history of capitalism. For if we want to establish a philosophical groundwork for Hume's arguments for free trade in the *Political Discourses*, we must be able to trace the persistence of his political views in the *Treatise*. Yet here we at once face a new range of interpretive problems.

The *Treatise* turned out to be Hume's first and last effort to present his "science of man" in a single work. He started writing essays in the same year he finished the manuscript of book III. His original plan was to join with his friend Lord Kames to compose and publish weekly essays patterned after *The Spectator*, a popular periodical once published in London by Joseph Addison (1672–1719) and Richard Steele (1672–1729). When that plan fell through, Hume proceeded on his own, and his intellectual reputation in the eighteenth century would be made on the basis of writings he published over the course of the next two decades. First, two volumes of *Essays Moral and Political*, published in 1741–42 and expanded in 1748. The first and last books of the *Treatise* were rewritten and published separately as *Philosophical Essays Concerning Human Understanding* (later known as the first *Enquiry*) and *An Enquiry concerning the Principles of Morals*. The *Political Discourses* appeared in 1752; this volume Hume later remembered as "the only work of mine, that was successful on the first publication." The first two volumes of his *History of Great Britain* were published in 1754 and 1756. In 1758, while in London to oversee publication of the third volume of his *History*, Hume also published his *Essays and Treatises on Several Subjects*, a very successful work that at that time represented the first edition of his collected philosophical writings.

Hume's turn to essay-writing marks an ambiguous moment in his career. With the exception of the *Enquiries*, the essays themselves have been at the center of a long-standing controversy about how best to approach the works Hume wrote after the

Treatise. On the one hand, there are contemporary historians of thought who have suggested that Hume's concern now shifted to educating his contemporaries in "the realities of modern European politics and the meaning of commercial civilization." While offering an array of new insights, this approach has been hard-pressed to honor with a straightforward explanation Hume's claim that the essays had clear ties to his original philosophical preoccupations.[54] Hume has had a great many readers who find no such ties. Indeed, in the eighteenth and nineteenth centuries, this absence prompted charges that he turned to essay-writing to gain personal fame and wealth rather than to pursue serious arguments. This questioning of Hume's motives has died out, but the tradition of viewing the essays as philosophically threadbare remains well-established. Indeed, apart from the *Enquiries*, the essays are avoided or ignored by most students of Hume's formal philosophy, presumably because they are off the main track of philosophers' interpretive debates about the key contrast between scepticism and naturalism in Hume's thinking.[55]

Hume himself thought that many of his essays were of central importance in clarifying his views, and he made this point quite clear in two belated acknowledgments of the *Treatise* he published at the end of his life. In the Advertisement he wrote for the 1777 edition of his essays, Hume said the following:

> Most of the principles and reasonings contained in this volume were published in a work in three volumes, called *A Treatise of Human Nature*, a work which the author had projected before he left College, and which he wrote and published not long after. But not finding it successful, he was sensible of his error in going to press too early, and he cast the whole anew in the following pieces. . . . Henceforth, the author desires that the following pieces may alone be regarded as containing his philosophical sentiments and principles.

There is no hint here that he saw the turn to essay-writing as an abandonment of his previous concern to show that human thought and action must be explained in terms of the complex workings of our instinctive predispositions. Instead, Hume emphasized that the essays had been written primarily to remedy defects in the presentation of his views. Or as he put it more succinctly in his other belated acknowledgment of the *Treatise* in *My Own Life:* the problem presented by his massive book had "proceeded more from the manner than the matter."[56]

A concern with the language of his argument in fact had troubled Hume deeply from the earliest days of the *Treatise*. In the spring of 1734, after he had temporarily given up work on the book and departed from Edinburgh, he had described the "greatest calamity" of his depressed life in a now well-known letter to Dr. George Cheyene. He seemed to have "no hopes of delivering my opinions with such elegance & neatness as to draw to one the attention of the world, & I wou'd rather live & die in obscurity than produce them maim'd & imperfect." One of the things Hume no doubt came to accept before he resumed work on the *Treatise* in France was that a thoroughgoing commitment to his naturalistic view of man entailed the formulation of a new and difficult language. But during the early 1740s he remained perplexed by yet another issue: the practical significance of his new "science of man." We have noted already his anonymous public efforts to draw attention to the originality of the *Treatise*. Privately, Hume voiced far more tempered assessments of his achievement. In the same letter that told Hutcheson of the "momentous" nature of his discovery that morality "was determined merely by sentiment," he also described the *Treatise* as a philosophical work "more useful by furnishing hints & exciting people's curiosity than as containing any principles that will augment the stock of knowledge that must pass to future ages."[57]

Taken together, Hume's disavowals and reservations concerning the *Treatise* conceded, in effect, that much of his "science of man" had been an overly abstract private game whose originality he had exaggerated. Hume never quite gave up his view of himself as novel thinker, but it is evident that in many of his essays, particularly those on political themes, he later tried to avoid presenting arguments in terms of the deep philosophical puzzles he had first raised in the *Treatise*. For example, "Of the first principles of government" (1741), one of his earliest political essays, omitted book III's elaborate query into the "artificial" nature of justice. But otherwise it reiterated, in a highly condensed argument, the view of justice set out in the *Treatise*. The same was true of the last essay Hume wrote for publication, in 1774, "Of the Origin of government," arguably the best précis of the positive principles of his political philosophy. Here again the chief purpose of law and government was, as Grotius had first argued, maintaining "peace and order" in a society of property-owning men. Again there was the characteristically Humean observation that such a society is rooted in "necessity," "natural inclination," and "habit," not in an abstract obligation of our reason.[58]

As Ernest Mossner has suggested, much of Hume's intellectual career after the *Treatise* can be understood as an attempt to defend and rewrite his first work.[59] The two main targets attacked by the "science of man" had been rationalist and theologically-based views of man that had dominated Western thought prior to the eighteenth century. These too remained objects of Hume's criticism to the end of his life, and the latter would be a recurring source of troubles for him in Scotland. In fact, he used his essays to launch his first open attacks on Christianity and natural religion. And it would be these attacks, together with his unflattering accounts of the "fanaticism" of the Scottish Reformation in the first volume of his *History of England*, that finally provoked the strict Presbyterian wing of the Scottish Kirk to call for a public censuring of his brazen "infidelity." Hume's name also remained anathema in Scottish universities. Glasgow rejected his application to secure the Chair of Logic, which Adam Smith vacated in 1752 to succeed to the Chair of Moral Philosophy. At Edinburgh, James Balfour (1709–95), Professor of Moral Philosophy from 1754 to 1764, concluded each academic session with six lectures directed against the errors of Hume's philosophy.[60]

Many of Hume's essays, then, were fully consistent with the central "principles and reasonings" set out in the *Treatise*. But it would be a vast oversimplification to say Hume's entire career ought to be understood in terms of purposes and problems to be found in his first work. As early as the first volume of his essays, it is clear that Hume had conceived a variety of new applications for his naturalistic view of man. One of the most important of these has been mapped out brilliantly by Duncan Forbes. He has shown that in many of the essays written between 1741 and 1748, and later in the first two volumes of the *History of Great Britain* (1754–56), Hume set himself against what he saw as a "chauvinism and limitation of outlook" in Whig doctrines that dominated Britain in his day. By contrast, he sought to develop a political standpoint that was "not Anglocentric but Europocentric." For example, his *Essays*, carrying forward the theory of political obligation expounded in book III, could accommodate the absolute monarchies of the continent in ways that the then "fashionable" Lockean account of an original contract could not. One of Hume's recurring messages was that it was not the English alone who had achieved liberty and security of the individual under the rule of law. The English prided themselves on their government's being a "matchless constitution," a government of laws, not men. But in Hume's view, the "civilized monarchies" of the continent were also governments of laws. For they, too, now provided that security of property and order in economic affairs which Hume took to be the essence of a law-governed individual liberty.

This breaking down of insular political opinion was one of Hume's central concerns in developing a "modern" view of politics that championed moderation both in domestic and foreign affairs.[61] But equally important to Hume was setting out specific positive prescriptions for policy that followed from this view. It was largely this concern that gave rise to the economic essays in the *Political Discourse*. Hume remarked at the outset of this collection that he would argue principles "which are uncommon, and which may seem too refined and subtle for such vulgar subjects" as commerce, money, interest, and the balance of trade. Hume's tendency to exaggerate the novelty of his thinking remained with him long after the *Treatise* was published. I want to show that the arguments of the discourses were in certain fundamental respects consistent with those of the first work. Yet it should also be noted at the outset that those arguments were not quite so uncommon as Hume suggested. The "vulgar" economic subjects he spoke of had been matters of intense and sophisticated dispute in both England and France since the early decades of the seventeenth century. If we begin by examining Hume's economic essays against the background of that dispute, it will become clear that the *Political Discourses* did not represent a wholly new departure in the discussion of commerce. The main dispute about commerce in early modern thought centered on the state's competence in directing economic affairs. In mid-eighteenth-century Europe, there was nothing unfamiliar in Hume's arguing both that government intervention hampered rather than encouraged economic activity and that a policy of free trade was the best way of achieving economic growth. Fixing the historical beginnings of those arguments, however, is not our main interest here.[62] Instead, we will explore what earlier students of Hume have largely overlooked: the great extent to which his economic writings may be understood in terms of certain moral and political assumptions that were already fully articulated in Hume's *Treatise*. Hence, as we turn to the *Political Discourses*, it will be their connection with those earlier philosophical assumptions that I wish to uncover.

Historians of economic ideas have provided what remains the most familiar account of the dispute the *Political Discourse* addressed: a struggle for influence between two opposite doctrines of policy-making known as mercantilism and classical free trade. Yet the opposition here was not fundamental in every respect.[63] First of all, mercantilist and free trade theorists alike focussed on the same broad question of policy regarding commerce—when and how was the pursuit of individual economic goals consistent with the pursuit of national wealth and strength?—because both schools agreed that the economic interests of the government and its subjects were identical and, more broadly, that the power and prestige of the nation were dependent upon the prosperity of the people. Hume showed that he shared these views early in "Of Commerce," the first of his *Political Discourses*:[64]

> The greatness of a state, and the happiness of its subjects, how independent soever they may be supposed in some respects, are commonly allowed to be inseparable with regard to commerce; and as private men receive greater security, in the possession of their trade and riches, from the power of the public, so the public becomes powerful in proportion to the opulence and extensive commerce of private men.

This is the sort of remark that has prompted comments about the *Political Discourses* as Hume "at his least skeptical."[65] But when viewed in historical context, it must also be seen as an example of Hume's describing what he took to be a conventional axiom of modern economic thinking, a truism for mercantilist and free trade thinkers alike we might say. The basic dispute among advocates of commerce, as Hume knew only too well, was the question of how much and what kinds of intervention were needed to ensure that "the greatness of the state" and "the happiness of its subjects" remained consistent.

The mercantilist reply to this question was based on a broad collection of ideas and practices that again had much in common with views often associated exclusively with the free trade and laissez-faire positions. We know that while English and French mercantilists addressed their recommendations to different kinds of governments, both sought to increase national wealth by eliminating the vestiges of feudal economic views and practices that impeded the growth of trade and industry. One of the main broad purposes of early-modern writers who directed attention to political economy was to emphasize the fact that the glory of a nation, the wealth of its subjects, and the strength of its government were one and the same. The seventeenth-century French mercantilist Antoine de Montchrétien, who perhaps coined the term "*œconomic politique*," argued that work in the household and the market place was the source of public prosperity. He wrote to urge his king to become an economist, to base policy on the assumption that the first aim of government is the good management of the economy. Similar advice was offered to Parliament by a variety of English mercantilist writers that included William Petty, John Locke, Dudley North, and Bernard Mandeville.[66]

These aims, shared by mercantilist and free trade thinkers alike, no less clearly informed Hume's *Political Discourses*. In his economic essays—as the title of the volume that contained them suggests—Hume tried to shape contemporary policy. He sought to convince men with political power of the advantages that would follow from policies based on the assumption that "men and commodities are the real strength of any community." Individuals benefit from the increase in commodities in "so far as they gratify senses and appetites." The public at large also benefits because a "greater stock of labour is, by this means, stored up against any public exigency; that is, a greater number of laborious men are maintained, who may be diverted to the public service, without robbing any one of the necessaries, or even the chief conveniences of life." Throughout the *Political Discourses*, Hume insisted that the primary aim of government was to foster the "manufactures and commodities" that will spur its subjects to labor for more than "the necessaries of life." Hume again agreed with the mercantilists in seeing that the political advantage to the nation here was that rich countries could be governed more peacefully and securely than poor countries. It was assumed by mercantilist and laissez-faire thinkers that riches and strength were one and the same. Therefore wise policy-makers would see, in Hume's words, that trade and industry were "a stock of labour, which, in times of peace and tranquility, is employed for the ease and satisfaction of individuals; but in the exigencies of state, may, in part, be turned to public advantage."[67]

A second important element of continuity between free trade theorists such as Hume and their mercantilist rivals lay in their analysis of psychological foundations of a person's quest for wealth and profit. French mercantilists who stressed the consonance of public and private interest at the same time investigated particular passions involved in economic activity. In highlighting for policy makers the motives that drew subjects out of habit and laziness and spurred innovation and productivity, they remarked on the social utility of ambition and the unintended public good that would spring under certain circumstances from avarice. And as Nannerl Keohane has observed, in their ad hoc reflections on these subjects, French mercantilists offered counsels again remarkably similar to those later given by laissez-faire thinkers.[68] Again, Montchrétien was among the first to see the hope for private gain and profit as a way to draw talented individuals out of the ordinary mass and move them to refine their productive skills. He warned the king not to make the mistake of measuring the well-being of the nation "solely by virtue simply considered." Man is moved by the desire for gain and happiness, and his action in society is primarily concerned with selfish profit. Enlightened policy will not try to make such men into citizens and patriots. It will take men as they are and by skillful policy making insure that ambition and avarice contribute to the public good in spite of themselves.

These same beliefs were repeated by a number of French and English writers in the late seventeenth and early eighteenth centuries. We know from Hume's early letters and essays that he was familiar with much of their work, particularly La Rochefoucauld's *Maxims* (1665), Jean de La Bruyère's *Les Caractères, ou, les moeurs de ce siècle* (1688), and Mandeville's *Fable of the Bees* (1714). As a philosopher concerned with the proper delineation of passions, Hume had his disagreements with particular points made by each of these writers.[69] But when his purpose became to influence policy, he set aside most of those disagreements. His bold injunction in "Of Commerce" urging that "Sovereigns must take mankind as they find them" reiterated one of the conventional axioms of mercantilist thought. For Hume, as for those earlier advocates of economic improvement, the sovereign could not infuse into his subjects "a passion for the public good." The idealistic principles of civic humanist politics were "too disinterested and too difficult to support." We must "govern men by other passions and animate them with a spirit of avarice and industry, art and luxury." In "Of Interest," Hume wrote that the goal of policy, in fact, must be to make sure a subject "has gain so often in his eye, that he acquires, by degrees, a passion for it, and knows no such pleasure as that of seeing the daily increase of his fortune." This goal will be realized only if commerce and industry are allowed freedom to prosper. In Hume's view of human personality, it was "an infallible consequence of all industrious professions to beget frugality, and make the love of gain prevail over the love of pleasure."[70]

So far I have considered the extent to which the *Political Discourses* endorsed values and concepts already put forward by earlier mercantilist writers of whom Hume is usually taken to be a sharp critic. It remains to analyze the ways in which Hume, as a free trade theorist, introduced new elements into the discussions of commerce. Hume's view of the "love of gain," however, merits additional emphasis before we do so, primarily because it can help to trace a clear path to the particular philosophical novelty of the free trade position. In his study of the genesis of capitalism in early modern thought, we have seen already that Albert Hirschman has taken Hume's affirmative claims in behalf of the "love of gain" in "Of Interest" to be the culmination of a thorough reassessment of the place of passions in Western thought; and he has argued that Hume defended free commercial activity primarily because it encouraged a narrow but predictable "love of gain" to prevail over an insatiable and unpredictable "love of pleasure." Hirschman goes on to say at the end of his study that, from the vantage point of early-modern reflections on the passions, it would seem that contemporary critics of capitalism make an unfair accusation when they stress the way it inhibits the development of a full personality. For early-modern intellectual history reveals that capitalism was precisely expected and supposed to repress certain human drives and proclivities and to fashion a less multifaceted, less unpredictable, and more "one-dimensional" human personality.[71] We have just seen, however, that this position was in fact by no means the distinctive feature of arguments for free commerce in early-modern thought. Indeed, the policies of mercantilist and liberal political economists alike were supposed to accomplish the same result in narrowing the drives of individual subjects. Viewed in this historical context, it is evident that Hume's account of the "love of gain" and his related point at the end of his essay on "luxury"—i.e., that magistrates "cannot cure every vice by substituting a virtue in its place" and often "can only cure one vice by another"—only continued to endorse familiar views shared by all early-modern advocates of economic improvement.

What, then, was the new element in the argument for greater freedom of trade? Mercantilist and free trade thinkers agreed that it was unnecessary to sacrifice individual self-interest to the larger demands of the public good. The issue that decisively divided them was the mercantilist contention that political authority was necessary and able to insure that the widespread pursuit of self-interest resulted in the good of the nation as a whole. This division involved differences about the practical effects of particular economic policies. But it also brought to the surface fundamental philosophical disagreements regarding the role of government in human affairs. Hume made major contributions in both areas of this debate that will be reviewed here. It is chiefly in the second area, however, that we will find him employing certain moral and political assumptions he first argued in book III of the *Treatise*. Here, too, we will come to see how his moral philosophy has an important place in the intellectual history of capitalism.

One of the basic premises of mercantilism was that the world economy was a closed universe. In a world with inescapable material limitations, it could not be assumed that the untrammelled pursuit of self-interest automatically benefited the whole society. From this view it followed that while people should be taken as they are, they must also be "guided by wise measures in that direction which will enhance the well-being of the state." A strong and enlightened government alone could insure that individuals pursued their profit wisely.[72] The domestic politics of mercantilism were based on a view of man as a creature whose economic energies were to be stimulated and channeled by wise government policies. But it was also thought that, in a closed economic universe, competition among subjects of different nations required more than skillful manipulation. Untrammelled international trade might undermine national wealth and power. Hence, mercantilists thought it necessary to protect as well as strengthen a state's economy. The specific policies characteristic of mercantilism—the strict regulation of external trade in gold, silver, and essential raw materials, the requirement that all able-bodied men work, the disapproval of imported luxuries, and the general concern to prevent "strangers" from draining the national treasury—all followed from the assumption that "the greatness of the state" and "the happiness of its subjects" were necessarily opposed to those of other nations. The uniform success of these policies, moreover, also required a subject's patriotic and sometimes xenophobic attachment to his nation. Hence, with those dispassionate accounts of the psychological foundations of a subject's quest for wealth and profit came the crown-centered patriotism of French mercantilists and their counterparts' appeals to the glory of Englishmen.[73]

The opposing argument for free commerce made by thinkers such as Hume was in the first place a matter of showing why political supervision of economic activity ought to be eliminated. Hume's technical arguments in the *Political Discourses* against mercantilist policy regarding money, balance of trade, and taxation have been studied in detail by historians of economic thought, and there is no need to repeat their analyses here.[74] In pursuing the connection between Hume's political and economic views, however, two broad points about his arguments should be underlined. First, Hume's advocacy of free commerce stemmed partly from a rejection of the mercantilist view that the state could facilitate economic activity by means of regulating the actions of its subjects. In reality, regulation crippled rather than nurtured commerce. Hume also rejected the mercantilist view that trade among nations was a zero-sum activity. He assumed that the possibilities of world economic growth were open-ended. In such a world, as Hume argued in "Of the Jealousy of Trade," reasonable men must oppose the "narrow and malignant opinion" that all trading nations are rivals and cannot flourish except at one another's expense. The truth is that the "encrease of riches and commerce in any one nation, instead of hurting, commonly promotes the riches and commerce of all its neighbours; and that a state can scarcely carry its trade and industry very far, where all the surrounding states are buried in ignorance, sloth, and barbarism."[75]

Free trade thinkers also differed sharply from the mercantilists in their views about the competence of government in economic affairs. Hence, the first—and still the most well known—novel element that free trade thinkers introduced into their discussion of commerce was the call for the removal of the state's supervision of its subjects economic activity—"*laissez-faire, laissez-passer*," as the Physiocrats aptly put it. This disagreement about the competence of government in economic affairs also revealed that the free trade position carried with it a fundamentally different conception of the proper relationship between a state and its subjects. Throughout the *Political Discourses*, for example, Hume referred to mercantilist policies as the work of a "narrow and malignant politics," of an unfounded "jealous fear" among states.[76] By contrast, he developed a view of politics that saw no virtue in a subject's conscious and exclusive attachment to his state. He endorsed as emphatically as possible a cosmopolitan view of the world that was characteristic of theorists who advocated free trade. "I shall therefore venture to acknowledge," Hume concluded in "Of Jealousy of Trade," "that not only as a man, but as a BRITISH subject, I pray the flourishing commerce of GERMANY, SPAIN, ITALY, and even FRANCE itself." Put another way, Hume's attitude regarding the state's role in the economic activities of its subjects meant that he looked upon men as creatures whose economic energies should know no external nor internal boundaries. There was no danger to the state here, however, because subjects whose lives were given over to the pursuit of profit were also to be seen as inhabitants of a single system of interconnected national economies. In such a world, foreign merchants were not "strangers" who ravaged a state of its limited wealth. Their profits instead indirectly served the state by tempting other local "adventurers to become their rivals." Competition spawns "imitation" that leads domestic industry "to emulate" foreign improvements, and work up "every home commodity to the utmost perfection of which it is susceptible."[77]

Hume prized free commercial societies for enabling their subjects to see themselves as citizens of one world. But he also thought them to be founded on an accurate appraisal of what the state can demand of its subjects, and it was precisely in exploring this issue that he could sound again the central themes of the "science of man" set forth in the *Treatise*. In the *Political Discourses*, Hume was often concerned to criticize mercantilism for what he saw as inconsistencies in its understanding of human nature. In asking the merchant to be a patriot, mercantilists were not only being blind to the economic losses resulting from their xenophobia, they also were asking the merchant to undermine the logic of his vocation. If sovereigns were in fact to "take mankind as they find them," they would have to accept fully the view that "every thing in the world is purchased by labour; and our passions are the only causes of labour." The mercantilist project had been to release such passions, yet at the same time hold them in check by enforcing an artificial concern for national wealth and glory. For Hume, the two ends of this project were philosophically inconsistent; and he saw the attempt to achieve both ends at once as destructive of economic progress.[78]

For all of their claims to realism, then, mercantilists still held to what Hume saw as an outmoded view that human beings were in some manner political entities, creatures whose passions ultimately required checking by a rational conception of the larger needs of their nation or local community. Hume's alternative contention in the *Political Discourses* was that the purpose of government was to serve "private men," particularly to give them security in "the possession of their trade and riches." Because the "power of the public" is primarily dependent on "the opulence and extensive commerce of private men," there is no need for the state to instill subjects with an exclusive *amor patriae*. In free commercial societies, subjects may be relied upon to provide the nation with an abundance of industry and commodities. Hence, the state is left with only two matters of "public exigency." The first is peace—to provide military force adequate for national self-defense. This need, however, clearly promised to become less urgent as the advance of commerce extended the local interconnectedness of economic activity to the world as a whole. That left as the chief task for government the assurance of economic order. The main business of politics, according to Hume, was administration and enforcement of laws that protect private property and define rational economic transactions. Any additional concerns simply run counter to "the natural bent" of human nature.[79]

Again it should be acknowledged that Hume never used the phrase "laissez-faire" in the *Political Discourses*. Still, at the heart of his argument for free trade was a conception of the role of government in economic affairs that we can describe accurately enough with that phrase. His conception of government's role in the economy was also one whose particular language we have heard before, although in connection with a different project. Earlier in this chapter, we found that book III of the *Treatise of Human Nature* had also provided an account of law and government where men were seen to be governed and governable by their passions. There too it had been argued that man instituted governments not to realize a higher form of self or a positive community, but strictly for instrumental reasons. The rules of justice, which Hume had held governments must enforce, were a remedy for a specific "contrariety of passions." By nature, men were generous to family and friends. But this honorable passion was counterbalanced by each man's instinctive desire to know "what he may safely possess." Justice, then, sprang from our "limited generosity," and law and government must do no more than enforce a strictly procedural equality of treatment of self-interested men. Put another way, politics in the *Treatise* was above all an economic problem because rules of justice aim to order relationships among men considered exclusively as owners of property. And the practical goal of law-governed society, Hume had concluded in Book III, was to provide its subjects with security in obtaining the material goods they seek, not to go further and actively to guide that quest. All these ideas, it should be clear by now, would remain key philosophical supports of the liberal economic doctrines in the *Political Discourses*.

They remained, too, philosophical supports of the "Idea of a Perfect Commonwealth," the last essay of the collection published in 1752, also Hume's most systematic account of the form of government he thought appropriate for a commercial society. He began by stressing two features of his proposal different from previous utopian plans. His scheme supposed no "great reformation in the manners of mankind." Nor did it require an unnatural degree of material or moral equality. Instead, Hume's "perfect commonwealth" was a federal structure designed to serve a society of merchants, manufacturers, and financiers, as well as laborers, porters, and clerks in their employment. One hundred county assemblies formed the base of the ideal commercial polity. Every county would be divided into one hundred parishes. Qualified freeholders and urban householders in each parish would elect annually the members of their county assembly. These county representatives then would choose from among themselves both local magistrates and a member of the national senate. Defeated candidates for the senate who received more than one-third of the votes were to form an official opposition in what Hume called a "court of competitors."

Each new law would be debated first in the senate, but the county assemblies held ultimate legislative power. The senate held full executive authority. Senators would choose from among their number a protector, two secretaries of state, councillors of state, religion and learning, trade, laws, war, and admiralty, also six commissioners of the treasury and a first commissioner. This "perfect commonwealth" was to be defended by a militia composed of laborers made available for recruitment during wartime and financed by commercial profits that also would pay for subsidies to allies and for any necessary domestic political support. Finally, there would be a national church, presbyterian in structure, but in practice subordinate to the state since its ministers would be appointed by local county magistrates.[80]

The "perfect commonwealth" met the needs of a commercial society in at least two key respects. Hume stressed—as he had in previous essays in the *Political Discourses*—that the first goal of political authority in such a commonwealth was to provide for the personal security and private property of its subjects, to guarantee that individual liberty under law which allows for the peaceful pursuit of private interest. Secondly, he also emphasized—again repeating an earlier theme—that political authority here would not concern itself with the creation of virtue and community. In fact, in Hume's commonwealth, little more was expected from subjects than electing their representatives. Indeed, when Hume later revised new editions of the *Political Discourses*, he twice moved voting qualifications upwards, hoping to isolate a small electorate of "fortune and education."[81]

Now Hume acknowledged that even in his best of all polities some men would seek political power for its own sake. In creating the "court of competitors," however, Hume imagined an ingenious means of preventing competition for office among such men from interfering with the workings of commercial society. This institution not only eased the frustrations of defeated candidates for public office, it also allowed members of the court of competitors to initiate recall or impeachment proceedings against elected senators and magistrates. This last arrangement, coupled with provisions for annual elections, suggests that in Hume's "perfect commonwealth," those few men who mistakenly saw politics as mankind's highest concern "would have little time for any other aspect of public business than . . . indictments and trials of their fellow politicians."[82]

It should be clear by now that there was a playful irony in the "Idea of a Perfect Commonwealth." Hume's irony here, however, also served to express one of the recurring themes of all his political and economic writings. In commercial societies, "sovereigns must take mankind as they find them." Which in practice meant that the best policy for those with political power is to allow their subjects to pursue private economic concerns in freedom. The ironic variation on this theme that we find in the "Idea of a Perfect Commonwealth" is a form of government in which such a policy promises to be an unintended result of the pursuit of political power.[83]

In coming to terms with Hume as a social theorist, the discovery of a deep level of continuity in his conception of politics is important in at least two respects. It provides first of all additional and convincing evidence to support his claim, published in his "Advertisement" for the 1777 edition of his essays, that even after the *Treatise* failed to gain acclaim he held fast to its central "principles and reasonings." We may thus put to rest once and for all the view that after the *Treatise* Hume somehow abandoned serious philosophical argument by writing essays.

Yet there is something even more important here than the vindication of Hume's personal honor as a philosopher. The recognition of a deep level of philosophical continuity in Hume's vision of politics, taken together with an understanding of the central importance of a laissez-faire politics in Hume's advocacy of free commerce, provides a corrective to the familiar view that Hume was at best a sophisticated publicist of an emerging capitalist civilization. It should be said again that, in their views of government, Hume's arguments for free trade and laissez-faire were not *sui generis*. But neither were they philosophically threadbare nor, in Duncan Forbes's words, instances of Hume "at his least skeptical." In the *Political Discourses*, Hume repeatedly emphasized that the case of free trade turned on a realistic appraisal of the relationship between men and their governments. That appraisal had been ventured systematically first in the *Treatise*. Hume refashioned it, to be sure, in subsequent work, using simpler language to serve intentions less philosophically ambitious. But its essential elements never disappeared from Hume's thought. Given this fact, it should be evident by now that both the analysis and the endorsement of commercial freedom we find in Hume's work were founded on assumptions that in all respects were characteristic of him as a serious philosopher.

v   This chapter has tried to show how the liberal economic doctrines of Hume's *Political Discourses* were braced by philosophical conceptions of law and government that he first set out in the *Treatise of Human Nature*. This approach, of course, has not allowed me to do full justice to certain other interesting and important aspects of Hume's work. And it may be, as Duncan Forbes once observed, that the difficulties involved in tracing the full development of Hume's thought in the end are so plentiful that "a completely satisfactory interpretation would be little short of a miracle."[84] Two broad points which have been established in this chapter, however, should be emphasized in conclusion.

The first regards the precise philosophical context within which Hume viewed and approved the commercialization of Western society. We saw in the previous chapter that in Hutcheson there had been an uncoordinated variety of such contexts: ethical, theological, and political. In Hume, the context became predominantly a political one. Or, to put the point succinctly in his words, his approach to economic policy was "actuated by the prudent views of modern politics."[85]

Yet we have also discovered, secondly, that there were "philosophical" as well as "prudent" views of politics in Hume's economic arguments. Indeed, even when Hume's sense of prudence was misinformed, his philosophical perspective on the issue of relations betewen polity and economy remained much the same. In one of his economic essays, Hume portrayed the development of a system of public borrowing in Britain, which, together with the creation of the Bank of England and the spread of paper money, provided for the rapid growth of British military and economic power during his lifetime, to be "ruinous beyond all controversy." The warnings he sounded in "Of Public Credit," which would become almost shrill in additions he made to the essay in 1764, have been taken by some of Hume's students as evidence of pessimistic and nostalgic Tory attitudes that gradually eclipsed his earlier forward-looking "liberal" views. But, philosophically speaking, we ought not lose sight of the fact that Hume's fears in this much-debated essay were also grounded in essentially the same conceptions of government that informed the other economic essays in his *Political Discourse*. Those were essays, as we have seen, whose messages were hardly pessimistic or nostalgic or alarmist.[86]

Hume faulted public credit partly because it had prevented the development in Britain of a cosmopolitan view of world affairs that had been a key element in his argument for free trade. He thought the growth of public credit was due entirely to his nation's misguided involvement in foreign wars and colonial adventures.[87] Seen in this context, Britain's national debt was thus condemned as the main material support for one of those "narrow destructive maxims of politics"—"imprudent vehemence" in foreign rivalries—that the *Political Discourses* pointedly attacked. Equally important, Hume opposed the practice of mortgaging future government revenues for the sake of present glory for essentially the same reason he opposed other kinds of political intervention in any nation's economic affairs. The practice assumed that a government was competent to direct the economic activity of its subjects to benefit the nation as a whole. "I must confess," Hume wrote, "when I see princes and states fighting and quarrelling, amidst their debts, funds, and public mortgages, it always brings to my mind a match of cudgel-playing fought in a *China* shop." In the case of the national debt, the match required a skill that could never be mastered. It was not simply that servicing the debt required additional taxes that threatened to hurt commerce and industry. It more specifically entailed the ominous prospect of statesmen and ministers facing national economic fluctuations that required "continual alterations in the nature of taxes."[88]

Apart from its continuities with the other *Political Discourses*, "Of Public Credit" is also important in the last instance for showing Hume's awareness that certain pre-existing habits of mind and institutional barriers could prevent full implementation of liberal economic principles. But Hume's fear about the social and economic consequences of the national debt proved to be unfounded. That fear at the same time remained a minor theme in a collection of essays that otherwise represented a vigorous and confident call to reform. An accurate measure of the full extent of the gulf between practice and ideal was a task that Adam Smith would perform in the *Wealth of Nations*.

IV Adam Smith

Law and government . . . seem to propose no other object but this, they secure the individual who has enlarged his property, that he may peaceably enjoy the fruits of it. By law and government all the different arts flourish, and that inequality of fortune to which they give occasion is sufficiently preserved.—LJ (B), p. 210.

To expect, indeed, that the freedom of trade should ever be entirely restored in Great Britain, is as absurd as to expect that an Oceana or Utopia should ever be established in it.—WN, IV.ii.43.

i The previous chapters can be taken as an historical prolegomenon to *The Wealth of Nations*. Like Hutcheson and Hume before him, Adam Smith thought that the case for economic freedom turned on an accurate appraisal of the relationship between men and their governments. I do not mean by this that Smith's argument for a free market economy must be understood only in terms of his political affiliations with Hutcheson and Hume. The *Wealth of Nations* also was held together by a series of theoretical couplets—productive/unproductive labor, production/consumption, town/country, commerce/agriculture, East/West, ancient/modern—designed to provide a multiplicity of perspectives, not all of them positive, on man's pursuit of wealth. And the intellectual drama in Smith's massive treatise was less its analytical rigor and comprehensiveness than the nuance and complexity of its rethinking of certain well-established eighteenth-century arguments for free trade. Reaching toward Smith from the world of his immediate Scottish predecessors will unfold only part of the intellectual context from which the *Wealth of Nations* emerged. Nonetheless, this is intricate terrain that remains largely unexplored.

The main objective of this chapter, as of the preceding two, will be to see economic doctrines primarily against the background of a system of thought intended to provide regulations for all aspects of life. Here my initial concern will be to show how Smith approached issues studied before him by Hutcheson and Hume. My broader purpose, however, will be to trace the main outlines of his moral philosophy. As we have noted already, Smith, unlike Francis Hutcheson, argued his views on ethics, politics, and economics in separate works. Yet his goal was the same as that of his teacher: to coordinate his views in a single, internally coherent system of thought. Smith remarked in the *Wealth of Nations* that moral philosophy was preeminently concerned with investigating and explaining the "connecting principles" in common life.[1] The present chapter will attempt to show what Smith took his own connecting principles to be. The task is more complicated and intriguing than most of his students have been ready to concede.

Smith's relationships with his two great Scottish predecessors often have been misunderstood, and this misunderstanding partly accounts for the neglect of his grand designs as a thinker. Historians of thought who conceive of ethics as an autonomous field of inquiry sometimes combine these figures as a "school" of Scottish philosophers of feeling or sentiment.[2] Usually, this interpretation maintains that Hutcheson raised the question of how morality "is more properly felt than judged of," Hume gave the most powerful and original answer to that question, and Smith then pursued refinements of his answer. This view is correct in emphasizing a general unity of approach among the three Scottish thinkers, which we will need to consider in this chapter. But it also overlooks certain larger correlations in their purposes. Indeed, if we wish to view Smith as a successor to Hutcheson and Hume, it is more accurate historically to regard his work within the framework of their highest ambitions, which were those of moral philosophizing in both the classical humanist and Grotian natural law traditions. That is the approach this chapter will take, and it will produce other conclusions about Smith's views.

One of our main tasks here must be to define the scope of Smith's debts to and criticisms of certain arguments in Hutcheson and Hume. Smith, like Hume, rejected the "moral sense" theory, partly for reasons that owed much to book III of the *Treatise*. But seen from another angle, Smith was much closer to Hutcheson than to Hume. For one thing, he was not above writing an avowedly didactic or pedagogic account of "virtue." The *Theory of Moral Sentiments*, partly based on lectures Smith gave as Professor of Moral Philosophy at Glasgow from 1752 to 1764, often glowed with that "warmth in the cause of virtue" which Hutcheson had looked for in vain in book III. Nor did Smith ever see any reason to dispense with a theory of "rights" in his accounts of law and government. This is not to say, however, that Smith shunned Hume's problems and theories. His account of "sympathy" in the *Theory* and his historicized explanation of rights in the *Lectures* were deeply informed by his reading of Hume. Still, if our main object of inquiry is the broader spirit and purpose of Smith's work, the predominant intellectual influences must be traced back to the Glasgow moral philosophy curriculum that Smith studied at the feet of Francis Hutcheson.

In the end, there are also interesting and important ironies in Smith's relationships to his predecessors. Some have been noted and accounted for in the previous two chapters; new ones will be explored here. First, Hutcheson: he celebrated the humanist ideal of "virtue," yet also provided a view of the relationship between reason and passion that undermined that ideal. Second, Hume: he prided himself on developing the first systematic, nonteleological account of human nature, yet also came to champion a view of human life that forcefully endorsed the free pursuit of "trade and riches." But the greatest (and most significant) irony of all may be in Smith. Through six editions of the *Theory*, he spent much of his intellectual energy struggling to answer a question Hume once had declared unanswerable. What connections can be drawn between the new naturalistic view of man as a creature moved by feelings, sentiments, and passions and the traditional humanist view of man as aspirant to all-encompassing virtue? Smith pursued this question at the same time he argued a view of economic affairs which has suggested to many of his readers that virtue was either reducible to enlightened self-interest or simply irrelevant to human purpose. In the *Wealth of Nations*, warmth in the cause of virtue seemed to dissolve in an account of human nature that set man above the animals primarily because human passions were uniquely channelled by an instinctive willingness "to give this for that."³ On this view of man, Smith built a massive economic treatise that seemed to stand apart from the traditional, interconnected concerns of moral philosophy and thereby herald the subsequent development of a now-autonomous discipline known as economics.

Smith's technical economic arguments have been picked to pieces by generations of scholars. The approach to Smith taken in this study does not require a lengthy repetition of this familiar operation. In fact, there are some positions regarding Smith's views of commerce that I intend to avoid. In the first place, we impoverish Smith if we see his case for economic freedom as argued mainly on the grounds that the fundamental explanation of man's conduct can be found in the rational, persistent pursuit of self-interest. This approach simply tells us to ignore all that Smith had to say about the "levity and inconstancy" of human nature and about the morally ambiguous kinds of social interdependence created by an economy based on specialized labor.⁴

Secondly, while we should welcome scholarly interpretations demonstrating the inadequacies of "laissez-faire" as a translation of all that Smith meant in arguing a "natural system of liberty," I want to resist the current fashion of doing without this famous yet slippery term. Donald Winch is quite right to emphasize that the *Wealth of Nations* was concerned to record the losses as well as the gains that came with the commercialization of society. But Smith did so partly by way of reformulating a key element in established contemporary arguments for free trade—namely, a particular view of government's role in economic affairs that in fairness can be translated "laissez-faire."⁵

Finally, it should be said again that, whatever approach one takes to the book, the *Wealth of Nations* remains complex and puzzling. There were, to be sure, significant similarities between Smith's book and Hume's *Political Discourses*. Both sought to persuade eighteenth-century lawmakers to change current economic policies, and Smith's justifications of those changes reiterated many of Hume's earlier arguments. Eliminating mercantilist regulations, Smith wrote, promised to "enrich both the people and the sovereign."⁶ Moreover, he saw those regulations to be ineffective as well as misinformed. In Smith's view, beneath the privileged orders of monopolies and corporations, mercantilism had given rise to an underground world of successful, petty lawbreakers.[7] At the same time, it had prevented the development of a cosmopolitan spirit that would grow naturally out of "the liberal system of free exportation and free importation."[8] But in another sense, Smith's project was very different from Hume's. The *Political Discourses* were essays; the *Wealth of Nations* a treatise of almost half a million words spread through five books often markedly different in tone and purpose. And while Smith often praised and cited Hume in his famous book, he had planned to inscribe the work to the French economic theorist and reformer François Quesnay.[9] In the end, Smith appeared to see only the Physiocrats as sharing his mode of his discourse.

The question of the historical significance of the *Wealth of Nations* has been the subject of endless dispute, and I will offer my answer to it at the end of this chapter. For the moment, however, I simply want to note that a great many doors lead into Smith's mind. Here I presume to open only some of the previously unnoticed ones.

ii   Adam Smith was born in the spring of 1723, at Kirkcaldy in the Scottish county of Fife, into a prosperous and eminent family. His father, the Comptroller of Customs for Fife, died a few months before his birth. But through his mother, Margaret Douglas, daughter of a wealthy gentry family in the county, young Adam Smith remained assured of a social position and economic security. From 1737 to 1740, he studied moral philosophy under Francis Hutcheson at the University of Glasgow, and the affiliation with Glasgow then begun was to be lifelong. In April 1752, Smith would become the second successor to Hutcheson in the Chair of Moral Philosophy, a post he held until his resignation in February 1764. Later, in November, 1787, after election to the honorary position of University Rector, he wrote in his acceptance letter that no one "can owe greater obligations to a society than I do to the University of Glasgow." It was also in this letter that he offered his famous tribute in memory of "the abilities and virtues of the never to be forgotten Dr. Hutcheson."[10]

Smith's studies with Hutcheson first developed what became an abiding interest in defining virtue and explaining how it arose from inherent sentiments. His long-standing commitment to moral philosophy also stemmed from this early training, in which Hutcheson taught him to see ethics, politics, and trade and finance as issues that should be drawn together into one internally coherent system of thought.

It would of course be foolish to suggest that by 1740, at the age of seventeen, Smith was a thinker whose purposes were fixed. He entered Balliol College, Oxford, on scholarship as a Snell Exhibitioner in the fall of 1740. While a victim of poor health and anti-Scottish prejudice during six years at Balliol, he nonetheless discovered new interests there that went beyond Hutcheson's moral philosophy. Returning to Edinburgh in 1746, he was prepared to deliver lectures on a great variety of topics. For example, during the years 1748–51, Henry Home (later Lord Kames) sponsored Smith in a series of public lectures on rhetoric and belles-lettres. Both of these were topics he later would repeat and develop at Glasgow. The Edinburgh lectures also contained Smith's first efforts in the history of philosophy, a concern that would appear again in both the *Theory* and the *Wealth of Nations*, as well as in posthumously published essays on the history of ancient logic and metaphysics.

The Edinburgh lectures established Smith's intellectual reputation in Scotland, and in January 1751 this remarkable young polymath was appointed to the vacant post of Professor of Logic at Glasgow. When he began his teaching in the following autumn, Smith also was asked to take over part of the moral philosophy courses taught by Thomas Craigie, the first successor to Hutcheson, who was seriously ill. When Craigie died a short time later, he was appointed to succeed him. At the age of twenty-nine, Adam Smith had ascended to the most prestigious academic position in Scotland.

Many commentators have speculated about the importance of Glasgow intellectual life in shaping Smith's views, and for a variety of good reasons. In his acceptance letter of 1787, Smith remarked that his thirteen years as a teacher at Glasgow were "by far the happiest and most honourable period in my life."[11] They were also by far his most productive. At the time of his resignation in February 1764, Smith had published two editions of the *Theory;* pursued in his lectures major innovations in the Grotian tradition of natural rights theorizing he first learned from Hutcheson; fashioned in those same lectures views that would later appear in books III and V of the *Wealth of Nations;* written a long first draft of his now-classic account of the division of labor in book I; and, finally, pursued in some detail arguments defending the view that "Britain should by all means be made a free port" and that "there should be no interruptions of any kind made to foreign trade."[12]

Two preliminary points of caution should be made here, however, to avoid a misleading stress on the importance of the Scottish context of Smith's thinking. First, like Hume, Smith was deeply committed to a cosmopolitan standpoint. And it is clear that this aspect of his character was often frustrated by the provincialism of eighteenth-century Scotland. For example, in February 1759, Smith wrote the following in a letter to a Scottish peer living in London:

> This country is so barren of all sorts of transactions that can interest anybody that lives at a distance from it that little entertainment is to be expected from any correspondence on this side the tweed: Our epistles to our friends at the capital commonly consist more in inquiries than in information. I must therefore put your Lordship in mind of the promise you was so good as to make me of some times letting me hear from you of what passes in the Great World, either at home or abroad.[13]

The audience for which Smith wrote was more in "the Great World," than in Scotland. Like Hume, he sought to influence the conduct of men who had power and place; and after the union of Scottish and English parliaments in 1707, there were few such men left in Scotland. Moreover, although many of the ideas in the *Wealth of Nations* can be traced back to Glasgow, the book itself, most of which Smith wrote in London, was the fruit of ten years of concentrated effort made possible by an English aristocrat's largess. Charles Townshend, most famous in history for proposing the taxes that led to the Boston Tea Party in 1773, also lured Smith away from Glasgow in 1764 to serve as the travelling tutor of his stepson, the Third Duke of Buccleuch. Smith received a yearly salary of £500; and when the Grand Tour was completed in 1766, Townshend gave him a pension for life of £300 a year. With that income, Smith could devote himself entirely to writing his huge book.

Second, and more important in the context of this study, Smith also was a proud and independent thinker, conversant with and perplexed by views Hutcheson and Hume thought exaggerated or mistaken. For example, although Smith never accepted Mandeville's view that a person's desire to accumulate wealth resulted primarily from vanity, he nonetheless was haunted by those moral shortcomings in commercial society Mandeville had delighted in unmasking. And if "private vices" were the necessary foundation of "public benefits" brought by greater wealth, how could Smith avoid affirming that the pursuit of wealth must be seen as the modern alternative to the pursuit of virtue, that traditional humanist ideal he had refashioned and defended in his *Theory of Moral Sentiments?* This was a serious issue, as was Rousseau's different account of the genealogy of commercial morality in the *Discours sur l'inégalité*, a work Smith himself first brought to the attention of Scottish readers in a 1755 letter to the *Edinburgh Review*. There was no natural harmony of selfish interests, Rousseau warned, the morality of commercial society taught men to get the better of one another by deceiving, betraying, and supplanting one another. Profit came at the expense of some other person, which meant that the "progress" of commercial societies must spawn radical inequality and dependency.[14]

We will consider later in this chapter how the views of Mandeville and Rousseau influenced the development of Smith's views on eighteenth-century commercial activity. During those first "happy and honourable" years at Glasgow, however, the question of commerce was not among his primary concerns. Most of his program of thought in fact was prefigured for him in the Glasgow moral philosophy curriculum, and his academic responsibilities initially involved him in more conventional sorts of formal philosophical questions. Indeed, here his main concerns were the same issues we explored in studying Hutcheson's thought in chapter II: virtue, rights, and justice.

During his first seven years at Glasgow, Smith devoted much of his energy to a comprehensive analysis of virtue that he would publish in 1759 as *The Theory of Moral Sentiments*. This book quickly established his reputation among educated Europeans, and its argument can be understood partly in terms of Smith's view of Francis Hutcheson. Like Hume, Smith saw Hutcheson's major achievement was launching the first rigorously philosophical defense of the view that man was moved to make moral judgments by particular "sentiments and feelings," not by reason or self-love. In fact, Smith's praise for Hutcheson on this count was of a kind that modern historians of philosophy have reserved for Hume. "Dr. Hutcheson had the merit of being the first who distinguished with any degree of precision in what respect all moral distinctions may be said to arise from reason, and in what respect they are founded upon immediate sense and feeling," Smith wrote, "and, in my opinion, so unanswerably, that, if any controversy is still kept up about this subject, I can impute it to nothing, but either inattention to what that gentleman has written, or to superstitious attachment to certain forms of expression, a weakness not very uncommon among the learned. . . ."[15]

For all that, Smith also found reasons to fault his former teacher's thinking on these matters. He saw that the original purpose of the "moral sense" argument had been to show that "the principle of approbation" was founded in "a peculiar power of perception, somewhat analogous to the external senses." But Smith also thought Hutcheson had missed the illogical consequence of his particular adaptation of Locke's theory of knowledge. Locke's account of "reflex or consequent" senses had sought to explain the general ideas the mind employs to order experience out of antecedent perceptions in our external senses. For example, "to perceive the harmony of sound, or the beauty of a colour, we must first perceive the sound or the colour." Smith argued, however, that it was a mistake to suppose moral judgments might also spring from faculties of this kind. The mistake here was simply that any moral qualities belonging to the objects of our faculties cannot "without the greatest absurdity, be ascribed to the sense itself." If one does not call "the sense of seeing black or white, the sense of hearing loud or low, or the sense of tasting sweet or bitter," it would be "equally absurd to call moral faculties virtuous or vicious."[16]

Two key points in Smith's account of virtue in the *Theory* followed from his claim that moral qualities belong to the objects of our faculties, not to our faculties themselves. In the first place, his analysis of moral "approbation and disapprobation" would not treat them as "emotions of a particular kind distinct from every other." Smith remarked that if "we attend to what we really feel when upon different occasions we either approve or disapprove, we shall find that our emotion in one case is often totally different from that in another, and that no common features can posisbly be discovered between them." Moral praise prompted by "a tender, delicate, and humane sentiment" was quite different from that prompted by "great, daring, and magnanimous" sentiment. The same was true of moral disapproval: horror in the face of cruelty is hardly the same as contempt for a mean-spirited action.[17]

Second, Smith's recurring stress on the essential heterogeneity of moral sentiments also hinted at the broader purpose his analysis of "sympathy" had been designed to serve. For Smith never took sympathy to be synonymous with instinctive benevolence. The term actually had a number of technical twists, which in some places are difficult to sort out. Still, the original general intention of the analysis remained clear: to explore the workings of sympathy by means of a careful examination of the various kinds of circumstances that gave rise to it. For Smith, the particular situation of another person was the primary object of moral judgments. This fact also suggested to him that sympathy was best understood in the form of distinct judgments passed on passions at work in different actions that we may witness.[18]

In the *Theory*, Smith would come to break the various moral sentiments encompassed by the term "sympathy" into at least four distinct kinds. In the first place, he observed that whenever we observe the conduct of others, we have a strong inclination to "sympathize with the motives of the agent." Yet, second, we also will seek to "enter into the gratitude" of those who benefit from that agent's action. Moral approbation, then, must begin with "an imaginary change of situations," and this change allows us to "enter into" the sentiments of others by allowing ourselves to be influenced by their feelings. This two-part ability to share the feelings of others was what Smith later had in mind when he called sympathy "the correspondent affection of the spectator."[19]

But this affection, he also went on to note, explained only *how* moral judgments were possible in the first place. It remained to show both why such judgments were necessary and why they take the forms they do. Smith saw himself breaking new ground in answering these questions, and he did so partly by fashioning two additional (and more complex) definitions of sympathy. He began by observing that however we happen to "enter into" the sentiments of others, the act of sympathizing ultimately remained a self-conscious, not a Lockean "reflex," action. As spectators, in other words, we inevitably come to compare our own reactions to those of others. For the passions of people whose conduct we evaluate always remain distinct from the sympathetic passions they evoke. In the face of this discrepancy, we are moved to decide whether or not their passions are appropriate to the situation at hand.

It was to explain this process of deciding what the original passions *ought to have been* that Smith fashioned his final two definitions of sympathy. Now he came to consider sympathy, as Knud Haakonssen has observed, to be something mutual among men, something given and received. Smith argued that in observing the conduct of others we express moral approval precisely when we find that another person actually intended his actions to benefit others. But the particular degree of our sympathy will be determined by the extent to which those actions promote the well-being of the individual or of the society at large. So moral judgments were, for Smith, essentially comparisons—comparisons between, on the one hand, particular feelings of people whose conduct we observe, and, on the other, our own sympathetic responses as spectators of their conduct. If these feelings or sentiments are in agreement, we approve of the actions of the person concerned; if not, we disapprove.[20]

There was, however, another important side to Smith's years in Glasgow, and to understand it we will have to consider the equally important influence of David Hume. During those years, Smith's view of Hume was compounded of many factors, not all of which can be traced simply by a careful reading of the *Theory* and the student notes on Smith's lectures on jurisprudence. Their admirable, life-long friendship probably began in the late 1740s, when Smith delivered his public lectures in Edinburgh. But for several years after his appointment to the Glasgow Chair of Moral Philosophy, that friendship largely was kept hidden from public view. The reasons for this are complicated.

In the first place, as we found in the previous chapter, Hume was seen in Scotland in the 1750s as a dangerous philosophical maverick. And Smith surely knew that open association with him would have jeopardized his standing in the university community. Indeed, in November, 1751, after Hume had been suggested as his replacement in the Chair of Logic at Glasgow, Smith wrote privately to one of his colleagues: "I should prefer David Hume to any man for a colleague; but I am afraid the public would not be of my opinion; and the interest of society will oblige us to have some regard to the opinion of the public."[21] Twenty-five years later, Hume's death moved Smith to write one of the most eloquent eulogies in the history of Western letters. The publication of that eulogy in Edinburgh, however, also set off an angry controversy that doubtless reminded Smith of the cost of disregarding the opinion of the Scottish public.[22]

Hume's infamous reputation in Scotland also probably accounts for one of the minor mysteries of the *Theory:* Hume was never mentioned by name in any of its six editions, even though his views were scattered throughout the work. Nonetheless, there can be no doubt that Smith had Hume in mind when he twice mentioned in the *Theory* the views of "an ingenious and agreeable philosopher."[23] The student notes on Smith's lectures in law and government also show that by the 1760s, he was ready to praise Hume by name, although only as the author of the *Political Discourses* and the *History of England*.[24]

I will postpone to the following two sections a more detailed discussion of the ways in which Hume's logic and grammar shaped Smith's thinking. Two broad points, however, can be made here, First, Smith never found in Hume's naturalistic view of man those dangerous implications for "virtue" and "justice" that troubled Hutcheson and many other eighteenth-century Scottish philosophers. In fact, Smith once remarked in the *Theory* that the new issue which had so excited Hume—explaining how moral judgments arose from passions and sentiments—was in the last analysis "a mere matter of philosophical curiosity."[25] The question of defining the substance of virtue remained predominantly important in his mind. Second, and more significant in the context of this study, while bringing many of Hume's ideas and questions into his moral philosophy, Smith at the same time set out to encompass Hume for his own purposes. This matter has to be put somewhat cryptically for the moment: Smith tried to assimilate Hume's naturalism to the normative and didactic discourse of Hutcheson's more traditional moral philosophy. His approach, both in the *Theory* and in the jurisprudence lectures, assumed that an account of human nature founded on the primacy of passions and sentiments could be developed so as to allow a moral philosopher to say specifically what men must actually do to pursue virtue, to enforce justice, and to respect the rights of others. One of my main concerns in the sections that follow will be to show how Smith's economic doctrines emerged precisely from this framework of philosophical concerns.

iii We have explored enough of the *Theory* to see that its analysis of virtue was an intricate exercise. The practical import of that analysis also has been an issue much-argued among scholars concerned with Adam Smith's grand designs as a thinker. According to Joseph Cropsey, Smith saw free and self-interested commerce as a "substitute for virtue," and that for two reasons. In the first place, he admired free commerce because it made freedom in the political sense possible, not because it was freedom. That so-called "system of natural liberty" set out in the *Wealth of Nations* represented, even with its considerable and fully acknowledged shortcomings, the liberation of man's natural instinct of self-preservation. Second, Cropsey argues that the *Theory* can be read as a defense of freedom on moral grounds, calling for an "emancipation from the reign of virtue"—if we allow "virtue" to mean an authoritative, traditional morality resulting from the joint discipline of Church and State.[26] Yet Cropsey's brilliant and influential essay is only one among many very different approaches to the apparent problem of how Smith linked virtue and commerce. A long line of scholars have stressed the important place of "prudence" in his account of virtue, and then have gone on to argue that prudence contributes a particularly virtuous dimension—usually described as "frugality"—to self-interested economic activity.[27] Finally, Albert Hirschman has recently unveiled a new portrait of Smith as a radical simplifier of human drives. Hirschman's outline of Smith's grand designs as a thinker may be expressed as follows: in the *Theory*, Smith first presented an account of human nature that collapsed all sentiments into the drive for an "augmentation of fortune"; in the *Wealth of Nations*, he proceeded with an investigation of the conditions under which man's fundamental desire to improve his material well-being could be best achieved.[28]

It may be better, however, to start by taking Smith at his word. Whatever its connections to the *Wealth of Nations*, the *Theory* was, in the first instance, the work of a thinker deeply concerned to define the source and substance of a virtuous life. "In treating of the principles of morals there are two questions to be considered," Smith observed: "First, wherein does virtue consist? . . . And, secondly, by what power or faculty in the mind is it, that this character, whatever it be, is recommended to us?"[29] We have seen already that Smith followed Hutcheson and Hume in arguing that men are moved to make moral judgments by particular "sentiments and feelings," not by reason or self-love. But it would be misleading to approach the *Theory* primarily as the work of an uncritical disciple of Hutcheson or a later minor follower of Hume. Smith felt he had accounted for major complexities in moral life that had been overlooked by his two great Scottish compatriots. On the one hand, he opposed Hutcheson's view that passions prompting moral judgments ought to be treated as "emotions of a particular kind, distinct from every other." On the other, while he followed Hume's argument in the *Treatise* that a sympathetic perception of another person's passion was the starting point of all moral judgment, he emphasized a related issue that Hume had not considered: the object of sympathy (i.e., another person's passions) must be distinguished from the cause of sympathy—namely, the whole set of circumstances that gave rise to the original passion. This point was to be of the greatest importance in understanding what Smith meant when he stressed that in practice virtue was a matter of "propriety." For it raised yet another consideration that Hume had not explored: in making moral judgments, we find that they spring from a capacity for sympathy that will be constrained by a realization that circumstances are always such that we cannot fully "enter into" the passions and feelings of others. Thus, sympathy is significantly more complex than the analogical inference Hume had posited. Indeed, sympathy for Smith was no longer the starting point of moral judgment, but rather its very essence. For to express sympathy was not only to respond to a particular situation; it was also, and more importantly, to judge what passions ought to be at play given the situation at hand.[30]

Now all of these points would require further detailed investigation if it were clear that Smith had meant the *Theory* to serve as a philosophical groundwork for the *Wealth of Nations*. There are, however, three problems involved in the assumption frequently made that he sought to explain the pursuit of economic self-interest in terms of "virtue," as he understood that term. In the first place, there would be only one instance in the *Wealth of Nations* where Smith seems to stress explicitly the moral benefits of free trade. In book IV, in his "Digression concerning the Corn Trade and Corn Laws," he argued in an attack on legal restrictions on the grain trade, that the operations of the law of supply-and-demand in a free grain market would serve to instill "thrift and good management" in the "inferior ranks of the people." The price mechanism, in other words, was here depicted as an instrument of moral restraint, specifically because it forced individuals into propriety. In a free market, Smith wrote, men will be bound to control their desires so as to consume grain strictly in proportion "to the supply of the season."[31] Yet, as we shall see, this was only one of several arguments Smith used to defend the elimination of corn laws. Elsewhere in the *Wealth of Nations*, his discussion of the "prudence" that a free market demands would stress only its material rewards: "An augmentation of fortune is the means by which the greater part of men propose or wish to better their condition.

It is the means the most vulgar and the most obvious. . . ." No longer one of the cardinal virtues, "prudence" became for Smith a principle that guided improvement in a narrow, and at best morally neutral, economic sense.[32]

A second and greater problem lies in Smith's discussion of self-interest within the *Theory of Moral Sentiments*—a discussion that was fascinatingly complex, but not directly relevant to understanding arguments he would press home in the *Wealth of Nations*. Now there is no reason to dispute whether Smith was concerned with the morality of commercial society: the point seems too obvious; Mandeville left a deep mark on him here. The larger question is to determine whether we can extract a moral justification for the pursuit of wealth, a specific stress that one's pursuit of things necessarily entails a virtuous code of conduct. Sometimes in the *Theory* Smith did say that certain kinds of self-interested activity were either virtuous or morally neutral. As we have seen, he also described sympathy, the mainspring of moral judgment, as a self-conscious, not a reflex, action. Smith urged that in the pursuit of virtue a person should always compare his private reactions to those of others. Total sympathy was an unnatural sentiment, then, largely because it reflected a failure to inject one's own self-interest in one's response to the conduct of others. But of course this is not the economic "self-love" that Smith thought governed conduct in the market place.[33]

More often, and more clearly, Smith tried in the *Theory* to come to terms with his awareness that when wealth tempts men to ignore the cause of virtue, they usually will do so. He always made it clear that he could fashion no unambiguous moral defense of that particular aspect of self-interest that drives men to pursue riches: vanity. Echoing Mandeville, Smith observed that the primary motive in the pursuit of wealth was not a desire to live better so much as a desire to live better than our fellow man. "It is chiefly from this regard to the sentiments of mankind," Smith insisted, "that we pursue riches," and thus "it is the vanity not the ease, or the pleasure, which interests us." The same vanity, however, was also the source of an instinctive admiration for the rich that Smith thought was felt by most men, and here its effects were morally pernicious.

For while vanity may be the crucial motive of economic activity, it also caused many men to mistake wealth and greatness for virtue and wisdom. This state of affairs, Smith concluded, was "the great and most universal cause of the corruption of our moral sentiments."[34]

Perhaps what can be said about the direct philosophical connections between the *Theory* and the *Wealth of Nations* has been said best by Thomas Horne: Smith simply was "unwilling to rescue virtue and commercial society by making unrealistic claims on their behalf."[35] What he intended to explore in the *Theory* was a middle ground between proposals that he thought over-estimated the immorality of self-interest and those that were blind to the usefulness of some kinds of self-interest. Otherwise, this book, for reasons we will consider in a moment, dealt with concerns that Smith wished to treat separately from those he took up in the *Wealth of Nations*.

Finally, it is of the greatest importance in approaching Smith's texts that we respect his own account of his intellectual intentions. In the first place, he emphasized at the conclusion of the first edition of the *Theory* that his understanding of law and government, not his account of the dynamics of virtue, formed the precise intellectual context within which he conceived his economic doctrines:

> I shall in another discourse endeavour to give an account of the general principles of law and government, and of the different revolutions they have undergone in the different ages and periods of society, not only in what concerns justice, but in what concerns police, revenue, and arms, and whatever else is the object of law. I shall not, therefore, at present enter into any further detail concerning the history of jurisprudence.[36]

This promise said a great deal about Smith's grand designs as a thinker. It said that in his mind publication of the *Wealth of Nations* would make good only part of this large promise—a point he later explicitly acknowledged in the last edition of the *Theory*.[37] It also said, more importantly, that Smith's discussions of "police, revenue, and arms" in the *Wealth of Nations* presupposed a particular understanding of the "general principles of law and government" that had not been fully explained in that book. To be sure, Smith emphasized that his economic theory was an object of law, or, as he described it at the outset of book IV, "a branch of the science of a statesman or legislator."[38] But two large questions were left unanswered in the *Wealth of Nations*. Why were economic affairs best approached in legal and political terms, rather than moral ones? And how did the specific policies recommended in that book follow from a proper understanding of the history and purpose of law and government?

These, in the end, are the questions crucial to understanding the framework of philosophical concerns from which Smith's famous treatise emerged. Yet they are at the same time questions that Smith never succeeded in answering to his own satisfaction. Shortly before his death on July 17, 1790, and at his own request, sixteen folio volumes of his unfinished manuscripts were burned; and among them probably was a draft of his promised account of the history and principles of law and government.[39] Smith had done a vast amount of work on these issues, however, in the lectures on jurisprudence that were a major part of his responsibilities as Professor of Moral Philosophy at Glasgow. We have recovered detailed records of that work in the form of two sets of students' notes. Since the analysis that follows will make considerable use of these notes, I should register here the usual caveat of other recent scholars who have studied them. They are of course invaluable as records of Smith's legal and political philosophy. But they are also in the end students' notes, so there are some risks involved in basing one's reading of Smith on them. The accounts are often sketchy and sometimes frustrating in their much too abbreviated renderings of Smith's views. But there are also ways of testing the value of these notes. Winch and Haakonssen, for example, have explored explicit and implicit cross-referencing between the lectures and the *Theory* and the *Wealth of Nations*.[40] In the section that follows here, I will try to locate Smith's views on law and government in that same tradition of Grotian natural law jurisprudence that, in the previous chapters, served to clarify the theories of Hutcheson and Hume. In the final section, I want to show how this approach sheds new light on the *Wealth of Nations*, both as part of Smith's larger enterprise as a moral philosopher, and as a fundamentally important document in the intellectual history of capitalism.

iv Seen from one angle, there is not much to distinguish the message of Smith's *Lectures on Jurisprudence* from what we previously found in Hutcheson's natural rights theory. Every man is possessed of "perfect" and "imperfect" rights, Smith declared. Perfect rights are "those which we have a title to demand and if refused to compel another to perform"; imperfect rights correspond to "those duties which ought to be performed to us by others but which we have no title to compel them to perform." The most important of man's perfect rights is *dominium:* "the full right to property," which gives him "the sole claim to a subject, exclusive of all others, but can use it himself as he thinks fit, and if he pleases abuse or destroy it." Finally, and most importantly: the "first and chief design" of governments that respect the "rights" of their subjects will be to enforce "commutative justice," since governments should act only when a subject is "deprived of what he had a right to and could justly demand of others."[41]

All this sounds entirely like Hutcheson. And in drawing distinctions in Smith's approach to jurisprudence, it is essential never to lose sight of the fact that the Glasgow *Lectures* presupposed precisely the same Grotian scheme of philosophical terms and values Smith had learned as a student of the "never to be forgotten Dr. Hutcheson." Again we encounter the central importance of a categorical distinction between "perfect" and "imperfect" rights. And again this distinction between things political and moral provided the philosophical foundation for a theory of law and government that described the public concerns of men primarily as negative duties to respect what belongs to others. The basis of order in any community, Smith observed, was our desire to defend ourselves and our things against the possible "encroachment" of our neighbors. Hence, law and government ought to "propose no other object but this, they secure the individual who has enlarged his property, that he may peaceably enjoy the fruits of it."[42]

The fate of these familiar views in Smith's *Lectures*, however, is a very complicated matter. The study of jurisprudence, in Smith's treatment, required the pursuit of two broad lines of inquiry. Each had distinctive concerns that can easily become confused because of Smith's procedure and his students' sometimes sketchy accounts of his lectures. The first was an account of "the general principles of law and government," where Smith saw his jurisprudence as an argument made to explain certain abstract principles of justice and rights that "ought to be the foundation of the laws of all nations." The other was a documented story of the "different revolutions" those same principles had undergone in the "different periods" of history, where Smith both narrated and evaluated a detailed history of efforts actually made and—more often—not made to instate them.[43] The confusion lies partly in the fact that in Smith's account the two lines of inquiry often ran so closely parallel that they seem indistinguishable. Keeping them distinct, however, is critical to understanding Smith's purposes in the *Lectures*.

Here a contrast with Hutcheson can be a useful initial guide to his thinking. Their main difference lay in the question of how men come to have proper ideas of law and government. For Hutcheson, as we saw in chapter II, the question was usually answered as for all Grotian natural law and natural rights thinkers before him: by considering what kinds of arguments reasonable people might have made in the process of establishing their government. Smith could only follow him part of the way here. At the outset of the 1762–63 *Lectures*, he remarked, "The first thing to be considered in treating of rights is the original or foundation from whence they arise." Among our "perfect" rights were those pertaining to personal integrity and reputation. These were sometimes also called "natural" rights, because they would be recognized at once by reasonable men as those "competent to man merely as a man." It should be noted that Smith, like Hutcheson before him, placed the right to "commerce" in this group.

Property, however, was a right whose origin was not "altogether plain." It was an "acquired" perfect right, and thus one that Smith felt needed a more elaborate explanation than Hutcheson and his predecessors in the natural law tradition had provided. He observed, first of all, that in their discussions of property it "does not . . . appear evident that . . . any thing which may suit another as well or perhaps better than it does me, should belong to me exclusively of all others barely because I have got it into my power." Reason, in other words, simply gave us equally strong justifications for the two contrasting natural law views of property as that which is rightfully one's own (*ius in re*) and that which is rightfully one's due (*ius ad rem*).[44] It must be emphasized, however, that Smith's solution to this problem, which he raised at the outset of the 1762–63 *Lectures*, did not require a new definition of property. Like Hume before him, while doubting the strength of reason as guide and motive in human conduct, Smith never doubted that property must be understood, as Grotius had first argued, as a person's exclusive title to enjoy and use the things he happens to possess. And again like Hume's, his concern thus was more narrowly a matter of explaining what in human nature or experience prompted us to accept that view of property.

Smith's initial approach to this issue was to re-explain what natural law thinkers had in mind when they talked of the five ways by which men come to possess their goods—namely, by occupation, by accession, by prescription, by succession, and by voluntary transfer. At the outset, the logic of his argument followed Hume's very closely. For Smith, as for Hume, no theory of property could have content if it were not supplemented by an explanation of how instinctive human sentiments participated in the creation of a political community where the mere possession of something was taken to give the possessor a right to the thing exclusive of everyone else. How was it, Smith asked, "That a man by pulling an apple should be imagined to have a right to that apple and a power of excluding all others from it—and that an injury should be conceived to be done when such a subject is taken from the possessor?" Reason could never explain such a right. But an account of the workings of human sentiments could show how this virtually automatic association was made. Property acquired by occupation, Smith declared, must be an exclusive right simply because there was a "sympathy or concurrence" between the spectator and the actual possessor. Put another way, an impartial spectator entered into the possessor's thoughts as he occupied part of the world and always concurred in his opinion that "he may form a reasonable expectation of using the fruit or whatever it is in what manner he pleases."⁴⁵

This essentially Humean argument, however, was only a preliminary "foundation," Smith emphasized. Three additional issues required attention. The first was a technical question of "at what time property is conceived to begin by occupation—whether it be when we have got sight of the subject, or when we have got it into our actual possession." Again, neither reason nor a theory of sentiments can help us here. It was enough to say, however, that both approaches agree that in most cases property commences when "we have actually got possession of it." And the final crucial issues, at any rate, lay elsewhere: in linking property with occupation, a theorist must be able to show "how long and in what circumstances" property actually continues and "at what time is it supposed to end."⁴⁶

These last two issues were crucial for Smith partly because they required unveiling what he took to be a new scene of thought within the natural law and natural rights tradition. Once again, neither an appeal to universal reason nor an abstract theory of sentiments could respond to the problems raised here. What Smith had in mind instead was an inductive historical investigation which could explain the fact that, while property was everywhere seen as an exclusive right, those goods men have allowed to be property varied considerably "according to the state or age society is in at that time." For Smith, there were four distinct stages through which mankind passed—"1st, the Age of Hunters; 2dly, the Age of Shepherds; 3dly, the Age of Agriculture; and 4thly, the Age of Commerce." And much of the material he incorporated into his Glasgow *Lectures* would be organized to show precisely how and why the character of property—as well as the nature of governments established to protect property—had evolved through these stages.⁴⁷

The analysis that followed from plotting the history of mankind in four stages has provoked an intense and protracted controversy in modern studies of Smith's work. Some scholars have treated this scheme of stages as a contribution to a materialist vision of history. Smith here is seen as a theorist of social change primarily concerned to trace the emergence of his own commercial age in terms of stages characterized by a particular mode of subsistence. There can be no question that this interpretation, chiefly associated with Ronald Meek, captures much of the historical dimension of Smith's thinking. It distinguishes his approach to law and government from the more deductively organized speculations of Hutcheson and Hume. It also has the perhaps more important merit of linking the *Lectures* to the *Wealth of Nations*. Meek himself has conceded, however, that the "theory of four stages" would have a relatively small role to play in Smith's economic treatise.[48] Even if we restrict our focus to the *Lectures*, there also is room for disagreement about Smith's purpose in using the "stages" sequence. In the first place, the habit of seeing Smith as a materialist historian has obscured what we have just established in a detailed examination of the questions that gave rise to the four stages scheme: namely, that the language, presuppositions, and main arguments Smith employed at the outset of the *Lectures* make them a recognizable contribution to the Grotian tradition of natural law and natural rights speculation that Hutcheson had taught him at Glasgow.[49]

Seen from this angle, we also might say that Smith's historical approach to property served a didactic purpose. It is clear that one of his overriding concerns in using the four stages scheme was to teach his Glasgow students when and why "sentiments" regarding property had been subject to change. For example, in referring to "succession" or inheritance as an occasion of property, Smith wrote: "There is no point more difficult to account for than the right we conceive men to have to dispose of their goods after their death. For at what time is it that this right takes place? Just at the very time that the person ceases [to have] the power of disposing them. . . ." Here again, reason is an unreliable guide, because it cannot explain why we should prefer "the person made heir in the testament to the heir at law if he has one." Smith noted that this question had proved so vexing to the great rationalist natural law thinker Pufendorf that he abandoned reason and "called into his assistance the immortality of the soul." However, if we view human sentiments in historical terms, we need not go this far. An instinctive regard "we all naturally have to the will of a dying person" will be sufficient to explain testamentary succession if we see the situation as follows: "Piety to the dead," Smith declared, "is a pitch of humanity, a refinement on it, which we are not to expect from a people who have not made considerable advances in civilized manners." Thus, we discover that "it is pretty late" before the right of testamentary succession was introduced in most countries.[50]

Surely the point of this entire line of inquiry is missed if we represent the arguments as parts of a materialist view of history. Smith's main concern was not to grasp a story whose underlying factors are predominantly economic. It was, instead, to furnish his students with an answer to the philosophical question of how human sentiments come to shape our understanding of the purpose of law and government. Seen in this light, it also seems clear that the four stages scheme served for Smith to mediate between the different proposals of Hutcheson and Hume regarding property and justice that we explored in the previous two chapters. On the one hand, Hutcheson's conventional natural law approach to government had its philosophical foundation in a doctrine that defended and ordered the "private rights" of rational men; so did Smith's. On the other, Hume had wanted to build a new theory of human nature whereby the primary role of instincts and sentiments in all human endeavours would be made clear; that too was one of Smith's aims. The "four stages" allowed Smith to reconcile these apparently different purposes by viewing rights as products of sentiments that were subject to change and development. Thus, while, like Hume, Smith retained an essentially Grotian view of justice and property in his stress on the primacy of "sentiments" in human conduct, he saw no reason to follow Hume in eliminating all reference to "rights." Instead, Smith saw rights as the objects of a "natural progress" in human sentiments. And hence, the history of the four stages in the *Lectures* turned out to be both a history of a greater refinement and complexity in sentiments—i.e., a transition from barbarous to increasingly "civilized" societies— and a history of changing modes of subsistence.[51]

These points can be illustrated briefly by showing how the "four stages" served to buttress Smith's Grotian definitions of property and justice. In the 1762–63 *Lectures*, which Smith began with an account of rights, it is evident that his discussion at the outset presupposed Grotius's definition of property as an exclusive right and then used the "four stages" primarily as a means of demonstrating how changes in the economic organization of a society gradually alters or, in the word Smith used repeatedly, "extends" our notion of what we may be entitled to designate exclusively our own. In a society of hunters, where "the only thing amongst them which deserved the appelation of a business would be the chase," property began and ended with actual "possession." The prizes of past and present chases would be each hunter's "immediate property." In a society of shepherds, where men come to tame wild animals and bring them up "about themselves" in flocks and herds, property must be "extended" a great deal further. The specific extension made was to view animals as "the property of their master as long as they could be distinguished as his." Although a considerable amount of time may have passed since those animals actually had "come into his power," they nonetheless were now to be considered as fully his property. The single most important "extension" of property, however, accompanied the introduction of agriculture, for here property came gradually to include the land itself, now divided into "particular properties." Smith also noted, however, that a person in a society of hunters or shepherds would not easily conceive that "a subject of such extent as land is, should belong to an object so little as a single man." So even after the invention of agriculture, a great deal of time passed before land was divided into individual plots. One of Smith's later and most important purposes in the *Lectures* would be to explain why and how the character of this particular species of property had been limited, and still remained so, in the different nations of Europe.[52]

Smith's argument worked essentially the same way in the 1766 lecture notes, where he began by discussing government rather than property. Here he presupposed a Grotian view that government had strictly negative responsibilities. It was concerned, in Smith's words, only to preserve "the public quiet and safety of the individuals" in its realm—and here the four stages scheme helped him to describe precisely why and how these responsibilities were "extended" over time. Not unlike the inhabitants of later more civilized societies, tribes of hunters "who live in the same village and speak the same language" agreed to keep together primarily for the sake of "mutual safety." Because there was almost no property among hunters, the one action that disturbed the "public quiet" here was depriving any of them of his game. Yet since the whole society must have taken interest in this offense when it occurred, there was "no regular government" among hunters, and they thus lived in the closest accord with the laws of nature.[53] In a society of shepherds, however, "mutual safety" would become a new and pressing matter of securing wealth and defending the rich from the poor. For with flocks and herds came an "inequality of fortune" among men, and property of this sort in turn made regular government inescapable:

> When once it has been agreed that a cow or a sheep shall belong to a certain person not only when actually in his possession but wherever it may have strayed, it is absolutely necessary that the hand of government should be continually held up and the community assert their power to preserve the property of individuals.

Smith's stress on the key role of economic inequality in giving rise to a regular system of government was partly an expression of Rousseau's influence on his thinking. In fact, it was in the context of discussing this question that Smith offered a definition of the state that sounds exactly like a précis of Rousseau's position in the *Discours sur l'inégalité:*

> Laws and government may be considered . . . in every case as a combination of the rich to oppress the poor, and preserve to themselves the inequality of the goods which would otherwise be soon destroyed by the attacks of the poor, who if not hindered by the government would soon reduce the others to an equality with themselves by open violence.[54]

But we should be careful not to exaggerate Rousseau's influence here. He was never mentioned by name in the Glasgow *Lectures,* and Smith's brief meditation on the prospects of economic class warfare was by no means his only comment on the issue of inequality. Prior to the discussion we have considered here, Smith had made it clear that he, unlike Rousseau, wanted to record the benefits as well as the dangers of economic inequality. From one perspective, a man who in the eighteenth century consumed an annual income of £10,000 might be taken as "the most destructive member of society we can possibly conceive." For he seems to have spent entirely on himself what might have supported 1,000 ordinary men and their families. But from another, this account is entirely misleading. For the value of particular goods wealthy men happened to consume was trivial in significance when compared to that increase in "work and manufacturing" their demands for those goods must occasion. Thus, even if it had not been their intention, rich men act in ways that turn out to be of great advantage to society. Any attempt to limit their fortunes, while it might "render all on an equality," would also render the nation very poor and therefore unable to provide for or defend itself in times of emergency.[55]

In addition to stressing practical benefits, Smith also emphasized that the problems posed for government by inequalities of property would change as the economic structure of a society changed. In the age of shepherds, the negative responsibilities of government could be defined very simply: punish theft and robbery with the utmost rigor. In the later ages of agriculture and commerce, however, those responsibilities grew more complex. For while the main purpose of governments remained the protection of their subjects' exclusive rights to use and enjoy their personal property, the new general "opulence" that accompanied agricultural and commercial improvement added at least two new historical variables. First, beginning with the age of agriculture, governments witness a steady increase in the number of their subjects who can be considered owners of property. Laws must be multiplied in proportion to protect their rights and their various economic activities. Second, and perhaps more significant, governments now must also assure that any existing inequalities in property rights do not jeopardize continued economic improvement.[56]

It will be necessary, of course, to return to the question of what kinds of inequality Smith had in mind here. For the moment, however, I want to draw attention to a slightly different issue. None of this detailed counter-argument stressing a traditional natural law, rather than a novel materialist, side of Smith's "four stages" sequence perhaps would have been necessary if previous students of the *Lectures* had accepted his contention that his jurisprudence was, in the first instance, an account of the normative principles of justice and rights that "ought to be the foundation of the laws of all nations." There may be, however, a somewhat misleading interpretive illusion in this approach. I noted earlier that jurisprudence for Smith in fact involved two lines of inquiry that often ran very closely parallel. What we have explored in the *Lectures* thus far has isolated the first line at the expense of the second. Moreover, as we have just begun to see, Smith was not interested in history simply because it allowed him to link the old natural law language of rights with the new Humean stress on the primacy of sentiments. In fact, one of his arguments on this last point was slightly bizarre; the rest were often sketchy. The bizarre argument was in the 1766 notes, where Smith explained the right of testamentary succession in terms of our ability to enter into a person's dead body and "conceive what our living souls would feel if they were joined with his body, and how much we would be distressed to see our last injunctions not performed."[57] The sketchiness may be due, of course, to the inattentiveness of his students. But their notes also show us, more importantly, that Smith usually hurried on to a more practical question that, in the last analysis, seems to have concerned him most of all in the *Lectures:* whatever the method of his argument, how can a thinker propound natural law principles of rights and justice in the face of the obvious fact that past and present history deviated from, or sometimes simply violated, the norms he prescribed?

It was in raising and answering this question that Smith made his most important new contribution to traditional natural law jurisprudence. Here again the "stages" scheme had an important role to play in clarifying his argument. Yet that role cannot be appreciated if we treat Smith as some sort of economic determinist. For the historical study of jurisprudence now became a program of legal criticism and reform, an explicit plea, as Smith put it, that certain outdated "remains of the old jurisprudence should be removed."[58]

Smith answered his question by taking two slightly different approaches. The first was to present the "different revolutions" that legal and political principles had undergone through the different periods of history as a story of fitful, often unintended, but nonetheless steady progress toward the realization of more rational systems of law and government. Seen in this perspective, Smith's "natural jurisprudence" can be read partly as an historical sociology of law.[59] He had declared in the *Theory* that "Every system of positive law may be regarded as a more or less imperfect attempt towards a system of natural jurisprudence, or towards an enumeration of the particular rules of justice."[60] In the *Lectures*, natural law and natural rights theory in practice would be used as a guide for understanding past and present history. In Smith's view, all abandoned or outdated legal practices or political forms could be understood in terms of normative ideals they temporarily or imperfectly realized.

In this heuristic jurisprudence, the four stages again served as a didactic device whereby Smith located and illustrated for his students the precise historical origins of particular laws and forms of government. Once again, Smith's main concerns were property and the rules of justice. Legal principles such as primogeniture and entail, he observed, emerged during that period of violence and uncertainty which followed upon the defeat of Rome, an agricultural and commercial society, by the invading Northern tribes. With the fall of the Roman empire, the "public quiet" suddenly had come to depend exclusively on the power of a local lord, and nothing could have been worse for society in "those early times" than a division of landed estates. The strength of feudal lords, therefore, was necessarily based on grossly unequal landholding. Moreover, the extreme circumstances of the times dictated a specific legal "extension" in the notion of landed property held by right of "succession": feudal estates became indivisible, with inheritance based on a quality that was "altogether indisputable." For if it "were to be given to wisdom and valour, there might be great disputes, but among brothers there can be no contest who is the oldest." Smith would employ a similar historical analysis in accounting for the practice of entail, "the greatest of all extensions of property" which gives legal power to control one's property "to the end of the world." When viewed historically, an entail could be seen as a further attempt to secure feudal estates. Once there was a "notion of the will of the deceased directing his succession for one step," it would be "no difficult matter to suppose that it should extend farther."[61]

The concern for historical origins was also one of Smith's main interests in discussing changing forms of governments. Democracies, feudal societies, republics, and monarchies, all could be understood as variations on one theme: the need to prevent violence and disorder in societies where property was the primary value and inequality of wealth threatened to disrupt the "public quiet." The four stages, in this context, pinpointed moments when strategies designed to meet this need had to change in the face of military, commercial, and technological improvements. Certain forms of government were simply impractical prior to such improvements. The civic-mindedness of ancient Athens, for example, was the product of a unique confluence of historical factors. Inhabitants of the Greek province of Attica had created a prosperous commercial society in a time when men in most other nations remained hunters and shepherds. This of course made them an especial temptation to their more primitive neighbors. To secure their safety, the Greeks found it more expedient to fortify the city of Athens than the frontiers of their entire province. Yet once they agreed to live in the city, the old chieftains of their tribal clans quickly lost authority and the government of Attica turned republican.[62]

Smith told essentially the same kind of story in tracing the origins of modern forms of government, although here the number of factors at play increased and their interrelationship was somewhat more complex. In feudal society, national government was largely a stalemate of three powerful interests: the king, the feudal lords, and the Church. Feudal noblemen fought each other and the king; the clergy, united in their special spiritual mission, and often wealthier than the feudal lords, were more successful in resisting the king. This stalemate was broken only gradually as the king discovered an unexpected ally: the burghers in the towns. He granted them trading privileges and later extended those privileges to include self-taxation and thereby self-government. These policies, which established "order and good government" in the towns, assured that their inhabitants would also become independent of the king's two main rivals. They also greatly facilitated the townspeople's expanded pursuit of wealth and property. For it was under the king's protection that they first began to pursue foreign commerce and new sources of raw materials. Commerce and manufacturing, in turn, provided an expanding market for the produce of the country, and it was this last development that sealed the doom of the feudal nobility. Now wealth they had previously spent to maintain their dependents was spent on new goods manufactured in the towns, and the nobility thereby lost all their retainers except a "few menial servants" who gave them no influence.[63]

From this point, Smith's historical narrative proceeded along several paths as he sought to describe the subsequent course of events in the developing monarchies and principalities of Europe. But his general outline of the political history of Western Europe remained generally the same in each case he explored. First, "regular government" came to be established in the countryside as well as in the cities. Second, and more important, "regular government" did not dictate a particular form of government, but rather a situation where nobody had sufficient power to disturb a government's operations either in the countryside or in the city. It meant, in sum, a variety of governments grown powerful enough to secure that "public quiet" without which a society's economic activity could not continue to prosper.[64]

The second answer Smith gave to the question of how the abstract ideals of his natural law jurisprudence were to be defended in the face of history provided the context for his first open and sustained attacks on the economic laws and policies of his day. It should be recalled here that in his investigations of the history of law and government Smith never wanted his students to lose sight of the fact that his natural law jurisprudence was more than a heuristic inquiry into the origins of law and government. One of the most important purposes of his lectures was to show where and when positive laws fall unacceptably short of his ideals. Following him in this work will take us directly to his earliest pronouncements on economic policy, and it is work in which the "four stages" had a subtle but important part to play.

Smith was emphatic in his denunciations of those particular "remains of the old jurisprudence" that "must be removed," and many of his arguments here later would be carried over almost verbatim into the *Wealth of Nations*. But it is important to note at the outset that his main concern was with laws governing property and commercial activity. For beyond tracing the social and historical origins of different forms of governments, he thought little more could be said with any great assurance about the ideal forms of a polity. "No government is quite perfect," Smith declared, "but it is better to submit to some inconveniences than make attempts against it." Duncan Forbes has shown that, like Hume, Smith too was determined to avoid what he took to be the overly parochial perspectives of English political thinkers. And there is an abundance of evidence in the *Lectures* showing how deeply his thought was influenced by the political essays Hume published in the 1740s. For Smith, as for Hume, a government that respected the "liberty" of its subjects provided each of them with a sense of security under the rule of law. And he too thought this could be done by an enlightened absolute monarchy as well as by a parliamentary one.[65]

Reforming the "old jurisprudence," then, was entirely a matter of specifying which laws governing the property and the economic activities of subjects needed to be eliminated or rewritten, which inequalities of property were no longer justified. Smith never minced his message on this point, but it is useful to distinguish among the kinds of arguments he made in attacking outdated laws. He attacked primogeniture, for example, on both historical and practical grounds. In the first place, Smith emphasized that "circumstances" justifying its existence had changed entirely. In eighteenth-century Europe, where the law protected small as well as great estates, primogeniture simply had forfeited its original rationale. Second, primogeniture was also a practical hindrance to further improvements in agriculture: "if the whole estate were divided among the sons, each would improve his own part better than one can improve the whole. Besides, tenants never cultivate a farm so well as if it were their own property."[66]

The atack on entails in the *Lectures* raised similar points. But it also added a passionate appeal to principle that would appear again in book III of the *Wealth of Nations*. Smith began by conceding that a man's claim to determine what shall be done with his goods after his death was "agreeable to our piety to the deceased." But he then denounced as "the most absurd thing in the world" the view that a person also had a power of determining how those goods shall be disposed "on in infinitum." Then followed an early version of what later became one of the more famous points in book III of the *Wealth of Nations:*

> There is no maxim more generally acknowledged than that the earth is the property of each generation. That the former generation should restrict them in their use of it is altogether absurd; it is theirs altogether as well as it was their predecessors in their day.[67]

Finally, Smith included among laws of property that he considered harmful and outdated those he called "exclusive privileges." Unlike primogeniture and entail, however, not all such privileges were to be condemned. In Smith's view, the right of inheritance, as originally understood, was an exclusive privilege that arose naturally from the development of human sentiments. Moreover, a few types of exclusive privileges created by law were relatively harmless in their effects. If limited in time, an inventor's patent was an acceptable reward for his ingenuity; by serving as an "encouragement to the labours of learned men," an author's copyright also served a good purpose. Nonetheless, through the course of legal history as Smith depicted it, most exclusive privileges in fact had been detrimental to the well-being of society. And the worst among them were those of the still powerful monopolies and corporations that controlled economic life across Europe. Smith sharply criticized both institutions for failing to meet the one criterion that originally had appeared to justify their creation: public utility. By increasing "the difficulty with which the several necessaries of life are procured," monopolies had served to impoverish their nations. For the economic logic of any monopoly always dictated as follows: reduce the quantity of goods made, raise prices nearly in proportion, and by these means "make great profit at a less expense of material and labour than can be done when many have the same liberty." Similarly, the exclusive trading privileges of urban corporations had worked in the end to make "all sorts of necessaries so much more uncomeatible."[68]

It is hard to find a place for Smith's frequently pursued interest in criticizing and re-writing "old constitutions" in the familiar view of him as a thinker who treated political and legal institutions as epiphenominal to underlying economic forces. Both Donald Winch and Knud Haakensson have suggested recently that we come much closer to understanding Smith's intentions in the Glasgow *Lectures* if we honor his claim that inquiries into the principles and history of jurisprudence—taken in conjunction—would provide the basis for a new "science" of legislation. In Smith's mind, as Haakensson puts it, natural law jurisprudence in itself was ultimately a "political challenge."[69] In this connection, it also might be noted finally that one of the most important and concrete functions of the four-stages scheme was to provide Smith with a clear understanding on what that challenge involved. For nowhere in the *Lectures* or in the *Wealth of Nations* did he ever make use of the four-stages scheme as a linear sequence describing man's inevitable economic progress. The allowances for primogeniture and entail that remained written in eighteenth-century law, after all, were troubling evidence that European society had become arrested in certain areas of its development. The continuing power of corporations and monopolies also showed that a "natural progress" through the four stages in fact had been reversed: here the "civil constitution" had favored "commerce" over "agriculture," and this situation had yet to be remedied as far as Smith was concerned. In short, Smith knew that his ideal account of human principle and purpose was one thing, and his parallel story of actual human events often something else entirely. As we turn to the *Wealth of Nations*, this aspect of Smith's thinking should be carefully borne in mind. For there, too, historical self-awareness was crucial to his message.

v   So far, we have studied Adam Smith as a thinker whose work continued and reformulated major themes explored by Francis Hutcheson and David Hume. Three considerations lie behind my choice of this perspective. In the first place, it provides what previous students of the three great Scottish philosophers have tended to overlook: an understanding of them as complete philosophers, thinkers whose main branches of inquiry—ethics, politics, and economics—explained each other and ought not to be lifted from comprehensive structures of thought. Here we also have found our way to Smith's economic doctrines as he himself did—namely, as a question initially approached by way of a categorical distinction between the norms of "ethics" and those of "jurisprudence." Because he thought law and government must aim only "to secure the individual who has enlarged his property, that he may peaceably enjoy the fruits of it,"[70] Smith argued—as Hume had before him—that the key to maintaining a well-ordered society did not lie in inspiring its subjects with a civic-minded virtue. The rules of justice, when observed or enforced represented a "negative virtue" that hindered us from hurting our neighbors.[71] Thus the key practical concern in a just society was to assure the proper ordering of relationships among men whose public concerns were mostly a matter of the pursuit and enjoyment of property. A just polity, in other words, can be understood as the protector of a rational system of commerce.

The second reason for emphasizing the "connecting principles" in Smith's thought is to suggest a corrective to a familiar but oversimplified approach to the study of arguments for capitalism in early-modern thought. That approach, chiefly associated with C. B. Macpherson, is based on the claim that arguments for free and self-interested commercial activity cannot be understood historically unless we consider them first in terms of a decisive break in the entire course of Western thought. The case for economic laissez-faire, Macpherson insists, must be seen as a reversal of assumptions, governing the West from Aristotle until the seventeenth century. During this period it had been "more usual to see the essence of man as purposeful activity, as exercise of one's energies in accordance with some rational purpose, than as consumption of satisfactions." But with the emergence of modern market societies in the seventeenth century, this traditional concept of man was "turned into almost its opposite": now the essence of rational behavior was held to lie in "unlimited individual appropriation," and thus "man became an infinite appropriator and an infinite consumer."[72] The story of Smith's intellectual career in Scotland, however, has uncovered a more complicated story. First of all, we have found in the Glasgow *Lectures* that the first weapons Smith used in arguing for free commerce were concepts drawn from a well-established tradition of legal humanism that dated back to Hugo Grotius. And those same weapons would be brought into battle again in the *Wealth of Nations*. In book IV, for example, in the "Digression on the Corn Trade," Smith's final argument against hindrances on free trade in grain was that the practice had sacrificed "the ordinary laws of justice" to much vaguer ideas of "public utility" or "reasons of state."[73] Laws imposing restrictions on manufacturers and farmers were denounced as "evident violations of natural liberty, and therefore unjust."[74] Apprenticeship laws were condemned not only on practical grounds, but also as "a manifest encroachment upon the just liberty both of the workman, and of those who might be disposed to employ him."[75] Essentially the same charge would be made against laws of settlement that had restricted the mobility of the poor. Finally, Smith himself sometimes used the phrase "the system of natural liberty" as a short-hand description of the entire argument of the *Wealth of Nations*. By this he meant that, if all systems of economic preference or restraint could be removed, "every man, as long as he does not violate the laws of justice," could in fact be left "perfectly free to pursue his own interest his own way." Smith's arguments for economic liberty, in short, were linked with an insistence on justice, and this for reasons any reader familiar with natural law jurisprudence might readily have understood.[76]

There is no question that some elements of what Macpherson has called "possessive individualism" can be traced back to the Grotian tradition of natural law thinking. Grotius himself may have been the first to argue notions of justice and rights based on a view of man as "owner" of his liberty and other moral attributes. He stressed, too, the primary significance of economic affairs in the good ordering of a polity. Thus, that decisive break in Western thought which Macpherson contends begins with Hobbes should be redated to begin with Grotius. There is, however, something more than a quarrel in historical scholarship involved in making this point. Placing Smith in the Grotian natural law tradition has helped us to uncover the exact sources of his understanding of justice, property, and rights. But it also allows us first to understand him in the same fashion we earlier understood Grotius, Pufendorf, Locke, Hutcheson, and Hume. Smith was, to be sure, a major character in a story of decisive intellectual change. But that story was not one that began simply as a radical break with all past Western values. Instead, the pattern of change we have uncovered has involved a restructuring or restating of the natural law tradition to fit new needs and ends. Hence, the notions of free trade and laissez-faire now appear far more compatible with the traditional assumptions of high-level Western thought than Macpherson and others have allowed.[77]

But the final reason for emphasizing those well-established philosophical values supporting Smith's argument for free trade is perhaps the most important. We can now conclude by attempting to measure the originality of that argument as it appeared in the *Wealth of Nations*. Explaining the purpose and achievement of this book surely is the main prize in any study of Adam Smith. There have been, of course, many interpretive strategies already tried in the effort to secure it. Most historians of economic thought agree that Smith's massive book was in some sense sui generis, but they have significant disagreements in explaining why the *Wealth of Nations* stands apart from all previous economic writing. In his classic *History of Economic Analysis*, Joseph Schumpeter distinguished between the development of economic analysis and economic policy-making. He remarked that the *Wealth of Nations* was not an original contribution to technical economic analysis, because it did not "contain a single idea, principle, or method that was entirely new in 1776." As an economic thinker, Smith was to be seen primarily as a systematizer who collated and ordered ideas inherited from others and made them available to even "the dullest readers." Only from the standpoint of policy, Schumpeter insisted, could it be said that Smith's book was an "epoch-making, original achievement," a "great performance" that was "thoroughly in sympathy with the humours" of its time and thus "fully deserved its success." Most modern historians of economic thought have been reluctant to accept Schumpeter's account of Smith's contribution to the development of formal economic analysis. Their usual counter-argument has been that nothing written before the *Wealth of Nations* matched its analytical rigor and comprehensiveness. William Letwin also has suggested that Schumpeter missed "the relations between system and science," thereby confusing the scientific character of Smith's book with its truth. The *Wealth of Nations* deserved its reputation, Letwin has argued, not as an ultimate statement, but as a turning point in the history of economic analysis: it was a "perfectly scientific" book in the sense that it exhibited its weak spots, invited testing, and so aided "the process of rejection and amendment by which a science approaches the truth."[78]

The on-going debate about Smith's merits as an economic analyst has framed the question of the originality of the *Wealth of Nations* in terms of its contribution to the development of economics as a discipline. There is no doubt that this approach focuses on one of the most important aspects of Smith's book. But it has prevented us from grasping what may be one of the most important keys to establishing its historical significance: the fact that both the technical economic analysis and the policy-making advice in the *Wealth of Nations* can be read as critical reassessments of previous arguments associated with the free trade position.

To offer this as the key to Smith's message is by no means to suggest that we may now unlock every door leading into his mind. Indeed, any reader coming "cold" to the *Wealth of Nations*, without context of any kind, would probably regard it as a book only because Smith happened to gather a huge and miscellaneous amount of material within one volume. The *Wealth of Nations* in fact is more like a small library than a real book inviting us to read straight through. William Robertson, who correctly predicted that Smith's book would become "a Political or Commercial Code to all Europe," also urged Smith in the second edition to add "a copious index, and likewise what the Book-sellers call *Side-notes*, pointing out the progress of the subject in every paragraph. This will greatly facilitate the consulting and referring to it."[79] And yet, if we put aside the question of a total structure, there are other ways to establish the unity of Smith's concerns in the *Wealth of Nations*. In what follows I want to sketch out only the major areas in which Smith was evidently concerned to reassess the key arguments for free trade. A detailed examination of all the areas in which he carried out this operation would help to account for the huge scale of the *Wealth of Nations*, and it perhaps would also provide a straightforward explanation of Smith's decision to publish this huge book separately from his even larger projected study of the principles and history of jurisprudence.[80] But there is not room for a full treatment of these issues here. What will concern us is the character of Smith's argument, not its breadth or rigor, and I want to show that this was a unique as well as a unifying element in the *Wealth of Nations*.

Probably the most important part of Smith's reassessment of technical arguments for free trade can be found in his account of that most powerful of all the new ideas championed in early-modern economic analysis: the conceptual model of an economic market place. Smith was not the first thinker to suggest that shipments of goods, trade of commodities, and exchange of bills were best understood in an intellectual model of trade relations where economic factors were clearly differentiated from their social and political entanglements. In England, we can date that idea back at least to the third decade of the seventeenth century.[81] What was remarkable in Smith's discussion, however, was his recurring emphasis of the view that this new paradigm in economic analysis remained very much beyond the intellectual grasp of his contemporaries.

One of the major reasons for this was the continuing influence in the late eighteenth century of the tradition of the "moral economy of the crowd." E. P. Thompson has shown that during Smith's lifetime, the urban and rural poor, and many artisans as well, rejected the emerging doctrine of free trade insofar as it applied to grain, meat, and bread. In the popular mind of the eighteenth century, an increase in the price of food was not caused by the impersonal operations of market forces, but by the greedy workings of forestallers (merchants who withheld goods from the market) and engrossers (those who sought to monopolize vital commodities). The defenders of the "moral economy" rejected the demand for freedom of trade in food as "the liberty of a savage." They instead upheld, at times by means of actual seizures of food supplies, an older ideal of an economy regulated by the state on behalf of its subjects.

The attack on the Corn Laws in book IV, chapter v, of the *Wealth of Nations* can be understood partly as a fierce criticism of this old moral economy of provision. Here that tradition was condemned as the embodiment of a misleading collection of the "prejudices of the public." Smith was not the first critic of the Corn Laws, yet he also understood the continuing strength of the popular prejudices that supported the Corn Laws more fully than Thompson has acknowledged in his account of Smith's attack on the "moral economy." According to Thompson, the criticism of the Corn Laws in the *Wealth of Nations* should be read "less as an essay in empirical inquiry than as a superb, self-validating essay in logic."[82] Let us see why this view will not stand examination.

Smith observed that in the minds of ordinary people in the eighteenth century, the processes of sales and exchange had yet to be disentangled from personal and concrete social relationships. A free trade market in grain was for them by no means the natural state of things. Indeed, Smith himself remarked that no trade was "so much exposed to popular odium" as the corn trade, and he emphasized that the effective operation of a free market in grain could be assured only by the vigilant protection of the law.[83]

None of this is to suggest that Smith doubted the merits of the argument for "entire freedom" in marketing goods such as grain. Indeed, while his "Digression concerning the Corn Trade and Corn Laws" in book IV voiced the cautions I've just underlined, it also contained some of his fiercest denunciations of the social and political direction of economic activity. "Famine has never arisen," Smith wrote, "from any other cause but the violence of government attempting, by improper means, to remedy the inconveniences of a dearth." And here too he denounced popular fears of engrossing and forestalling by comparing them to "the popular terrors and suspicions of witchcraft." And yet, whatever the logical merits in the argument for a free market in grain, Smith was also ready to concede that this same argument flew in the face of conventional wisdom. He allowed that the interest of a grain merchant and that of the "great body of the people" at first glance did appear opposite—especially in years of scarcity when the merchant's profit would be seen as no more than avarice. And even in the late eighteenth century, Smith noted, the "popular odium" on this point remained so powerful that "people of character and fortune" still were reluctant to enter into the trading of grain as a full-time business.[84]

Given these views, it is hardly a surprise that the following sentences were the outcome of Smith's discussion of the Corn Laws:

> The laws concerning corn may every where be compared to the laws concerning religion. The people feel themselves so much interested in what relates either to their subsistence in this life, or to their happiness in a life to come, that government must yield to their prejudices, and, in order to preserve public tranquility, establish the system which they approve of. It is upon this account, perhaps, that we so seldom find a reasonable system established with regard to either of these two capital objects.[85]

Smith here struck combined notes of sarcasm and realism that he would strike again and again in the *Wealth of Nations*. And we simply miss this aspect of his thinking if we consider the book, as Thompson has suggested, "less as an essay in empirical enquiry than as a superb, self-validating essay in logic." Smith's book unquestionably was a counter-argument directed at the "moral economy of the crowd." But it was not one that ever assumed its merits were self-evident or "thoroughly in sympathy with the humors" of its time.

Smith's view that his technical arguments, however carefully presented, remained beyond the grasp of his contemporaries also appeared in his attack on mercantilism as a doctrine governing international market relations. At the outset of book IV, chapter 1, he began his effort to distinguish the true "wealth" of a nation—i.e., its supply of labor and commodities—from its supply of gold and silver with a characteristic concession: "That wealth consists in money, or in gold and silver, is a popular notion which naturally arises from the double function of money, as the instrument of commerce, and as the measure of value." It followed from this, Smith remarked, that the "great affair" in all commercial societies always must be "to get money." In the "common language," the rationale was that "when we have money we can more readily obtain whatever else we have occasion for." Smith was not ready to dismiss out of hand the conventional view that "to grow rich is to get money." But he made his counter-argument here far more pointedly than in his criticism of the Corn Laws. One of the obvious errors in the mercantilist identification of wealth and specie, he observed, was drawing an analogy between a rich country and a rich man. A nation's heaping up of gold and silver was thereby taken to be the readiest way of enriching itself. Smith's reply came in one of the more subtly ironic passages in the entire *Wealth of Nations*:

> For some time after the discovery of America, the first enquiry of the Spaniards, when they arrived upon any unknown coast, used to be, if there was any gold or silver to be found in the neighbourhood? By the information which they received, they judged whether it was worth while to make a settlement there, or if the country was worth the conquering. Plano Carpino, a monk sent ambassador from the king of France to one of the sons of the famous Gengis Khan, says that the Tartars used frequently to ask him, if there was plenty of sheep and oxen in the kingdom of France? Their enquiry had the same object with that of the Spaniards. They wanted to know if the country was rich enough to be worth the conquering. Among the Tartars, as among all other nations of shepherds, who are generally ignorant of the use of money, cattle are the instruments of commerce and the measures of value. Wealth, therefore, according to them, consisted in cattle, as according to the Spaniards it consisted in gold and silver. Of the two, the Tartar notion, perhaps, was the nearest to the truth.[86]

But Smith's ironic tone here should not distract us from grasping the larger issue that lay behind this passage. For clearly his discussion again has been shaped by the view that the logic of free trade had yet to find the way into the common language of his time. Schumpeter claimed that in the *Wealth of Nations* Smith "disliked whatever went beyond plain common sense," that he never "moved above the heads of even the dullest readers," and even that he "led them on gently . . . making them feel comfortable all along."[87] It should be evident by now, however, that one of Smith's intentions was to emphasize that only for its proponents was the so-called "system of natural liberty" a matter of "plain common sense." Indeed, they seemed to be, in his mind, the Tartars of their age.

What we have uncovered thus far in Smith's economic analysis will surprise only those who still subscribe to the view that, in making his argument for the free market, Smith chose to ignore the mores and mentality that obstructed the "natural progress" toward productivity and attended to purely technical issues such as the accumulation of capital, the extension of the market, and the increase in the division of labor. Joyce Appleby declares, for example, that because classical economists such as Smith "took it for granted that human beings would make rational economic choices, they were able to explain the transition from a feudal order to a modern one in terms of impersonal processes." For Smith, she argues, "society as a force that shaped the behavior of its members did not figure in explanations of change."[88] But this familiar interpretation is based partly on a non sequitur. It simply does not follow from the fact that Smith assumed individuals would make rational economic choices in a projected free market that he must have been blind to established obstructions of such choices in the existing directed market. Furthermore, there is an abundance of textual evidence in the *Wealth of Nations* suggesting that one of Smith's overriding concerns was to show that the transition from a feudal economic order to a modern one was still in progress and that it was neither a "natural" nor an "impersonal" process.

Smith knew, for example, that operations of the market place were influenced by pre-existing social and economic hierarchies. At the outset of book I, chapter VIII, he discussed in great detail how those operations were to be understood, given a fundamental conflict between the interests of "masters" and "workmen." There could be no doubt, Smith observed, about which party had the advantage in any dispute and thus "could force the other into a compliance with their terms." Because they are fewer in number, masters can combine far more easily; in addition, the law "authorizes, or at least does not prohibit their combinations, while it prohibits those of the workmen." The upshot is that masters are "always and every where in a sort of tacit, but constant and uniform combination not to raise the wages of labor above their actual rate." Workmen, on the other hand, have no recourse but to "the loudest clamour, and sometimes to most shocking violence and outrage." Often they will be desperate and act with the folly and extravagance of desperate men, "who must either starve, or frighten their masters into an immediate compliance with their demands."[89] Smith thought the fruits of free trade would serve to diminish many of those conflicts between masters and workmen, but he also made it clear that economic growth would benefit the two parties in significantly different ways. No society could be flourishing and happy in which the greatest "part of the members are poor and miserable." But wages, he noted, obviously were not profits: they were for the workmen only that "share of the produce of their own labour" which allows them to be "tolerably well fed, cloathed and lodged." This would not change even with the coming of more widespread opulence.[90]

So Smith meant exactly what he said when he announced in the sub-title of book 1 that he wished to explore how the "produce" of a society was "distributed among the different Ranks of People." It is certainly a mistake to think of him as a writer whose account of a free market can in fairness be reduced to a formula of the harmony of abstract individuals pursuing their separate interests. Smith was an analyst of social conflict and change as well as an economist. And it was precisely this awareness of the disruptions that free commerce might bring to eighteenth-century societies that colored his policy advice to those legislators and statesmen who alone had the power to create a truly free market place. By comparison to Hume, for example, Smith was far more circumspect in his account of how economic improvement would come to serve both "the greatness of the state" and "the happiness of its subjects." He conceded that many of the most powerful subjects in existing societies already recognized that a government's adoption of a laissez-faire policy in the economic realm promised their failure. The elimination of apprenticeship laws, for example, would be both an act of justice and a practical benefit to the public, since the work of artisans would thereby become cheaper. But the old masters would of course be losers here, and "in the end, perhaps, the apprentice himself would be a loser." For under conditions of free market competition not only would the inefficient be driven out of business by the efficient. Those who remained in businesses where a trade was easily learned would have more competitors, and the outcome here would be that their wages "would be much less than at present." There was, in brief, always something of a zero-sum analysis in Smith's argument for free competition.[91] To be sure, in his mind the winnings in a laissez-faire policy outweighed the losses. But Smith was not blind to the fact that winners could only exist if losers existed, and in his vision of economic order, among the projected losers were those who then still had the power to foil his open and defiant plotting against them.

This last point was made in a slightly different way in Smith's discussions of the division of labor. The *Wealth of Nations* was by no means the first work to argue that an ever-increasing rationalization of human labor, together with a steady expansion of the market place, were the keys to economic growth. Schumpeter observed that the book was remarkable because "nobody, either before or after A. Smith thought of putting such a burden upon division of labor"; indeed, it was "practically the only factor in economic progress." But Smith's account of the division of labor was also remarkable in its willingness to measure the dangers that he thought would appear in an economy dependent upon highly specialized techniques of labor.[92] Where Hume linked a "quick march of the spirits" with commerce and manufacturing, Smith observed that labor in simple and unchanging tasks threatened to reduce a workman's capacity for invention and render him "as stupid, and ignorant as it is possible for a human creature to become. The torpor of his mind renders him, not only incapable of relishing or bearing a part in any rational conversation, but of conceiving any generous, noble, or tender sentiment, and consequently of forming any just judgement concerning many even of the ordinary duties of private life." In sum, while improving dexterity in one's particular line of business may be essential to productivity, it seems to be acquired at the expense of one's "intellectual, social, and martial virtues." This, Smith concluded, was a situation that government must "take some pains to prevent," and we shall consider his remedy in a moment.[93]

Jacob Viner once remarked that the historical importance of the *Wealth of Nations* could be explained partly by the fact that it was an "evaluating and crusading" book that later would be used by critics of existing society and government and by those who called for an end to political intervention in economic matters.[94] There is no doubt that this describes what became of Smith's book in the nineteenth century. But like many other scholars, Viner saw the issue of the historical importance of Smith's book only in terms of its success or influence. It should be evident by now that a complex intellectual drama unfolds within the *Wealth of Nations*, and this is a drama which it seems possible to understand only if we grasp Smith's recurring interest in "evaluating" the "crusade" that he had joined in writing the book.

Seen in this context, it should be noted, finally, that the main thrust of Smith's reassessment of the conception of government that supported "free trade" can be found in the three concluding paragraphs of book IV, chapter II. He declared at the end of this famous chapter that to expect freedom of trade would ever be entirely restored in Great Britain was "as absurd as to expect that an Oceana or Utopia should ever be established in it." This was by no means an off-hand remark; Smith went on in some detail to explain what he meant. He meant, above all else, that a policy of laissez-faire, whatever its considerable intellectual merits, ran far ahead of actual social developments in eighteenth-century Europe. Even in Britain, the most advanced of all European economies, "not only the prejudices of the public, but what is much more unconquerable, the private interests of many individuals, irresistibly oppose it." The "master manufacturers," Smith wrote, were not only opposed in principle to the doctrines of free trade and competition. In practice, their influence in most instances had been powerful enough to muffle those members of Parliament calling out for an end to legislated economic privileges. "The monopoly which our manufacturers have obtained against us," Smith declared, "has so much increased the number of them, that, like an overgrown standing army, they have become formidable to government and upon many occasions intimidate the legislature." The inevitable outcome was that members of parliament who had supported existing monopolies acquired "not only the reputation of understanding trade, but great popularity and influence with an order of men whose numbers and wealth render them of great importance." Those who opposed monopolies, in turn, had stood unprotected "from the most infamous abuse and detraction, from personal insults, [and] sometimes from real danger, arising from the insolent outrage of furious and disappointed monopolists."[95]

It should be said again that none of this is to suggest Smith himself doubted the intellectual soundness of the free trade and laissez-faire positions. Indeed, it was in the opening pages of this chapter that he offered what has become the most famous statement of those positions ever written: the doctrine that a man given freedom to pursue his own gain is "led by an invisible hand" to promote the growth of commerce and industry.[96] But his view, as we saw in examining Hume's *Political Discourses*, was in no way unique to Smith. In fact, it was more typical of Smith's approach throughout the *Wealth of Nations* to find him at the end of the chapter emphasizing that those who would defend or implement a laissez-faire policy necessary to establish free trade in the first place must see that this policy represented a radical challenge to an established socio-political order—and a challenge whose prospects of full success were at best uncertain.

Thus, Smith concluded book IV, chapter II, with a cautious program of practical advice for statesmen and legislators who might happen to embrace his views. In the first place, he remarked that any thoughts of suddenly laying open the domestic market to free competition were dangerous as well as utopian. While free competition would destroy the great manufacturers of Britain, Smith saw no cause to squander the capital they had invested in paying workmen and maintaining the material instruments of their trades. So the choice he posed was not regulations versus no regulations, but finding a reasonable way of eliminating the worst regulations. An "equitable regard" to the interests of monopolies and corporations, as well as the more "extensive view of the general good," required that changes be made piecemeal—or, in Smith's words, "slowly, gradually, and after a very long warning." And the task for government here clearly was not simply one of restraint. The market place, for Smith, was a world of preexisting adversary relationships where government must often play the role of disinterested yet pragmatic judge. On the question of monopolies, what he hoped for was not the utopian world of pure laissez-faire, but instead a more pragmatic concern "neither to establish any new monopolies of this kind, nor to extend further those which are already established."[97] The same spirit of pragmatism would later govern his remedies for the "mental mutilation" that was threatened by the division of labor. Education must be made compulsory for ordinary workmen, but Smith's curriculum was entirely functional in its intent—apart from the three Rs, there would be additional instruction only in "the elementary parts of geometry and mechanics."[98]

There is room here only for this truncated analysis of Smith's vast and complex book. Nonetheless, the arguments we have explored briefly serve to establish at least one major philosophical continuity between the *Wealth of Nations* and those earlier Glasgow *Lectures* out of which the book grew. It should be evident by now that Adam Smith was a thinker who argued for legal, political, and economic principles that he knew history had selectively endorsed or simply ignored. In the face of this recognition, he attempted to establish the basis for a reclarification of what those principles might yet hope to accomplish. In the case of the *Wealth of Nations*, Smith's strategy can be summarized as follows. In pursuit of an economic order whose principal objective was growth, to be realized partly through the free pursuit of self-interest and partly through vigilant political campaigns against privileged economic orders, Smith set out a policy that avoided utopian visions and mechanical formulas. Yet he projected at the same time a single goal—the "system of natural liberty"—that was difficult, audacious, but also imaginable as a guide for eighteenth-century policy. Free trade and laissez-faire in Smith's mind presented a series of demanding lessons that statesmen and legislators would learn more painfully, gradually, and incompletely than its previous exponents had recognized. In pursuit of what he understood to be justice and economic freedom, Smith was an historical realist and a political pragmatist. Taken together, those two aspects of his thinking may describe best what was sui generis in his extraordinary book.

V Epilogue: The Man of 'Public Spirit'

i Few people in the nineteenth and twentieth centuries have paused to consider the pragmatic, self-scrutinizing character of the argument for free trade in the *Wealth of Nations*. Fewer still have seen that Smith's argument emerged from rigorous thinking about the philosophical issues that we have explored in this study. Modern critics of Adam Smith, at both ends of the ideological spectrum, have conditioned readers to ignore these aspects of the *Wealth of Nations*.[1] Self-styled disciples have developed a "science" of political economy with certain obvious resemblances to the analytical sections of Smith's book. Yet most of them have overlooked his cautiousness and ignored signs that said the book was only one part of his larger enterprise as a moral philosopher.

It was to this enterprise that Smith devoted most of his intellectual energy during the fourteen years that remained of his life after publishing the first edition of the *Wealth of Nations*. Before his death in 1790, he brought to press five new editions of his massive book. Yet in them he made only minor corrections and additions—the "side-notes" that William Robertson suggested awaited the efforts of later nineteenth-century editors such as William Playfair and J. R. McCulloch.[2] After 1776, Smith returned to more conventional philosophical reflection.[3] He made several major additions to the *Theory of Moral Sentiments*, and also resumed work on the draft of his promised "account of the general principles of law and government." His renewed thinking about these issues raises serious problems for those who take for granted that in the *Wealth of Nations* traditional questions of Western ethical and political theory had dropped from his sight. Indeed, it seems to provide final confirmation of what I have tried to show throughout these pages—namely, Adam Smith's economic doctrines developed with substantial continuity from ethical and political concerns he first confronted while a student of Francis Hutcheson.

This study must stop with the *Wealth of Nations* because my main project has been to trace some of its more important yet neglected sources in the history of Western thought. I have not made many forward glances in this book, partly for the sake of greater historical accuracy, partly in the interest of analytical rigor. Nonetheless, what we have discovered about the distinctive character of Smith's argument also provides a means of developing a more complete understanding of new uses to which the *Wealth of Nations* would be put after his death. Before I summarize the main points of this study, I want to sketch the general outlines of that understanding by way of exploring one of the more important additions to the sixth edition of the *Theory*.

To explain what was to become of the *Wealth of Nations*, we must examine historical landmarks lying outside of Smith's texts. They include the factory, the locomotive, and the steamboat, as well as the violent and portentous coming of the democratic age in 1789. Smith himself seemed to sense this last rupture more keenly than the first. In one of the longest of the final additions he made to the *Theory*, he began with an apparent allusion to the French Revolution. Smith spoke of an abrupt end to "peaceable and quiet" times when the respect for established social and political institutions had been compatible with the desire to improve the condition of one's fellow citizens. He also talked of developments that compelled men to choose between two different approaches to the task of improving society. On the one hand, there was a "spirit of system" which had mixed itself with, and thereby corrupted, the old "public spirit" of progressive men. The typical adherents of this new "spirit of system," Smith wrote, were prone to "the madness of fanaticism"; their leaders, even if they wished to maintain restraint, dared not disappoint their followers and thus always refused "all palliatives, all temperaments, all reasonable accommodations." On the other hand, there remained the traditional reformer whose "public spirit" still partook of "humanity and benevolence." He respected "the established powers and privileges even of individuals, and still more those of the great orders and societies, into which the state is divided." He was not a man of faction, but contented himself "with moderating what he often cannot annihilate without great violence," with ameliorating the wrong when he cannot establish right. And, finally, unlike the man of system who was "so enamoured with the supposed beauty of his own system" that he would never suffer "the smallest deviation from any part of it," the public-spirited man, when unable to establish the best system of laws, would "endeavour to establish the best that the people can bear."[4]

Smith sent these remarks to his printer in December of 1789. Because he made no specific reference to events in France, we cannot be certain that he meant the distinction between "public spirit" and "spirit of system" to be used primarily to measure the magnitude of the huge historical divide that had been thrown up by the French Revolution during the last months of his life. We can be certain, however, that the sketch of the man of "public spirit" was an account of Smith's own method of speculation, a self-description confirmed in all its details by the analysis of the *Wealth of Nations* presented at the end of the previous chapter. We can be certain, too, that Smith wanted the idea of free trade championed by men of "public spirit" who shared his understanding that to "insist upon establishing, and upon establishing all at once, and in spite of all opposition, every thing which that idea may seem to require, must often be the highest degree of arrogance."[5]

Yet Smith could not yoke together his central doctrine and his distinctive method of arguing for it. The *Wealth of Nations*, when read, was to be understood and hence reinterpreted by its readers in historical contexts that gave urgency or new meaning to only certain parts of the book. In fact, it is fair to say that many of the earliest admirers of the *Wealth of Nations* were driven by the very "spirit of system" that its author had disavowed. In the decade immediately following Smith's death, a number of thinkers associated the success of revolutionary ideas in France with the spread of his doctrines. In part I of *The Rights of Man,* Thomas Paine cited the *Wealth of Nations* in a defense of the new French constitution that promised "no more monopolies of any kind, that all trades shall be free, and every man free to follow any occupation by which he can procure an honest livelihood." In part II, Paine began a statement of his vision of a democratic civilization with an account of the primacy of the division of labor and exchange in human affairs that, as Elie Halévy pointed out, sounded much like book 1 of the *Wealth of Nations*. Men in society, Paine insisted, performed most of what traditionally had been ascribed to their government. The "mutual dependence and reciprocal interest which man has upon man, and all parts of a civilized community upon each other," he explained, actually "create that great chain of connection which holds it together."[6] For Paine, as for other champions of the French Revolution such as Condorcet, Mackintosh, and Wollstonecraft, such views justified dismantling an established order based on privilege and custom and framing a new constitution that more equally divided the exercise of political power and the enjoyment of wealth among all men.[7]

But the *Wealth of Nations* was to be tied only briefly to the cause of radical political reform. Four years after Paine's pamphlet, in *Thoughts and Details on Scarcity*, Edmund Burke proclaimed his support for Smith's principles at the same time as he launched a fierce attack on reform schemes engendered in Britain in the wake of the French Revolution. J. R. Poynter has observed that Burke's obsession with social order and hatred of revolution "led him to elevate Smith's system of economic liberty into a dogmatic faith which the author might scarcely have recognized."[8] Yet Burke was hardly alone in his intolerance of change. In the first edition of *Essay on the Principle of Population* (1798), Thomas Malthus too sought to discredit radical democratic ideals of progress and equality by arguing that competition between the means of subsistence and population was a first and immutable law of nature. This Malthusian doctrine would be taken up by those who resisted efforts to redistribute power and wealth as interferences with the God-given laws of life in society.

In the end, however, it was to be the transformation of Britain from an agricultural to an industrial economy, rather than ideological debates surrounding the French Revolution, that provided the historical context within which the *Wealth of Nations* gained its greatest historical significance and again took on meanings that went beyond what Smith had originally intended. In at least two realms, Smith's text provided an indispensable guide for those who sought to explain, accelerate, and complete the industrialization of Britain in the first half of the nineteenth century. First of all, the triumph of industrial capitalism required an intellectual reordering of reality. An economy filling with new machines and factories and reaching unprecedented levels of productivity and population had to be placed within an understandable context. Books I and II of the *Wealth of Nations* provided a crucial point of departure for this work. The nineteenth-century "political economists" who first defined the general outlines of Britain's new economic reality were preoccupied, as Smith had been, with economic growth. They too assigned capital accumulation the dominant role in this process. In seeking to explain the causes and consequences of growth, they also refined many of Smith's analytical concepts: the division of labor, the theory of value, the tripartite division of national income into rent, profits, and wages, and the concept of progress toward a stationary state. In brief, Smith provided nineteenth-century political economists with a text that became the foundation for a mode of economic discourse that was more dogmatic and deductive, yet also more urgent and rigorous, than the *Wealth of Nations* had been.[9]

The second contribution that Smith's text made to the triumph of industrial capitalism lay in his argument for free trade and the conception of the proper relationship between polity and economy that underpinned this argument. There is no question that Smith was the hero of proponents of free trade in the first half of the nineteenth century. Yet why did his disciples dismiss his caveat of free trade as a utopian ideal? And did they misinterpret his argument in doing so? The answer to both questions requires repetition of some points that I made in the first chapter.

It is important to remember that Smith's concept of his eighteenth-century commercial society cannot simply be equated with that of modern industrial capitalism. But at the same time we should not overdraw the distinction between Smith's economic world and that in which the buying of human labor to power the operation of machines became the essential characteristic of Western economies. For in the first decades of the nineteenth century, as in Smith's day, the global network of British economic activity still remained largely within politically defined channels, limited by traditional privileges and prerogatives guaranteed by the state. Before capitalist relations came to dominate industrial production, the political supervision of economic activity had to be eliminated in some areas, curtailed in others. Monopolies of all kinds had to be abolished because they hampered the reproductive capacity of capital. Those with political authority were also asked to understand that the demands of capital accumulation required the state to surrender its control over the movement of raw materials. This is, of course, precisely what Smith had in mind in attacking monopolies, apprenticeship restrictions, laws of settlement that impeded the mobility of the poor, and regulations of free trade in grain. He also understood that not all demands made in the name of free trade required a diminishment of state power. Smith stressed—as would nineteenth-century free traders—that state assistance was necessary to open up new markets as well as to protect nascent industries from external competition or internal subversion. Finally, he made it clear that the success of free trade also depended on state investments to create "public works and institutions" that would benefit a free commercial society without demanding significant outlays from it. But even here Smith's political message was of one piece: law and government must be servants of economic activity; they must also give the greatest possible freedom to men who engage in trade and manufacturing.

This was of course the message that the makers of industrial capitalism in nineteenth-century Britain seized on as the most compelling proposal in all of the *Wealth of Nations*. Ultimately, there is no great problem in explaining why they dropped Smith's caveat on free trade as a utopian quest. In their significantly changed economic setting, it seemed only too obvious to them that Smith had greatly underestimated the strength of his most important argument. But what, then, are we to make of the loss of that distinctive "public spirit" that informed the *Wealth of Nations?* Its disappearance is perhaps best taken as a reminder of the limits of scholarly studies (such as this one) concerned primarily with restoring Adam Smith to the intellectual world where his ideas were initially formed. There is no question that Smith's own intentions as a thinker have been ignored for too long. But in the end, they simply do not contain all possible readings of his work. Or put another way, Smith's understanding of himself must be seen as only one among several, and it should never come to monopolize our efforts to determine the historical significance of his work.

ii It remains to furnish some afterthoughts on what I have said about the sources of Smith's extraordinary book. First, I hope this study has clarified the much-argued, but often misunderstood, link between classical liberal economic doctrines and some of the recurrent concerns in Western moral philosophy. The *Wealth of Nations* developed partly in answer to one of the oldest and most important questions in Western thought: what is the nature of a just state? For Smith, the bracing pillars of "free trade" were particular conceptions of justice and rights that I have traced back, through Francis Hutcheson and David Hume, to Hugo Grotius. It would be misleading, of course, to characterize the *Wealth of Nations* merely as a tract in natural law and natural rights politics. What I have tried to show is that we understand its message more fully when we recognize that this tradition taught Smith to see politics primarily as an economic problem and at the same time provided him with a vocabulary of moral and political terms to explain why that must be so.

Secondly, we have, I think, a deeper appreciation of the extent to which the terms "free trade" and "laissez-faire" in the eighteenth century were calls for legal reform. Although the calls were made in somewhat different ways by the three figures studied here, their arguments also reveal at least one centrally important continuity. There was a developing awareness, beginning in the last pages of Hutcheson's *Inquiry* and culminating in books IV and V of the *Wealth of Nations*, that the realm of justice—even when confined to a Grotian concept of commutative, rather than distributive, justice—would become more extensive and complex as the commercialization of society continued. It would also, as Smith often emphasized, require sovereigns to campaign soberly against old habits of thought and traditional privileged institutions.

Thirdly, the familiar identification of "free trade" as the doctrine of a new "middle class" requires much deeper examination. Probably there is more error than truth in the connection, at least before the French and Industrial Revolutions. This connection also was not one our thinkers were much concerned to emphasize. As Donald Winch has observed, if all of Smith's criticisms of the landed aristocracy were assembled, they would not add up to an endorsement of acquisitive middle-class values. Moreover, as we have seen in one of his additions to the sixth edition of the *Theory*, Smith clearly did not see his economic doctrines as part of a program for liberal democratic reform. His was the cautious, pragmatic "science of a statesman or legislator" he spoke of at the outset of book IV. Its goal was to "enrich both the people and the sovereign," not to fashion a new, universal "science of legislation" that was later pursued by Jeremy Bentham and James Mill.[10]

For historians of thought, my final point may be particularly interesting and fruitful. It regards the sharp distinction between things moral and political—"right" in private and public senses, kept sharply distinct—that was central to Adam Smith's understanding of moral philosophy. I have tried to show in these pages why understanding this distinction is important in grasping the philosophical foundations of the doctrine of free trade. I have traced its origins to Grotius's *De Iure Belli*. This work overthrew the notion that a just polity should create a society of virtuous men, and it fashioned, at the same time, an alternative conception of justice that stressed the right of individuals to use the world for their private purposes. In this study, the use of Grotius's thought as a key landmark in the history of Western moral philosophy has allowed me to by-pass some of the more well-worn yet problematic routes into the *Wealth of Nations*. It may also suggest a promising line of inquiry for examining the fate of free trade and laissez-faire doctrines in the hands of certain great Western thinkers in the nineteenth century. In this widely studied age of industrial expansion and political reform, there are still important gaps between research in moral and political theory and economic ideology. More work could be done on the Utilitarians along lines pursued in this book. To approach Hegel and his followers in this fashion might also lead to some new insights.

At the end, I am left with the feeling that Adam Smith is, for those concerned with the current problems of capitalism, the most relevant of our three thinkers. That is hardly a surprising judgment, but it follows primarily from my admiration for those aspects of Smith's thought that he described as typical of the man of "public spirit." The irony here is that Smith has been famous for ideas that were not originally his own, while his subtle method of defending those ideas has largely been forgotten. He did not see the *Wealth of Nations* as a book that would transform the popular mentality. Nor did he write it with the intention of providing a founding faith for a new intellectual discipline—economics.[11]

Today, the *Wealth of Nations* should be studied more for particular insights than for vast practical remedies. Apart from helping us to grasp certain conceptions of law and government that were crucial to the triumph of capitalism, Smith remains relevant because of the modern, disillusioned cast of his mind. Indeed, for a late-twentieth-century audience, what is most profoundly interesting in Smith may be his awareness that historical events are not commanded by ideas alone, that they might take courses very different from those for which he argued. In the last analysis, Hutcheson's abstract arguments linking commerce with virtue, justice, and rights are of interest mostly to intellectual historians. Hume's injunction—"Sovereigns must take mankind as they find them"—will satisfy only those who take the values of commercial society for granted. Smith remains an eminent companion for those who ponder the limits as well as the achievements of largely free commercial societies, and wonder why there is no better practical arrangement to serve the common public purpose. Smith does not provide answers for all our present concerns. But his thinking still defines the general outlines of our predicament. The project of capitalism, as he envisioned it, is for self-seeking men to create a prosperous world in which economic activity serves individual needs and desires, not those shaped by religion, nation, government, or privileged social and economic institutions. This is an unheroic and unromantic view of life, and there are of course other nobler visions of our purpose. Smith's achievement was to see that there is nonetheless a great and difficult project here, one that men will never pursue consistently. In an age when capitalism has facile champions and dogmatic critics in equal abundance, Adam Smith remains lucid and realistic about a world he only helped to create.

Notes

Preface

1 *Corr.*, Letter 154 from Adam Ferguson, 18 April 1776, p. 193.
2 Quoted in John Rae, *Life of Adam Smith* (London, 1895), p. 286.
3 Walter Bagehot, "Adam Smith as a Person," in *Biographical Studies*, ed. R. H. Hutton (London, 1881), p. 280.
4 Donald Winch begins his careful study of *Adam Smith's Politics* (Cambridge, 1978), with a survey of established interpretations of Smith's achievements and shows how they have neglected the eighteenth-century context within which the *Wealth of Nations* was conceived; see pp. 1–27. On the slowness of the process by which Smith's economic doctrines gained intellectual predominance, see Kirk Willis, "The Role in Parliament of the Economic Ideas of Adam Smith, 1776–1800," *History of Political Economy* 11 (1979): 505–44.
5 Quoted in *Corr.*, p. 46n.
6 For a useful survey of the original literature on *das Adam Smith Problem*, see Glenn R. Morrow, *The Ethical and Economic Theories of Adam Smith* (New York, 1923), pp. 1–12. On the perfunctory treatment of this scholarship in recent studies of Smith, see my "Rethinking *Das Adam Smith Problem*," *Journal of British Studies* 20 (1981): 106–110.
7 *Lectures on Justice, Police, Revenue, and Arms*, ed. Edwin Cannan (Oxford, 1896). The new student notes are more thorough and detailed in their account of Smith's notions of property, rights, and justice. They show, too, that Smith's economic doctrines grew out of the Western natural law tradition to a much greater extent than has previously been imagined. Both sets of notes are now printed in *Lectures on Jurisprudence*, ed. R. L. Meek, D. D. Raphael, and P. G. Stein (Oxford, 1978). Yet another set of very brief lecture notes recently has been printed and discussed in R. L. Meek, "New Light on Adam Smith's Glasgow Lectures on Jurisprudence," *History of Political Economy* 8 (1976): 439–77.
8 Among useful works that isolate one aspect of Smith's thought are T. D. Campbell, *Adam Smith's Science of Morals* (London, 1971); Peter Stein, "From Pufendorf to Adam Smith: the Natural Law tradition in Scot-

land," in *Europäisches Rechtsdenken in Geschichte und Gegenwart: Restschrift für Helmut Coing* (Munich, 1982), pp. 667–79; A. W. Coats, "Adam Smith and the Mercantile System," in *Essays on Adam Smith*, ed. A. S. Skinner and T. Wilson (Oxford, 1976), pp. 218–36. Knud Haakonssen's *The Science of the Legislator: The Natural Jurisprudence of David Hume and Adam Smith* (Cambridge, 1981), contains a much-needed textual analysis of the Glasgow *Lectures*, but there is little concern here with tracing Smith's debts to seventeenth-century natural law jurists.

9   J. Ralph Lindgren, *The Social Philosophy of Adam Smith* (The Hague, 1973), provides a careful and often stimulating examination of various strands of Smith's thought. But, for reasons that will become clearer as this study proceeds, two of Lindgren's assumptions are very questionable. The first is that Smith's view of history is not "part of the central core of his social philosophy" (p. xiii); the other is that Smith saw his natural jurisprudence as "a branch of ethics" (p. 63).

10 Alexander Murdoch, *"The People Above": Politics and Administration in Mid-Eighteenth Century Scotland* (Edinburgh, 1980), pp. 1–27. Also see John M. Simpson, "Who Steered the Gravy Train, 1707–66?" in *Scotland in the Age of Improvement*, ed. N. T. Phillipson and Rosalind Mitchison (Edinburgh, 1970), pp. 47–72.

11 Within two months of the publication of the *Wealth of Nations*, Smith received letters of enthusiastic praise from his Scottish friends David Hume, Hugh Blair, Joseph Black, William Robertson, and Adam Ferguson; see *Corr.*, Letters 150–54, pp. 186–95. On criticism of Smith in Scotland, see Salim Rashid, "Adam Smith's Rise to Fame: A Reexamination of the Evidence," *The Eighteenth Century* 23 (1982): 70–79.

12 I borrow this defense of the biographical approach from Daniel J. Singal, *The War Within: From Victorian to Modernist Thought in the South, 1919–45* (Chapel Hill, 1982), pp. xii–xv.

13 Earlier studies have focussed primarily on the contributions these figures have made to the development of technical economic discourse. See E. Cannan's introduction to the *Lectures*; W. R. Scott, *Francis Hutcheson* (London, 1900), pp. 230–45; and W. L. Taylor, *Francis Hutcheson and David Hume as Predecessors of Adam Smith* (Durham, N.C., 1965). In a more recent provocative essay, Istvan Hont and Michael Ignatieff stress, as I do in this study, the deep significance of the Western natural law tradition in understanding the economic doctrines of Hume and Smith. But they have overlooked the important ways in which Hutcheson spurred each of them to restructure the philosophical assumptions that informed the tradition. See "Needs and justice in the *Wealth of Nations*: an introductory essay," in *Wealth and Virtue: The Shaping of Political Economy in the Scottish Enlightenment*, ed. Hont & Ignatieff (Cambridge, 1983), pp. 1–44.

1 Introduction

1 This study will not contribute to an on-going debate about whether the label "mercantilism" is a useful one in describing economic writing in the sixteenth and seventeenth centuries. Most economic historians have concluded that Adam Smith was misleading in speaking of a "mercantile system" in book IV, *WN*. But it is still plausible to use the term "mercantilism" in describing the general interests and outlook of economic thinkers before Adam Smith, many of which would find their way into his thinking as well. The concept of mercantilism as state-building is primarily associated with Gustav Schmoller, *The Mercantilist System*, trans. W. J. Ashley (London, 1902).
2 The deficiencies of the label "laissez-faire" as a description of the argument of *WN* have been explored in Jacob Viner, "Adam Smith and Laissez-Faire" in *The Long View and the Short* (Glencoe, Ill., 1958); Winch, *Adam Smith's Politics*, ch. 1; A. S. Skinner, *A System of Social Science* (Oxford, 1979), ch. 9.
3 *Philosophical Letters*, trans. Ernest Dilworth (New York, 1961), pp. 39–40.
4 For Marx's classic statement, see *Manifesto of the Communist Party* (1848) in *The Marx-Engels Reader*, ed. Robert C. Tucker, 2nd ed. (New York, 1978), pp. 469–500; Max Weber, *The Protestant Ethic and the Spirit of Capitalism*, trans. Talcott Parsons 1904–6; rpt. (New York, 1958). For a recent useful evaluation of Weber's intentions, see Ehud Sprinzak, "Weber's Thesis as an Historical Explanation," *History & Theory* 11 (1972).
5 See esp. Louis Dumont, *From Mandeville to Marx: The Genesis and Triumph of Economic Ideology* (Chicago, 1975), and Joyce Oldham Appleby, *Economy Thought and Ideology in Seventeenth Century England* (Princeton, 1977). In her exploration of English economic literature of the seventeenth century, Appleby argues that some writers then created the first imaginative model of commerce based partly on the view that human nature led to uniform behavior in the market place, and partly on the assumption that human beings pursued their self-interest in an orderly, rational way. This provocative study also reminds us that there was sophisticated economic writing long before Adam Smith. On this point, also see William Letwin, *The Origins of Scientific Economics* (Garden City, N.Y., 1964).
6 See J. G. A. Pocock, "Virtue and Commerce in the Eighteenth Century," *Journal of Interdisciplinary History* 3 (1972): 119–34; *The Machiavellian Moment: Florentine Political Thought and the Atlantic Republican Tradition* (Princeton, 1975), esp. pp. 423–505; and "The Mobility of Property and the Rise of Eighteenth-Century Sociology," in *Theories of Property: Aristotle to the Present*, ed. Anthony Parel & T. Flanagan (Waterloo, Ont., 1979), pp. 141–66.

7 This was one of the concerns that gave rise to the so-called "four-stages" theory of human history; see Pocock, *The Machiavellian Moment*, pp. 497–505, and "The Mobility of Property . . . ," pp. 155–64. But there are other contexts within which that theory might be understood. See Hans Medick, *Naturzustand and Naturgeschichte der burgerlichen Gesellschaft* (Gottingen, 1973); R. L. Meek, *Social Science and the Ignoble Savage* (Cambridge, 1976); James Moore, "Locke and the Scottish Jurists" (unpublished paper presented to the Faculty Seminar in Political and Social Thought, Columbia University, January 24, 1979).

8 Quentin Skinner, *The Foundations of Modern Political Thought: Volume One, The Renaissance* (Cambridge, 1978), pp. 73–74, 108–9.

9 Albert O. Hirschman, *The Passions and the Interests: Political Arguments for Capitalism before Its Triumph* (Princeton, 1977); also see Nannerl O. Keohane, *Philosophy and the State in France: The Renaissance to the Enlightenment* (Princeton, 1980), esp. pp. 151–68, 350–57.

10 In the last paragraph of the first edition of *TMS*, Smith announced his intention of writing another book that would "give an account of the general principles of law and government, and of the different revolutions they have undergone in the different ages and periods of society, not only in what concerns justice, but in what concerns police, revenue, and arms, and whatever else is the object of law" (*TMS*, VII. iv. 27). Later, at the start of the sixth edition, Smith noted that *WN* "partly executed this promise; at least so far as concerns police, revenue, and arms." He was still at work on his projected "theory of jurisprudence" when he died in 1790 (*TMS*, p. 3).

11 C. P. Kindleberger, "The Historical Background: Adam Smith and the Industrial Revolution," in *The Market and the State: Essays in Honour of Adam Smith*, ed. Thomas Wilson and Andrew S. Skinner (Oxford, 1976), pp. 24–25.

12 Smith combined two views of labor. The first argued that a commodity's value is what it has cost the laborer in time to produce; the second said that a commodity's value is determined by what it will exchange for and how much of the products of other men's labor it will purchase (*WN*, I. v. 1–2). The two views cannot be logically reconciled, but it is not surprising that Smith should have subscribed to both views, given the fact that his world was still dominated by merchants and small-time manufacturers. In the nineteenth century, a controversy began about which view of labor was the appropriate guide to the realities of a new industrial capitalist economy, and Smith was often faulted for a lack of clarity and consistency. This controversy has no direct bearing on my argument here, but see P. H. Douglas, "Smith's Theory of Value and Distribution," in J. M. Clark et al., *Adam Smith, 1776–1926* (Chicago, 1928), pp. 77–115, for a useful introduction to this issue.

13 Harold Perkin, *The Origins of Modern English Society, 1780–1880* (Lon-

don, 1969), esp. chs. VII and VIII, explores these views as elements of "the triumph of the entrepreneurial ideal" in the nineteenth century.

14 My account of "capitalism" here follows Maurice Dobb, *Studies in the Development of Capitalism* (New York, 1947); and E. J. Hobsbawm, *The Age of Revolution, 1789–1848* (New York, 1964), chs. 2 and 9, and *Industry and Empire* (Hammondsworth, 1969), chs. 1–4. Also see Eric R. Wolf, *Europe and the People Without History* (Berkeley, 1982), part three.

15 One of the earliest and more profound expressions of this feeling was made in the work of another eighteenth-century Scottish philosopher; see Adam Ferguson, *An Essay on the History of Civil Society*, ed. Duncan Forbes (1767; rpt. Edinburgh, 1966), esp. pp. 16–19. But the classic critique remains Marx's "Economic and Philosophic Manuscripts of 1844," in *The Marx-Engels Reader*, pp. 66–125.

16 I cite this as the most plausible modern philosophical defense of capitalism. In the first half of the nineteenth century, a free commercial society did have a moral vision imputed to it. John Cobden and other proponents of self-respect and international peace found in laissez-faire a new variation of Christian ethical teaching. "To buy in the cheapest market and sell in the dearest," Cobden once said, meant that one was "giving to mankind the means of enjoying the fullest abundance of earth's goods, and in doing so, carrying out to the fullest extent the Christian doctrine of 'Doing to all men as ye would they should do unto you.'" Quoted in Crane Brinton, *English Political Thought in the 19th Century* (London, 1933), p. 105. Utilitarians such as Bentham and James Mill also found the "political economy" of free trade to be a science that would enlighten self-interest, substituting for hedonism the virtues of thrift and self-denial. See William Thomas, *The Philosophical Radicals* (Oxford, 1979), esp. chs. I and III.

17 On the social and historical background of the Scottish Enlightenment, see H. R. Trevor-Roper, "The Scottish Enlightenment," *Studies in Voltaire and the Eighteenth Century* 58 (1967): 1635–58; Nicholas Phillipson, "Culture and Society in the Eighteenth Century Province: The Case of Edinburgh and the Scottish Enlightenment," in *The University in Society*, ed. L. Stone (Princeton, 1974), II, 407–48, and "The Scottish Enlightenment," in *The Enlightenment in National Context*, ed. R. Porter and M. Teich (Cambridge, 1981), pp. 19–40. Also see the recent collection of essays in *The Origins and Nature of the Scottish Enlightenment*, ed. R. H. Campbell and A. S. Skinner (Edinburgh, 1982).

18 On the Scottish "Moderates" see Ian Clark, "Moderatism and the Moderate Party in the Church of Scotland, 1752–1805" (Ph.D. diss., University of Cambridge, 1963); and Richard Sher, *Church and University in the Scottish Enlightenment* (Princeton, 1985). John Dwyer, "The Heavenly City of the Eighteenth Century Moderate Divines," in *New Perspectives*

on the Politics and Culture of Early Modern Scotland, ed. J. Dwyer, R. A. Mason, and A. Murdoch (Edinburgh, n.d.), pp. 291–318, explores the ways in which moderate divines borrowed from Smith's *Theory of Moral Sentiments*. The economic ideas of the English Latitudinarians have been examined recently by Margaret C. Jacob, *The Newtonians and the English Revolution* (Ithaca, 1976), esp. pp. 51–54, 181–94.

19 Winch, *Adam Smith's Politics*, pp. 36–44, 70–72, provides a reliable account of Montesquieu's role in Smith's work; I think the argument he makes here applies equally well to Hume. But also see P. E. Chamley, "The Conflict between Montesquieu and Hume: A Study of the Origins of Adam Smith's Universalism," in *Essays on Adam Smith*, ed. A. S. Skinner and T. Wilson (Oxford, 1975), pp. 274–305. On Ferguson and Kames, see Ronald Hamowy, "Adam Smith, Adam Ferguson, and the Division of Labor," *Economica* 35 (1968): 249–59, and David Lieberman, "The Legal Needs of Commercial Society: the Jurisprudence of Lord Kames," in *Wealth and Virtue*, ed. Hont and Ignatieff, pp. 203–34.

20 *Short*, p. 1; here Hutcheson described his moral philosophy as a matter of providing regulations for the whole of life. *Treatise*, xv–xvi, sets out the details of Hume's all-encompassing "science of man."

21 *TMS*, VII. ii. intro. 1.

22 Two of the clearest discussions about the place of "passions" in Western thought can be found in Anthony Levi, *French Moralists: The Theory of Passions, 1585–1649* (Oxford, 1964), and Keohane, *Philosophy and the State in France*, esp. chs. 4–7, 9, 10, and 12. I am much indebted to both of these invaluable studies.

23 See Keohane, *Philosophy and the State in France*, pp. 183–88, 283–312.

24 *Enquiry*$_2$, appendix II, 254, p. 302.

25 I will also explore aspects of Smith's politics different from those discussed in Winch, *Adam Smith's Politics*, and Duncan Forbes, "Sceptical Whiggism, Commerce, and Liberty," in *Essays on Adam Smith*, pp. 179–201. These important studies are concerned primarily with charting Smith's positions on eighteenth-century political issues and ideologies. My concern in this book is to uncover the broader philosophical assumptions that underpinned those positions.

26 C. S. Montesquieu, *The Spirit of the Laws*, trans. Thomas Nugent (1748; rpt. New York, 1949), book XX, 2, p. 317.

27 Hutcheson is a central figure in Albert Hirschman's provocative account of thinkers who saw money-making as a "calm passion"; see *The Passions and the Interests*, pp. 63–66.

28 "Of Civil Liberty," *Essays*, 1, p. 160.

29 *Inquiry*, p. 265.

30 Ibid., p. 228.

31 Smith's analysis arguably was the more profound of the two; cf. *TMS*, I. iii. 3 and *Treatise*, II. 1. x., pp. 309–16.

32 In his *Discours sur les sciences et les arts* (1750), Rousseau lamented the

fact that while "ancient politicians spoke incessantly of morals and virtue; ours speak of nothing but commerce and money." *Social Contract and Discourses*, trans. and intro. G. D. H. Cole (New York, 1950), p. 161.

33 Eli Heckscher, *Mercantilism*, trans. M. Shapiro (London, 1935), argued that mercantilist and laissez-faire doctrines were in agreement on these issues. In a later, briefer essay, he observed that mercantilist writers "actually harped upon 'freedom,' especially freedom of trade." See his essay, "Mercantilism" in *Revisions in Mercantilism*, ed. D. C. Coleman (London, 1969), p. 32. For a useful case study of the application of mercantilist principles, see J. F. Bosher, *The Single Duty Project: A Study of the Movement for a French Customs Union in the Eighteenth Century* (London, 1964), esp. chs. I–III.

34 The crown-centered loyalties of French mercantilists have been explored in Keohane, *Philosophy and the State in France*, pp. 151–68. Joyce Appleby, "Ideology and Theory: The Tension between Political and Economic Liberalism in 17th-century England" *AHR* 81 (1976): 499–515, explains the persisting appeal of English mercantilism partly as the result of its view of England as "an interlocking set of producers and distributors." In the balance-of-trade model, for example, subjects of the national economy were not viewed as isolated individuals but as common participants in England's collective enterprise of selling goods abroad. Self-interest and competition here always remained subordinate to nationalism, and the "symbolic cohesion" of England was thereby maintained.

35 "Of Commerce," *Essays*, 1, p. 292.

36 The scholarship on the natural law tradition is voluminous. The best introduction is still A. P. d'Entrèves, *Natural Law: An Historical Survey* (London, 1951). I have also found helpful discussions in Leonard Krieger, *The Politics of Discretion: Pufendorf and the Acceptance of Natural Law* (Chicago, 1965); Robert Derathé, *Jean-Jacques Rousseau et la Science Politique de Son Temps* (Paris, 1970), pp. 63–99; and Duncan Forbes, *Hume's Philosophical Politics* (Cambridge, 1975), ch. 1. Also see Isaiah Berlin's account of natural law theorists criticized by Vico, in *Vico & Herder* (New York, 1977), pp. 39–78.

37 *Letters*, 1, to Francis Hutcheson, 17 Sept. 1737, p. 34.

38 The following discussion draws largely from the recent invaluable accounts of Grotius's ideas in Richard Tuck, *Natural Rights Theories: Their Origin and Development* (Cambridge, 1979), esp. pp. 58–81, 156–77; and James Tully, *A Discourse on Property: John Locke and his Adversaries* (Cambridge, 1980), esp. pp. 70–72, 81–85, 112–14, and "The Framework of Natural Rights in Locke's Analysis of Property: A Contextual Reconstruction," in *Theories of Property*, pp. 114–38.

39 Tully, "The Framework of Natural Rights," pp. 120–23, and *A Discourse on Property*, pp. 65–70.

40 *De Iure Belli*, I. 2. 1. 5, as quoted in Tully, *Discourse on Property*, p. 81.

41 *De Iure Belli*, I. I, IV–VIII, as quoted in Tuck, *Natural Rights Theories*, p. 74.
42 Tully, *A Discourse on Property*, p. 69. For the full statement of Grotius's view of property, see *Of the Law of War and Peace, in Three Books*, trans. F. W. Kelsey (Oxford, 1927), book 2, ch. 2. Also Richard Schlatter, *Private Property: The History of an Idea* (London, 1952), and Forbes, *Hume's Philosophical Politics*, ch. 1.
43 Tully, "The Framework of Natural Rights," pp. 123–24. Pufendorf's definition of property comes from his *The Law of Nature and Nations*, 4. 4. 2. (1672), as quoted in Tully, *Discourse on Property*, p. 72.
44 *De Iure Belli*, Prolegomen, 8–10, as quoted in Tuck, *Natural Rights Theories*, p. 73.
45 Tuck, *Natural Rights Theories*, pp. 77–79.
46 *Inquiry*, p. 176.

II Francis Hutcheson

1 On Smith's debts to earlier English economic writers, see Joseph A. Schumpeter, *History of Economic Analysis* (New York, 1963), pp. 183–93; William A. Letwin, *The Origins of Scientific Economics* (Garden City, N.Y.), 1964; and Joyce Appleby, *Economic Thought and Ideology in Seventeenth-Century England* (Princeton, 1978), pp. 271–79. On his relationship with the Physiocrats, see Ronald Meek, *The Economics of Physiocracy* (Oxford, 1962), ch. 8, and Elizabeth Fox-Genovese, *The Origins of Physiocracy* (Ithaca, 1976), pp. 10–12, 78, 101–2, 272, 302, 313.
2 Smith taught books II and III of Hutcheson's *Short Introduction to Moral Philosophy*, those books which concerned natural jurisprudence and politics. This circumstance has been uncovered by R. L. Meek, "New Light on Adam Smith's Glasgow Lectures on Jurisprudence," *History of Political Economy* 8 (1976): 454–55, n. 29.
3 G. De Crecenzo, *Francis Hutcheson e il suo Tempo* (Turin, 1968), is the only full-scale study of Hutcheson's work. John D. Bishop, "The Moral Philosophy of Francis Hutcheson" (Ph.D. diss., University of Edinburgh, 1979), is a useful study of the first two books of the *System*, but it overlooks Hutcheson's ties to earlier seventeenth- and eighteenth-century natural law theorists.
4 John Dunn, "The Identity of the History of Ideas," *Philosophy* 43 (1968): 87–88, has explored problems involved in approaches to intellectual history that fail to consider "talking and thinking" as complicated instances of social activity. But given a thinker's sometimes explicit emphasis on writing an internally coherent body of thought—as with each of the three figures studied here—Dunn's distinction between thinking as "an effortful activity on the part of human beings" and thinking as "simply a unitary performance" may be a bit overdrawn.

5 *Inquiry*, pp. 256–63.
6 W. R. Scott, *Adam Smith as Student and Professor* (Glasgow, 1937), pp. 112–14. Also see E. Cannan's introduction to his edition of the Glasgow *Lectures*.
7 J. Rae, *Life of Adam Smith* (London, 1895), p. 13; W. L. Taylor, *Hutcheson and Hume as Predecessors of Adam Smith* (Durham, 1965), pp. 43–44. Also see Henry W. Spiegel, *The Growth of Economic Thought* (Englewood Cliffs, N.J., 1971), pp. 228–32.
8 Scott, *Adam Smith as Student and Professor*, p. 235.
9 *System II*, 104–8, 320–21.
10 Donald Winch, *Adam Smith's Politics*, p. 66, is correct in stressing this point. But I think Winch exaggerates the differences in their treatments of law and government; see ch. 3 of this stimulating essay.
11 *System I*, 281.
12 The basic details of Hutcheson's life are drawn from W. R. Scott, *Francis Hutcheson* (London, 1900), and " 'When is it that the Colonies may turn Independent': An Analysis of the Environment and Politics of Francis Hutcheson (1669–1746)," *William and Mary Quarterly* 11 (1954): 214–51. But it should be said that Hutcheson remains an important and complex figure awaiting a definitive modern biography.
13 Much recent scholarship concerning Hutcheson has traced the influence of the moral sense argument in eighteenth-century America; see Morton White, *The Philosophy of the American Revolution* (Oxford, 1978), pp. 97–141, and Gary Wills, *Inventing America: Jefferson's Declaration of Independence* (Garden City, N.Y., 1978), pp. 192–206, 228–39. But the same argument also impressed continental European thinkers such as Kant and Mendelssohn; see A. Altmann, *Moses Mendelssohn* (University, Ala., 1973), pp. 125–26.
14 *Characteristics of Men, Manners, Opinions, Times* (London, 1773 ed.), II, 415; my discussion in this paragraph follows Alasdair MacIntyre, *A Short History of Ethics* (New York, 1966), pp. 162–64.
15 My account of Shaftesbury's response to Locke borrows from David F. Norton, "Shaftesbury and Two Scepticisms," *Filosofia* 46 (1968): 1–12.
16 Leslie Stephen, *English Thought in the Eighteenth Century* (1876, rpt. New York, 1962), II, 34. The problems Mandeville posed in eighteenth-century thought have been explored more recently by James Moore, "The Social Background of Hume's Science of Human Nature," in *McGill Hume Studies*, ed. D. F. Norton, N. Capaldi, and W. L. Robinson (San Diego, 1979), pp. 23–41, and Thomas A. Horne, *The Social Thought of Bernard Mandeville* (New York, 1978), esp. ch. 5, and "Envy and Commercial Society," *Political Theory* 9 (1981): 551–70.
17 *Inquiry*, pp. 181–82, 160–61.
18 The discussion here is indebted to David Fate Norton, "Hutcheson on Perception and Moral Perception," *Archiv Für Geschichte Der Philosophie* 59 (1977), 181–97, and "Hutcheson's Moral Sense Reconsidered,"

Dialogue 13 (1973): 3–23. Also see Norton, *David Hume: Common-Sense Moralist, Sceptical Metaphysian* (Princeton, 1982), ch. 2.
19 *Inquiry*, pp. 109, vii.
20 Norton, "Hutcheson on Perception and Moral Perception," pp. 185–88.
21 *Letters*, I, March 16, 1740, p. 40. Hume was also a great admirer of Shaftesbury; see his "Of the Dignity or Meanness of Human Nature," *Essays*, I, 154n.
22 *Inquiry*, pp. 195, 198–99. The following is a brief example of the argument: "The moment of evil, produced by any agent, is, as the product of his Hatred into his Ability or $\mu = H \times A$" (p. 173). All such formulae, however, were dropped from later editions of the book.
23 Quoted in Scott, *Francis Hutcheson*, p. 32.
24 See William T. Blackstone, *Francis Hutcheson and Contemporary Ethical Theory* (Athens, Ga., 1965), and Henning Jensen, *Motivation and Moral Sense in Francis Hutcheson's Ethical Theory* (The Hague, 1971).
25 My accounts of "humanism" and "virtue" draw from Quentin Skinner, *The Foundations of Modern Political Thought: Volume One, The Renaissance* (Cambridge, 1978), pp. 69–112. Skinner stresses the importance of recognizing a distinctively humanist moral and political ideology reemerging during the Renaissance. By "ideology," he means a particular mode of argument and speech available to a thinker during a particular historical moment. There are of course other ways of defining the term, but I follow Skinner in this study.
26 *Essay*, p. 175.
27 *Short*, pp. 65–67, 102–3; *TMS*, VI. iii.
28 *Short*, pp. 1–2; the *System* I, 1–2, began with a description of moral philosophy that directly linked it to natural law thinking.
29 *Short*, p. 63.
30 The argument that a virtuous man gets pleasure from virtuous activity dates back to Aristotle's *Nichomachean Ethics;* so too does the notion of virtuous choice as choice in accordance with a mean. The novel point in Hutcheson was his contention that such choices must be made by reason of our emotions and inherent capacities.
31 See Albert O. Hirschman, *The Passions and the Interests* (Princeton, 1977), pp. 7–66, and Anthony Levi, *French Moralists: The Theory of the Passions, 1585–1659* (Oxford, 1964).
32 Skinner, *Foundations*, I, 73–74, 108–9. In Renaissance Florence, the spirited defenses of opulence and trade by Leonardo Bruni (1369–1444), Poggio Braccioloni (1380–1459), and Leon Battista Alberti (1404–72) were made in the 1420s and 1430s. By mid-century, however, the growth of private wealth was seen as a corrupting force that had kept Florentine citizens from their traditional and more important obligations in military service.
33 Levi, *French Moralists*, pp. 10–26.

34 *Inquiry*, p. 176.
35 *Short*, pp. 252–53.
36 *Treatise*, III. 1. ii., p. 470.
37 *System*, I, 12; *Short*, pp. 94–98.
38 Hirschman, *The Passions and the Interests*, pp. 65–66.
39 Horne, *The Social Thought of Bernard Mandeville*, pp. 86–92.
40 *Short*, pp. 18–19.
41 *Inquiry*, p. 177; also see *Short*, pp. 139–40. My analysis of Hutcheson's views on rights draws mostly from the *Inquiry*; his views did not change significantly in later works.
42 *Inquiry*, p. 256.
43 *Inquiry*, pp. 256–67.
44 *Inquiry*, pp. 257–58.
45 *Inquiry*, p. 259.
46 *Inquiry*, pp. 259–61.
47 *Inquiry*, pp. 261–62.
48 David Brion Davis, *The Problem of Slavery in Western Culture* (Ithaca, 1966), p. 378; C. Duncan Rice, *The Rise and Fall of Black Slavery* (New York, 1975), p. 167.
49 Tuck, *Natural Rights Theories*, pp. 1–4. Schumpeter, *History of Economic Analysis*, p. 122, described book v, chs. 1–8 of Pufendorf's *De Iure Naturae et Gentium* (1672), as an "embryonic *Wealth of Nations*." This work was also the main source of Hutcheson's interest in technical economic questions such as interest, price, coinage, contracts, insurance, and debt.
50 *Inquiry*, pp. 262–63.
51 *Inquiry*, p. 263.
52 *Inquiry*, pp. 263–65.
53 *Short*, p. 323.
54 *Short*, pp. i–iv.
55 See Grotius, *Of the Law of War and Peace*, I. 1. 2. 5, and Pufendorf, *De Iure Naturae et Gentium*, trans. C. H. and W. O. Oldfather (Oxford, 1934), I, vii, 7–9.
56 For more on this aspect of Grotius's work, see J. T. Johnson, *Ideology, Reason, and the Limitations of War: Religious and Secular Concepts* (Princeton, 1975).
57 The discussion that follows here draws primarily from Leonard Krieger, *The Politics of Discretion: Pufendorf and the Acceptance of Natural Law* (Chicago, 1965); Tuck, *Natural Rights Theories;* and Tully, *A Discourse on Property*. Hont and Ignatieff, "Needs and Justice in the *Wealth of Nations*," in *Wealth and Virtue*, pp. 22–44, have uncovered a third context within which Grotius's ideas were applied. They see Grotius's account of justice—one stressing its expletive, rather than distributive, domain—as marking the beginning of a distinctively modern (i.e., seventeenth-century) approach to a long-standing concern in

natural law jurisprudence—namely, how would a society ensure that the absolute property rights of its rich subjects not deny the propertyless the means of satisfying their needs. Hutcheson, however, never figures in their analysis. And the critical overview of natural law thinking he provided for Adam Smith, as we shall see, stressed more broadly philosophical matters.

58 *Natural Rights Theories*, p. 173. Julian Franklin, *John Locke and the Theory of Sovereignty* (Cambridge, 1978), and Skinner, *Foundations*, II, 122, 239-40, 338-39, also provide careful accounts of how Locke's radical theories of popular sovereignty and resistance developed out of earlier sixteenth- and seventeenth-century debates.

59 See Tuck, *Natural Rights Theories*, chs. 4-6; and James Tully, "Current Thinking About Sixteenth- and Seventeenth-Century Political Theory," *Historical Journal* 24 (1981): 475-84.

60 Krieger, *The Politics of Discretion*, p. 121.

61 *De Iure Naturae et Gentium*, III, v. 3.

62 Tuck, *Natural Rights Theories*, pp. 159-62.

63 *De Iure Naturae et Gentium*, IV. iv. 3-4.

64 Tuck, *Natural Rights Theories*, pp. 165-67.

65 Locke, *Two Treaties of Government*, ed. P. Laslett (Cambridge, 1963), pp. 309-18, 327-44. Both Tuck *Natural Rights Theories*, pp. 168-73, and Tully, *A Discourse on Property*, pp. 168-74, agree in their descriptions of Locke's account of the right of resistance. Tully, however, argues that an important part of Locke's rights theory is not Grotian, but instead derived from the neo-Thomist rights theorists that Grotius had attacked. But here again I follow Tuck's account of Locke, primarily because his account of Locke is closest to Hutcheson's understanding of the *Second Treatise*. For another writer who stresses Locke's ties to Grotius and Pufendorf, see Karl Olivecrona, "Appropriation in the State of Nature: Locke on the Origin of Property," *Journal of the History of Ideas* 35 (1974): 211-30.

66 For more on Carmichael, see James Moore and Michael Silverthorne, "Gershom Carmichael and Scottish Natural Jurisprudence in the Early Eighteenth Century," in *Wealth and Virtue*, ed. Hont and Ignatieff, pp. 73-88; on Barbeyrac, see Robert Derathé, *Jean-Jacques Rousseau et la Science Politique de son Temps* (Paris, 1970), pp. 89-92, and Tuck, *Natural Rights Theories*, pp. 174-76.

67 Hutcheson's account of the "law of nations" is not directly relevant to the concerns of this study. His thinking here followed that of Grotius, Pufendorf, and Cornelius Van Bynkershoek (1674-1743), the last of the figures mentioned in the preface of the *Short Introduction*. Bynkershoek was a Dutch jurist, one of the founders of modern international law, and originator of the "three mile limit" rule. See Francis De Pauw, *Grotius and the Law of the Sea* (Brussels, 1965).

68 *System I*, 309, 330, 323-24.

69 *Short*, pp. 303–6.
70 Gary Wills, *Inventing America*, p. 238, makes this point in arguing that Hutcheson was the chief influence on Thomas Jefferson's thinking about morality and politics. But Wills ultimately overstates his case; see also the incisive discussion in Ronald Hamowy, "Jefferson and the Scottish Enlightenment: A Critique of Gary Wills' *Inventing America*," *William & Mary Quarterly* 36 (1979).
71 *Short*, pp. 303, 305.
72 See C. Robbins, " 'When is it that the Colonies may turn Independent': An Analysis of the Politics of Francis Hutcheson (1694–1746)," for an account of how this argument was used by American colonial rebels in the 1760s and 1770s. For Hutcheson's statement of when a colony may justly constitute itself as an independent state, see *Short*, pp. 316–17.
73 *Short*, p. 112.
74 *System I*, 288–96.
75 *Short*, pp. 122–24, 241–46.
76 *System I*, 222–23.
77 See James Moore, "Locke and the Scottish Jurists" (unpublished paper presented to the Faculty Seminar in Political and Social Thought, Columbia University, January 24, 1979).
78 *System I*, 331, 319–20; *Short*, p. 150.
79 *System I*, 281, 293–95.
80 Moore, "Locke and the Scottish Jurists."
81 *Short*, p. 119.
82 On Hutcheson as a classical republican or neo-Harringtonian, see C. Robbins, *The Eighteenth-Century Commonwealthmen* (New York, 1968), pp. 185–96, and D. Winch, *Adam Smith's Politics*, ch. 3. On Harrington and the civic humanist tradition in early-modern British thought, see J. G. A. Pocock, *The Machiavellian Moment: Florentine Political Thought and the Atlantic Republican Tradition* (Princeton, 1975), chs. XII–XIV.
83 Moore, "Locke and the Scottish Jurists." For more on the differences between the legal and civic humanist traditions, see Pocock, "Cambridge Paradigms and Scotch Philosophers," in *Wealth and Virtue*, ed. Hont and Ignatieff, pp. 235–52.
84 "Considerations on Patronage," in *Collected Works*, VII, pp. 449–70.
85 *System*, II, 282.
86 "Considerations on Patronage," pp. 458, 462.
87 *System*, I, 12; II, 24; *Short*, pp. 94–98. I follow the account of English latitudinarian theology in Jacob, *The Newtonians and the English Revolution* (Ithaca, 1976), pp. 51–54, 181–94.
88 Hutcheson himself seems to have been aware of the problem. The *System of Moral Philosophy* was a projected magnum opus that he chose to abandon. Published posthumously by his son, this work was based on a manuscript Hutcheson began in 1733. On June 15, 1741, however, in

private correspondence he wrote that he had "dropped the thoughts of some great designs I had once sketched out." He then remarked that he was "adding confusedly to a confused book all valuable remarks in a farrago." His subsequent attempt to abbreviate his project in the *Short Introduction* did nothing to clarify the confusion in his ideological commitments. See Scott, *Francis Hutcheson*, p. 114.

III David Hume

1 Thomas Reid, *Essays on the Active Powers of the Human Mind* (1788; rpt. Cambridge, Mass., 1969), p. 413, spoke for most of Hume's critics in Scotland when he said that any notion of justice must carry "inseparably along with it, a perception of its moral obligation." By contrast, Reid observed that Hume's view was unacceptably "confined" to accounting for the social utility of justice.
2 John Plamenatz, "Hume" in *Man and Society* (London, 1964), p. 299; J. S. Mill, *Selected Writings*, ed. Maurice Cowling (New York, 1968), p. 18.
3 Duncan Forbes, *Hume's Philosophical Politics* (Cambridge, 1976), p. 87; Donald Winch, *Adam Smith's Politics* (Cambridge, 1978), pp. 73–74, also endorses this view.
4 *Treatise*, III. II. ii, p. 489. Hume acknowledged his deep and important debt to Grotius in *Enquiry*$_2$, v, 257n, p. 307.
5 *Letters*, to Francis Hutcheson, Sept. 7, 1739, I, 33. The conclusion of the *Treatise*, III. III. v, pp. 619–20, pursued the point in more detail.
6 James Conniff, "Hume's Political Methodology: A Reconsideration of 'That Politics May be Reduced to a Science,'" *Review of Politics* 38 (1976): 88–108, and "Hume on Political Parties: The Case for Hume as a Whig," *Eighteenth Century Studies* 12 (1978/9): 150–73; Forbes, *Hume's Philosophical Politics* and "Hume and the Scottish Enlightenment" in *Philosophers of the Enlightenment*, ed. S. C. Brown (Sussex, 1979), pp. 94–109; James Moore, "Hume's Theory of Justice and Property," *Political Studies* 29 (1976): 103–19, "Hume's Political Science and the Classical Republican Tradition," *Canadian Journal of Political Science* 10 (1977): 809–39, and "The Social Background of Hume's Science of Human Nature" in *McGill Hume Studies* (San Diego, 1979), pp. 23–42.
7 N. K. Smith, *The Philosophy of David Hume* (London, 1941), p. 79. David Miller's recent *Philosophy and Ideology in Hume's Political Thought* (Oxford, 1981), focuses squarely on the "central puzzle" Norman Kemp Smith underlined, and thus now provides the best introductory guide to Hume's political philosophy. It offers a more extended and perhaps well-balanced analysis of Hume than I have room for here. Miller sees him as a philosophical voice for an open and progressive aristocracy, ready to accept newcomers into its midst and eager for improvement in

agriculture and industry. But I think Miller somewhat oversimplifies the "historical" dimensions of Hume's thought. He says too little about the natural law foundations of Hume's views of property and justice and about how Hutcheson spurred him to re-build those foundations. He misses, too, the great extent to which the *Political Discourses* drew from earlier economic writing.

8   Shirley Letwin, *The Pursuit of Certainty* (Cambridge, 1965), p. 39; Peter Gay, *The Enlightenment: An Interpretation*, 2 vols. (New York, 1966–69), I, 401–19.
9   *Treatise*, II. III. iii, p. 413.
10 *Enquiry*$_2$, VI. I. 193, p. 237; *Treatise*, III. ii. x, p. 558.
11 In fact, as George A. Kelly has argued in a different context, there is something misleading in attaching "isms" to any great thinker: "Serious philosophy—the creative deployment of systematic intellectual power—is scarcely conservative. In political theory, the real conservatives—Burke, de Maistre, Haller—are pseudo-philosophers." *Idealism, Politics, and History* (Cambridge, 1968), p. 323. Also see Miller, *Philosophy and Ideology in Hume's Political Thought*, pp. 187–205, for a provocative three-sided comparison of Hume, Adam Smith, and Burke.
12 Sheldon Wolin, "Hume and Conservatism," *American Political Science Review* 48 (1954): 1001. Giuseppe Giarrizzo, *David Hume politico e storico* (Turin, 1962), makes a careful argument to show that Hume's political views grew more "conservative" as he grew older. But also see the incisive criticisms of this book in a review by Duncan Forbes in *The Historical Journal* 6 (1963): 280–95.
13 *Letters*, to Henry Home, Lord Kames, March 4, 1758, I, 272.
14 E. C. Mossner, *The Life of David Hume* (London, 1954), provides most of the biographical details mentioned in this chapter.
15 See Hume's own vivid account of his crisis in *Letters*, to Dr. George Cheyene, March or April 1734, I, 12–18.
16 "Of Interest," *Essays*, I, 324.
17 *Treatise*, xxi, n. 1; *Letters*, I, 40.
18 *Treatise*, II. I. xi, pp. 316–20; Barry Stroud, *Hume* (London, 1977), pp. 196–98.
19 *Enquiry*$_2$, I, 138, pp. 173–75. The account of Hutcheson's achievement here follows a long note that Hume appended to Section 1, *Enquiry*$_1$, in its first two editions, 1748 and 1751. (Selby-Bigge's edition omits this important note; see *David Hume: The Philosophical Works*, ed. Green and Grose, II, 10–11.) On the influence of Descartes on eighteenth-century thinkers, see Aram Vartanian, *Diderot and Descartes: A Study of Scientific Naturalism in the Enlightenment* (Princeton, 1953), esp. ch. III.
20 *Letters*, to Francis Hutcheson, Sept. 17, 1739, I, 32. The distinction between "anatomist" and "painter" would be raised again at the conclusion of the *Treatise*, III. III. vi, pp. 620–21.
21 For Hutcheson's letter of April 1739, see Ian Ross, "Hutcheson on Hume's

Treatise: An Unnoticed Letter," *Journal of the History of Philosophy* 4 (1966): 69–72.
22 *Letters,* I, 39–40.
23 *Letters,* to William Mure, August 4, 1744, I, 58.
24 *My Own Life* (1776), rpt. in *Letters,* I, 2.
25 Mossner, *Life of David Hume,* p. 148. My interest in Hume's relationship with Hutcheson also explains why in this study I make much more use of the *Treatise* than the *Enquiry concerning the Principles of Morals.* The *Treatise* displays more fully the extent of Hutcheson's influence on Hume. It was also far more well-known and controversial in Scottish universities than Hume later remembered.
26 For a powerful critique of the use of influence-models in intellectual history, see Quentin Skinner, "The Limits of Historical Explanation," *Philosophy* 41 (1966): 199–215, and "Meaning and Understanding in the History of Ideas," *History & Theory* 8 (1969): esp. 24–27. Skinner has argued that the influence-model only rarely can be made to work, and that when it can be, there is hardly ever any point in doing so. I think the story of Hutcheson's 'influence" on Hume suggests that *einflussstudies* sometimes provide important information. But the broader issue needs careful study, and Skinner's argument awaits a more systematic reply.
27 *Treatise,* II. III. iii, p. 415; later in the *Treatise,* III. I. i, p. 458, Hume described passions as "original facts and realities, complete in themselves . . . 'Tis impossible, therefore, they can be pronounced either true or false, and be either contrary or conformable to reason."
28 *Letters,* to Francis Hutcheson, Sept. 17, 1739, I, 32–35.
29 Ibid., 33.
30 *Enquiry*$_2$, XII. III. 129, p. 161.
31 N. K. Smith, *The Philosophy of David Hume* (London, 1941), esp. pp. 3–46; Stroud, *Hume.* A. J. Ayer, *Hume* (New York, 1980), is now perhaps the best brief introduction to the technical issues in his philosophy, especially the theory of causation.
32 *Inquiry,* pp. 259–61; *Short Introduction,* p. 123.
33 *Treatise,* III. II. i, pp. 477–84. Hume's argument here echoed an objection to Hutcheson first raised in the "Dissertation on Virtue" by Dr. Joseph Butler (1692–1752). Butler, whom Hume also deeply admired, pointed out that Hutcheson was wrong in saying that our motive to justice arises from our noticing what is useful to others. Often we notice that some just acts are not for the good of others.
34 *Treatise,* III. II. i, p. 484.
35 *Treatise,* III. II. ii, p. 486.
36 *Treatise,* III. II. vi, p. 526.
37 *Treatise,* III. II. ii, pp. 484–501. I am much indebted to the lucid essay by James Moore, "Hume's Theory of Justice and Property," esp. pp. 104–12,

and to Stroud, *Hume*, pp. 199-218, for clarifications of technical details in Hume's theory of justice.

38 *Treatise*, III. II. ii, p. 489.
39 Moore, "Hume's Theory of Justice and Property," p. 108; *Treatise*, III, II. ii, p. 492.
40 *An Abstract of a Treatise of Human Nature: A Pamphlet hitherto unknown by David Hume*, rpt. and intro. by J. M. Keynes and P. Sraffa (Cambridge, 1938), p. 4.
41 The conception of Hume as the sceptic who brought to grief the empiricism of John Locke and George Berkeley no longer dominates current discussions of his place in the history of philosophy. Nicholas Capaldi, "The Problem of Hume and Hume's Problem," in *McGill Hume Studies*, pp. 3-21, provides a useful survey of recent changes in Hume's reputation among current philosophers and historians of philosophy.
42 Robert D. Cumming, *Human Nature and History*, 2 vols. (Chicago, 1969), esp. vol. II, 113-231; Keohane, *Philosophy and the State in France*, pp. 151-68, 35-57; Horne, *The Social Thought of Bernard Mandeville*; Pocock, *The Machiavellian Moment*, pp. 459-61; Winch, *Adam Smith's Politics*, pp. 167-71; Moore, "The Social Background of Hume's Science of Human Nature," in *McGill Hume Studies*, pp. 23-42.
43 Albert O. Hirschman, *The Passions and the Interests: Political Arguments for Capitalism Before Its Triumph* (Princeton, 1977), pp. 14-20.
44 Ibid., pp. 20-56.
45 *Treatise*, II. III. iv, pp. 418-22.
46 Hirschman, *The Passions and the Interests*, p. 26. Also see Miller, *Philosophy and Ideology in Hume's Political Thought*, ch. 6, for another recent account stressing the complexities of Hume's analysis of commercial society.
47 $Enquiry_2$ in *Philosophical Works*, ed. Green and Grose, II, 11 n.; Hirschman, *The Passions and the Interests*, p. 69.
48 *Treatise*, III. II, ii, p. 492.
49 Moore, "Hume's Theory of Justice and Property," pp. 111, 115.
50 $Enquiry_2$, III. 145, p. 184.
51 $Enquiry_2$, III, 154, p. 192. John B. Stewart, *The Moral and Political Philosophy of David Hume* (New York, 1963), pp. 133-36, provides an illuminating analysis of Hume's distinctions between ethics and politics, which I have made considerable use of here in examining Hume on justice and government.
52 Ibid., pp. 134-35.
53 *Treatise*, III. III. vi, pp. 619-20. Put another way, Hume's distinction suggested that while every instance of a "natural" virtue—such as parental affection or friendship—results in some specific benefit, the exercise of "artificial" virtues usually creates some benefit but does not always do so. Repayment of a loan from a wealthy man, for example, may not result

in the good of others, but the just act is nevertheless to repay the loan. In Hume's account, as in those of natural law theorists before him, just acts provide regularity and structure in public affairs. The novel thrust of his discussion here was to account for the insight that there are at times gaps in the social utility of particular acts exemplifying justice. Here, too, he demonstrated why the traditional natural law appeal to "right reason" was inadequate in explaining our motives to justice in instances where we approve of just acts that do not obviously help society as a whole.

54 See esp. Nicholas Phillipson, "Hume as Civic Moralist: a Social Historian's Perspective" in *Philosophers of the Enlightenment*, ed. S. C. Brown (Sussex, 1979), pp. 140–61, and Forbes, *Hume's Philosophical Politics*. Phillipson's approach, I think, does not explore fully enough the consistently antitheological character of Hume's work after the *Treatise*. Forbes observes that the term "philosophical" must change its meaning over time when used with reference to Hume's politics (see p. x). I attempt to show in this chapter, however, that there was a fairly consistent philosophical view of politics running through Hume's work.

55 For a more detailed account of the charges, see E. C. Mossner, "Philosophy and Biography: The Case of David Hume" in *Hume*, ed. V. C. Chappell (Notre Dame, 1968), pp. 6–34. Mossner persuasively refutes the charges, but never develops fully his alternative view that Hume wanted a popular vehicle for presenting his philosophical views. On the *Enquiries*, the general view now seems to be that they differed from the *Treatise* "more in emphasis than in argument" (Ayer, *Hume*, p. 6).

56 The Advertisement is quoted in *Treatise*, ed. and intro. E. C. Mossner (Baltimore, 1969), p. 19; *My Own Life*, p. 3. I should note that by "essays" here I mean Hume's writings on politics and economics after the *Treatise*. His other work covered a large range of topics including history, manners, and criticism that are not directly covered in this discussion.

57 *Letters*, I, 17, 39.

58 *Essays*, I, 113–17.

59 See Mossner's useful introduction to the *Treatise* (Baltimore, 1969), pp. 7–28.

60 Balfour's one claim to distinction as a philosopher rested on his *A Delineation of the Nature and Obligations of Morality, with Reflexions upon Mr. Hume's Book entitled "An Enquiry concerning the Principles of Morals"* (anon., 1753). The book defended religion and reason against the naturalistic theory of morals and attacked Hume for reducing virtue to a matter of the observer's "utility" and "humanity" (see pp. 123, 144, 164).

61 The key essays in Forbes's interpretation include "Of the first Principles of Government," "Of Liberty and Despotism," and "Of the Rise and Progress of Arts and Sciences." James Moore, "Hume's Political Science and the Classical Republican Tradition," has charted Hume's campaign

against the specter of that political tradition that had haunted Hutcheson in his latter works.

62 Pierre de Boisguilbert (1646–1714) was among the first to develop a fairly systematic theory of laissez-faire economics during the last decades of Louis XIV's reign. See L. Rothkrug, *Opposition to Louis XIV: The Political and Social Origins of the French Enlightenment* (Princeton, 1965), pp. 392–413.

63 Donald Winch, "The Emergence of Economics as a Science, 1750–1870," in *The Fontana Economic History of Europe*, ed. Carlo M. Cipolla (London, 1973), vol. 3, 511–28, provides a useful introduction to this issue.

64 "Of Commerce," *Essays*, I, 288–89.

65 See Forbes, *Hume's Philosophical Politics*, p. 87.

66 Some of my account of Montchrétien follows Keohane, *Philosophy and the State*, pp. 164–65. Keith Tribe has argued that Montchrétien's *Traité de l'œconomie politique* (1615) inaugurated a distinct tradition of discourse that conceived of "political economy" in terms of the "administration of an aggregated polity by a 'sovereign' or 'statesman,' whose presence is essential to the discourse in providing a unity which is otherwise dispersed among the instances of the economy of the categories that articulate these instances." Tribe also argues persuasively that this same tradition of discourse remained vital for more than 150 years after Montchrétien's text first appeared, and that the economic writings of both Hume and Adam Smith were governed by its key assumptions. See Tribe, *Land, Labour and Economic Discourse* (London, 1978), ch. 5.

67 *Essays*, I: "Of Money," 319; "Of Refinement in the Arts," 309; "Of Commerce," 294–95.

68 Keohane, *Philosophy and the State in France*, pp. 158–68.

69 See *Letters*, I, 46; *Enquiry*$_1$, I. 4, p. 7; "Of Refinement in the Arts," *Essays*, I, 308n. In *Enquiry*$_2$, p. 314n., Hume wrote that French thinkers had expressed the sentiment "pride" by the term amour propre, "but as they also express self-love as well as vanity by the same term, there arises thence a great confusion in Rochefoucault, and many of their moral writers."

70 *Essays*, I, "Of Commerce," 292, 294–95; "Of Interest," 325.

71 *The Passions and the Interests*, p. 132.

72 Eli Heckscher, *Mercantilism*, II, 293.

73 Joyce Appleby, "Ideology and Theory: The Tension between Political Economic Liberalism in Seventeenth-century England," *AHR* 81 (1976): 499–515, includes a more detailed discussion of the role of these ideas in English mercantilist doctrines. On the patriotism of French mercantilism, see Keohane, *Philosophy and the State in France*, pp. 158–68.

74 The best surveys remain A. Schatz, *L'Oeuvre économique de David Hume* (Paris, 1902), and Eugene Rotwein's long introduction to *David Hume: Writings on Economics* (Madison, 1955), ix–cxi.

75 *Essays*, I, 345–48. "Of Jealousy of Trade" first appeared in *Essays and Treatises on Several Subjects* (1758).

76 *Essays,* 1: "Of the Jealousy of Trade," 348; "Of Public Credit," 370n.
77 "Of the Jealousy of Trade," 348; "Of Commerce," 295.
78 "Of Commerce," 293–94.
79 Ibid., 295, 291.
80 *Essays,* 1: "Idea of a perfect Commonwealth," 480–90.
81 Ibid., 487.
82 Moore, "Hume and the Classical Republican Tradition," p. 837.
83 My reading by no means exhausts the *Political Discourses.* It is now well known that Hume's essays had a profound influence on arguments fashioned by Alexander Hamilton and James Madison in *The Federalist Papers.* See Douglas Adair, "That Politics May Be Reduced to a Science: David Hume, James Madison and the Tenth Federalist," *Huntingdon Library Quarterly* 20 (1957): 343–60; and, more recently, Gary Wills, *Explaining America* (New York, 1981).
84 Forbes, review of *David Hume, politico e storica,* by G. Giarizzo, *Historical Journal* 6 (1963): 295. John Robertson, "The Scottish Enlightenment at the limits of the civic tradition," in *Wealth and Virtue,* ed. Hont and Ignatieff, pp. 137–78, is a recent provocative reading of Hume, yet also attempts the impossible interpretive miracle which Forbes warns against. Hume's chief ideological project, Robertson argues, was to show that Europe's emerging commercial civilization would "make it possible for every individual to satisfy the material and moral requirements of citizenship." Because commerce "can ultimately bring sufficiency and independence to all, all may eventually attain that economic autonomy which in civic terms was the material condition of free political activity." The heart of Robertson's account of Hume is his attempt to show that this projected reconciliation of competitive economic individualism with citizenship was based philosophically on Hume's novel integration of natural law and civic humanist conceptions of liberty. But serious reservations about the reliability of this analysis set in when one discovers that Hume's ambitious synthesis of civic and jurisprudential concepts of liberty is to be found in the "Idea of a Perfect Commonwealth." The essay is just too slender to carry all the weight that Robertson assigns it. Hume's playful irony also has escaped his notice entirely.
85 "Of the Balance of Power," *Essays,* 1, 354.
86 Giarizzo, *David Hume, politico e storico,* pp. 69–71, 94–95, and I. Kramnick, *Bolingbroke and his Circle: The Politics of Nostalgia in the Age of Walpole* (Cambridge, 1968), pp. 82–83. But also see the persuasive critique of this approach in Forbes, *Hume's Philosophical Politics,* pp. 173–75, and the interesting analysis of the connections between Hume's views on the public debt and on the American colonial disturbances in J. G. A. Pocock, "Hume and the American Revolution: The Dying Thoughts of a North Briton," in *McGill Hume Studies,* pp. 325–43.
87 "Of the Balance of Power," *Essays,* 1, 354: "half our wars with France,

and all our public debts are owing more to our own imprudent vehemence than the ambition of our neighbours."
88 "Of Public Credit," *Essays*, I, 371, 368.

IV Adam Smith

1 *WN* v. i. f. 25.
2 James MacKintosh, *Dissertation on the Progress of Ethical Philosophy*, ed. W. Whewell (Edinburgh, 1836), is perhaps the earliest example of this approach. See also James Bonar, *Moral Sense* (London, 1930); D. D. Raphael, *The Moral Sense* (London, 1947); and A. MacIntyre, *Short History of Ethics* (New York, 1966), ch. 12.
3 *WN* I. ii. 2.
4 In *WN* I. x, Smith also discussed the role of "the imaginations of men" in determining economic careers and examined that "over-weening conceit which the greater part of men have of their own abilities."
5 Donald Winch, *Adam Smith's Politics* (Cambridge, 1978), pp. 13–14, 172–73. Cesare Beccaria (1738–94) defended the principles of free trade as professor of economics at Milan in his 1769–70 lectures. Joseph A. Schumpeter, *History of Economic Analysis* (New York, 1963), p. 179, called him "the Italian Adam Smith." A less well-known eighteenth-century free trade argument appeared in Charles Smith, *Three Tracts on the Corn Trade* (1766), a work that Smith sometimes cited in *WN*.
6 *WN* IV. intro. 1.
7 *WN* IV. i. 8–14. Smith's example here was the extensive smuggling of gold and silver in eighteenth-century Europe.
8 *WN* IV. v. b. 39. Like the *Political Discourses*, the *WN* was also partly a didactic exercise. About his discussions of the division of labor, the extension of the market, and the accumulation of capital in books I and II, Smith reminded his readers at one point, "I am always willing to run some hazard of being tedious in order to be sure that I am perspicuous" (*WN* I. iv. 18).
9 The plan was reported in Dugald Stewart, "Account of the Life and Writings of Adam Smith," ed. I. S. Ross, in Adam Smith, *Essays on Philosophical Subjects*, ed. W. P. D. Wightman and J. C. Bryce (Oxford, 1980), p. 304.
10 *Corr.*, Letter 274, to Dr. Archibald Davidson, 16 Nov. 1787, pp. 308–9. Most biographical details in this chapter are taken from John Rae, *Life of Adam Smith* (London, 1895), and W. R. Scott, *Adam Smith as Student and Professor* (Glasgow, 1937).
11 *Corr.*, p. 309.
12 *LJ* (B), p. 269.
13 *Corr.*, Letter 28, to Lord Fitzmaurice, 21 Feb. 1759, p. 28.
14 Mandeville's views were discussed at length in *TMS* VII. ii. 4. 1–13. Smith

included translations of selected passages from Rousseau's *Discours* in his letter, rpt. in *Essays on Philosophical Subjects*, pp. 242–56.
15 *TMS* VII. iii. 2. 9.
16 *TMS* VII. iii. 3. 8.
17 *TMS* I. i. 1. 1–9.
18 *TMS* I. i. 1. 10–12.
19 *TMS* I. i. 1. 3–6; VII. iii. 3. 16.
20 *TMS* I. i. 3. b. Knud Haakonssen, *The Science of a Legislator: The Natural Law Jurisprudence of David Hume and Adam Smith* (Cambridge, 1981), pp. 52–54. My account of Smith on "sympathy" has benefited greatly from Haakonssen's careful analysis, pp. 45–61.
21 *Corr.*, Letter 10, to William Cullen, Nov. 1751, p. 5.
22 Smith's eulogy first appeared in a letter to William Strahan, *Corr.*, Letter 178, 9 Nov. 1776, pp. 217–21. The letter was made public when included in the posthumous *Life of David Hume, Esq.: Written by Himself* (1777). Details of the controversy are discussed in Mossner, *Life of David Hume* (Oxford, 1954), appendix I, pp. 620–22; and D. D. Raphael, "Adam Smith and 'the infection of David Hume's society,'" *Journal of the History of Ideas* 30 (1969): 225–48.
23 *TMS* IV. i. 2. and IV. ii. 2. Hume apparently was not offended by Smith's reluctance to acknowledge his influence more explicitly. Indeed, Hume helped to distribute complimentary copies of *TMS* to leading literary and political figures in London. He also published a lengthy anonymous review in Smollett's *Critical Review* for May 1759. See David R. Raynor, "Hume's Abstract of Adam Smith's *Theory of Moral Sentiments*," *Journal of the History of Philosophy* 22 (1984): 51–79.
24 *LJ(A)*, vol. V, i. 5; *LJ(B)*, p. 252–53.
25 *TMS* VII. iii. intro. 3.
26 Joseph Cropsey, *Polity and Economy: An Interpretation of the Principles of Adam Smith* (The Hague, 1957), pp. 5–55, 92–101.
27 This view of Smith dates back to Richard Zeyss, *Adam Smith und der Eigennutz* (Tübingen, 1889), a study that figured prominently in the first discussions of "*das Adam Smith Problem*" among German scholars. In their recent introduction to *TMS*, p. 18, Raphael and Macfie also suggest that "the prudent man of *TMS* VI. i. is the frugal man of *WN*. II. iii."
28 Hirschman, *The Passions and the Interests*, pp. 100–112.
29 *TMS* VII. i. 2.
30 *TMS* I. i. 1: "Sympathy ... does not arise so much from the view of the passion, as from that of the situation which excites it." Haakonssen, *Science of the Legislator*, pp. 45–47.
31 *WN* IV. v. b.
32 *WN* II. iii. 28.
33 *TMS* I. i. 4. 7–10. Here I also argue against myself, for it now seems to me in my article, "Rethinking *Das Adam Smith Problem*," *Journal of British*

Studies 20 (1981): 116–18, I stressed economic implications in Smith's account of virtue that he had not meant to suggest.
34 *TMS* I. iii. 2. 1, and I. iii. 3. 1.
35 Thomas Horne, "Envy and Commercial Society: Mandeville and Smith on 'Private Vice, Public Benefits,'" *Political Theory* 9 (1981): 560. My discussion of economic themes in *TMS* is much indebted to Horne's thoughtful analysis.
36 *TMS* VII. iv. 37.
37 *TMS*, Advertisement added in sixth ed. p. 3.
38 *WN* IV. intro. 1.
39 For a more detailed discussion of this incident, see Adam Smith, *Lectures on Justice*, ed. and intro. Edwin Cannan (Oxford, 1896), pp. xxxi–xxxiv.
40 Winch, *Adam Smith's Politics*, esp. chs. 3–5; Haakonssen, *Science of a Legislator*, passim. Also see the discussion of connections between *LJ(A)*, *LJ(B)*, and *WN* in the many editorial notes to *WN*, esp. III. II. i.
41 *LJ(A)*, vol. i, pp. 14–16, 9–10, 17.
42 *LJ(B)*, p. 210; *LJ(A)*, vol. iv, pp. 21–23.
43 *LJ(B)*, p. 1; *TMS*, VII. iv. 37.
44 *LJ(A)*, vol. i, pp. 24–25.
45 *LJ(A)*, vol. i, pp. 35–37.
46 *LJ(A)*, vol. i, pp. 37–40.
47 *LJ(A)*, vol. i, p. 27.
48 R. L. Meek, "Smith Turgot, and the 'Four Stages Theory,'" *History of Political Economy* 3 (1971): 9–27; and *Social Science and the Ignoble Savage* (Cambridge, 1976), esp. ch. 4. Also see R. Pascal "Property and Society: The Scottish Historical School of the Eighteenth Century," *The Modern Quarterly* 1 (1938): 167–79.
49 For Smith, the immediate source of the "four stages" probably was Montesquieu's *Spirit of the Laws*, book XVIII; see Meek, *Social Science and the Ignoble Savage*, pp. 31–35. But one novelty in Smith's jurisprudence was surely his effort to combine Grotius with Montesquieu.
50 *LJ(A)*, vol. i, pp. 24–25, 149–53.
51 Both historical developments, however, comprised what Smith sometimes referred to as the "natural progress which men make in society," *LJ(A)*, vol. iv, p. 19.
52 *LJ(A)*, vol. i, pp. 27–30, 45, 106–7, 50.
53 *LJ(A)*, vol. i, pp. 28–30; *LJ(B)*, p. 32. With regard to the order in which Smith explored the principles of his jurisprudence, the differences between *LJ(A)* and *LJ(B)* have been examined carefully by Meek, Raphael, and Stein in their introduction to the Glasgow edition of the *Lectures*, pp. 22–32. But there were no major differences in the content of the lectures, so I use them interchangeably. Smith himself never clearly explained why he reversed his procedure in *LJ(B)* to begin by exploring the nature of government rather than property and rights.

54 *LJ(A)*, vol. iv, pp. 21-23.
55 *LJ(A)*, vol. iii, pp. 135-39.
56 *LJ(A)*, vol. i, p. 34. Also see the provocative account of Rousseau's influence on Smith in Michael Ignatieff's recent *The Needs of Strangers* (New York, 1985), pp. 108-26.
57 *LJ(B)*, p. 165.
58 *LJ(A)*, vol. ii, p. 41.
59 Haakonssen, *Science of a Legislator*, pp. 154-77, provides a detailed examination of this aspect of the Glasgow *Lectures*.
60 *TMS* VII. iv. 36. Essentially the same point was made at the outset of both *LJ(A)*, vol. i. i, and *LJ(B)*, p. 1.
61 *LJ(B)*, pp. 159-61: *LJ(A)*, vol. i, pp. 161-62.
62 *LJ(B)*, pp. 31-33.
63 *LJ(A)*, vol. iv, pp. 157-58.
64 *LJ(B)*, pp. 59-91; *WN* III, iv. 15.
65 *LJ(A)*, vol. v, p. 58. *LJ(A)*, vol. v, pp. 115-19, finds Smith reiterating Hume's critique of the view that political obligation must be founded on consent. For more detailed accounts of Hume's influence on Smith's opinions of political debates in his time, see D. Forbes, "Sceptical Whiggism, Commerce and Liberty," in *Essays on Adam Smith*, ed. Skinner and Wilson (Oxford, 1976), pp. 179-201, and Winch, *Adam Smith's Politics*, pp. 70-103.
66 *LJ(B)*, pp. 163-64.
67 *LJ(A)*, vol. i, pp. 164-67. *WN* III. ii. 6, later made essentially the same argument.
68 *LJ(B)*, vol. ii, pp. 27-37.
69 Haakonssen, *Science of a Legislator*, p. 188.
70 *LJ(B)*, p. 210.
71 *TMS* II. ii. I. 9.
72 C. B. Macpherson, *Democratic Theory: Essays in Retrieval* (Oxford, 1973), p. 5; also see his classic *The Political Theory of Possessive Individualism* (Oxford, 1962).
73 *WN* IV. v. b. 39.
74 *WM* IV. v. b. 16.
75 *WN* I, x. c. 12.
76 *WN* IV. ix. 51. Hont & Ignatieff, "Needs and Justice in the *Wealth of Nations*," in *Wealth and Virtue*, pp. 26-44, arrive at a similar conclusion by exploring how the discussion of commercial market relations developed within seventeenth-century natural law jurisprudence. But it is misleading to say that Smith "*left no doubt* that in crafting his argument for a 'system of natural liberty,' he was deploying terms whose provenance *had to be* traced to Grotius . . ." (p. 26, emphases added). This makes the *Wealth of Nations* appear to be mostly a tract in natural law and natural rights theorizing. It should be acknowledged, after all, that

Grotius was never once mentioned by name in the text of the *Wealth of Nations*.

77 For more detailed critiques of Macpherson's approach, see David Miller, "Hume and Possessive Individualism," *History of Political Thought* 1 (1980): 261–78; and Donald Winch, "The Burke-Smith Problem in Late Eighteenth-century Political and Economic Thought," *Historical Journal* 28 (1985): 231–48.

78 J. Schumpeter, *History of Economic Analysis* (New York, 1963), pp. 184–85. William Letwin, *The Origins of Scientific Economic Analysis*, p. 245. A more recent challenge to Schumpeter's appraisal of Smith as an economic analyst is Samuel Hollander, *The Economics of Adam Smith* (Toronto, 1973).

79 *Corr.*, Letter 153, from William Robertson, 8 April 1776, p. 193.

80 Robert D. Cumming, *Human Nature and History* (Chicago, 1969), 2: 174–78, 213–20, sees the decision as a result of Smith's overriding new interest in the unintended social consequences of human activity. But it is difficult to reconcile this view of the origins of the *WN* with Smith's obvious emphasis on the need for planned legal and economic reforms.

81 The extensive economic pamphlet literature of this period has been studied carefully in Joyce O. Appleby, *Economic Thought and Ideology in Seventeenth-Century England* (Princeton, 1978), esp. ch. 2.

82 E. P. Thompson, "The Moral Economy of the English Crowd in the Eighteenth Century," *Past & Present* 50 (1971): 91. During Smith's lifetime, the term "corn" was used to describe all cereals—wheat, rye, barley, etc.—used to produce bread. Most ordinary people were thought to live almost entirely on bread alone. Thus "the price of corn" was roughly synonymous with "the cost of living" or "the price of food." The main targets of the Corn Laws were forestallers and engrossers. Parliament repealed legislation against forestalling in 1772, but restrictions would be reimposed when Britain went to war against the armies of the French Revolution and again during the Napoleonic Wars.

83 *WN* IV. v. b. 3 & 7.
84 *WN* IV. v. b. 5 & 8.
85 *WN* IV. v. b. 40.
86 *WN* IV. i. 1–2.
87 Schumpeter, *History of Economic Analysis*, p. 185.
88 Appleby, *Economic Thought and Ideology*, p. 7.
89 *WN* I. viii. 12–13.
90 *WN* I. viii. 36.
91 *WN* I. x. c. 16.
92 Schumpeter, *History of Economic Analysis*, p. 187. Article "Épingle" *Encyclopédie* (Paris, 1755), v: 804–7, was the source of Smith's famous discussion of the eighteen operations in a modern pin-factory, a discussion that noted "it is even a trade by itself" to put pins into paper; *WN* I.

i. 3. This is perhaps an example of work that led to the mental torpor Smith later discussed in book v.
93 *WN* v. i. f. 50.
94 Jacob Viner, "Adam Smith," in *The International Encyclopedia of the Social Sciences* (Glencoe, Ill., 1968), 14: 325.
95 *WN* IV. ii. 43. This important passage stressing the utopian aspect of free trade doctrines has been overlooked in Frank E. Manuel and Fritzie P. Manuel, *Utopian Thought in the Western World* (Cambridge, Mass., 1979). In his classic *The Great Transformation: The Political and Economic Origins of Our Times* (Boston, 1944), pp. 3, 33, Karl Polanyi argued that the disastrous course of Western history in the first half of the twentieth century must be understood in terms of the "stark utopia" pursued by those who believed in the idea of a self-adjusting market. The followers of Adam Smith, Polanyi argued, discarded "the common sense attitude toward change" in favor of "a mystical readiness to accept the social consequences of economic improvement, whatever they might be." But only a very selective reading of the *Wealth of Nations* allowed Polanyi to make the same points about Smith himself.
96 *WN* IV. ii. 9.
97 *WN* IV. ii. 44.
98 *WN* v. i. f. 55. Again there was a cautious pragmatism in Smith's willingness to retain the Navigation Acts, which required all British trade to be carried on British ships. Although Smith made clear that these laws subjected Britain to a disadvantage in every branch of trade she did not monopolize, he also conceded that they provided a crucial reservoir of trained seamen in case of war. See *WN* IV. vii. c. 19–32.

V   *Epilogue*

1 The conditioning began with the anonymous writer of Smith's obituary in *The Times*, 24 July, 1790. "Being in a commercial town," he observed with a sneer, Smith had not resisted the temptation of changing "the Chair of Moral Philosophy into a professorship of trade and finance."
2 The most well known side-notes are those in Edwin Cannan's 1904 edition, still available in various contemporary editions of *WN*.
3 Smith also pursued a new career as Commissioner of Customs for Scotland beginning in January 1778. That same year, after the British defeat at Saratoga, he was consulted by Lord North's Solicitor-General, Alexander Wedderburn, on alternatives open to the government. His memorandum is reprinted in *Corr.*, appendix B, pp. 377–85. Also see the thoughtful discussion of his views on the American Revolution in Winch, *Adam Smith's Politics*, ch. 7.
4 *TMS* VI. ii. 2. 12–18. Ernst Cassirer, *The Philosophy of Enlightenment*, p. vii, saw Enlightenment thought in general as a renunciation of the *esprit de système* characteristic of seventeenth-century philosophy. Its

alternative aim was the *esprit systématique* that Jean D'Alembert first defined in the "Preliminary Discourse" in vol. 1 of the *Encyclopédie* (1751). There is no mention of Adam Smith in Cassirer's classic study, but this distinction is relevant to understanding Smith's method of thinking.

5   *TMS* vi. ii. 2. 18.
6   Thomas Paine, *The Rights of Man* (Garden City, N.Y., 1961), pp. 312–13, 399.
7   Elie Halévy, *The Growth of Philosophical Radicalism*, trans. M. Morris (London, 1955), still provides a useful introduction to the question of how Smith's ideas were assigned such different practical implications during the 1790s. Also see Gertrude Himmelfarb, *The Idea of Poverty: England in the Early Industrial Age* (New York, 1983), pp. 42–144. A more systematic treatment, however, can be found in Stefan Collini, Donald Winch, and John Burrow, *That Noble Science of Politics: A Study in Nineteenth-Century Intellectual History* (Cambridge, 1984), chs. I and II.
8   J. R. Poynter, *Society and Pauperism: English Ideas on Poor Relief, 1795–1834* (London, 1969), pp. 52–53.
9   On the development of technical issues in "political economy" between the publication of the *Wealth of Nations* and David Ricardo's reformulations of Smith's doctrines in the *Principles of Political Economy* (1817), see M. Blaug's classic *Ricardian Economics* (New Haven, 1958). Blaug also provides an introduction to the important question of how political economy was popularized as a new "science." But the social and institutional determinants that defined problems treated by "political economists" who saw themselves as disciples of Smith and Ricardo still await a full-scale study. Also, although there are many works dealing with individual authors and topics, we need an historical account of the genesis and popularization of "political economy" in nineteenth-century Britain.
10 Winch, *Adam Smith's Politics*, p. 181. Haakonssen, *Science of a Legislator*, pp. 67–74, has a thoughtful discussion of the role of utility in *TMS*.
11 Smith himself was skilled, of course, in the quantitative discourse of economic analysis. But he also thought of this skill as a "political arithmetic" in which he ultimately had "no great faith." See *WN* iv. v. b. 30, and *Corr.*, Letter 249, to George Chalmers, 10 Nov. 1785, p. 288.

Index

Addison, Joseph, 102
Aequum, 22
Annual Register, x
Appleby, Joyce, 163, 181 n.5, 185 n.34
Aquinas, Saint Thomas: and scholastic rights theorists, 22
Aristotle, 23, 46, 155
Armagh, 34
Athens, 150
Augustine, Saint, 14, 42
Avarice, 16, 18, 95
Ayr, 34

Bagehot, Walter, x
Balfour, James, 105, 196 n.60
Balliol College, 126
Bank of England, 119
Barbeyrac, Jean, 57; edition of Grotius, 64, 68; influence on Hutcheson, 68; place in natural law tradition, 64
Beattie, James, 11
Bentham, Jeremy, 177, 183 n.16
Blair, Hugh, 11
Blaug, Mark, 205 n.9
Bracciolini, Poggio, 3, 188 n.32
Bristol, 80
Britain, 3, 173, 174, 175
Bruni, Leonardo, 3, 188 n.32
Buccleuch, Duke of, 128
Burke, Edmund, x, 173
Butler, Dr. Joseph, 81, 194 n.33
Bynkershoek, Cornelius Van, 57, 190 n.67

Calvin, Jean, 42
Cambridge, 34

Cannan, Edwin, xi
Capitalism, xiii–xiv, xv, 178; and commerce, 6–8, 174–75; intellectual origins of, 2–4, 93–96; morality of, 9–10; politics of, 8–10. *See also* commerce; Hume, David; Hutcheson, Francis; Smith, Adam
Carmichael, Gershom, 35, 73; edition of Pufendorf, 64; place in natural law tradition, 64
Cassirer, Ernst, 204 n.4
Cheyne, Dr. George, 104
Christianity, 35, 42, 105
Church of England, 11, 74
Cicero, 21, 46
Civic humanism, 3, 20, 72
Civil society, 55
Classical republicanism, 3
Commerce, 6–8, 174–75; as a right, 56. *See also* Hume, David; Hutcheson, Francis; Smith, Adam; Virtue
Condorcet, Marie-Jean-Antoine-Nicholas de Caritat, Marquis de, 172
Coniff, James, 76, 192 n.6
Craigie, Thomas, 126
Cropsey, Joseph, 133–34

Davis, David Brion, 53
Descartes, René, 82
Division of labor, 6; Smith on, 165–66, 168
Dominium, 23–25, 139
Dublin, 35

Edinburgh, 80, 84, 126, 132

Index

Edinburgh, University of, 80, 84
Enlightenment, Scottish, 11–12

Ferguson, Adam, 11, 18
Forbes, Duncan, 76, 105, 118, 119, 152, 196 n.54, 202 n.65
Fortitude, 43
Free trade, x, xiii, 16, 157; and laissez-faire, 1–2, 5–8, 10; and mercantilism, 1–2, 18–20. *See also* Hume, David; Hutcheson, Francis; Smith, Adam
French Revolution, 2; Smith on, 171–73
Frugality, 16, 47, 93, 134

Gay, Peter, 77
Gerson, Jean, 22
Glasgow, 35, 44, 56, 132; merchants of, xiv; "tobacco lords" of, xv
Glasgow University, ix, xi, 30, 85, 105, 125. *See also* Smith, Adam
Glorious Revolution, 34
Great Britain. *See* Britain
Grotius, Hugo, 20, 57, 65, 92, 99, 176; absolutism of, 25–26, 58–59; ambiguity of, 58–64; criticism of Aristotle, 22–23, 59; *De Iure Belli ac Pacis*, 21, 23, 26, 58, 99, 177; on justice, 22–25; and natural law tradition, 21–26, 57–64; on property, 23–25, 62–63; on rights, 22–25, 62. *See also* Hume, David; Hutcheson, Francis; Smith, Adam

Haakonssen, Knud, 131, 138, 154
Halévy, Elie, 173, 205 n.7
Harrington, James, 57, 72, 73
Hegel, G. W. F., 177
Hirschman, Albert O., 93–96, 111, 134
Hobbes, Thomas, 38, 68, 156; absolutism of, 59; and Grotius, 59–61; place in natural law tradition, 58–61
Hont, Istvan, 180 n.13, 185 n.57, 202 n.76
Homer, x
Horne, Thomas, 137

Hume, David, 74–120; and capitalism, 77, 80, 93, 102, 112; conservatism of, 79; cosmopolitanism of, 113–14, 120; as critic of mercantilism, 77, 112–15; and Grotius, 99, 102; and Hutcheson, 81–83, 84, 85–88, 89; as innovator, 75; irony of, 76, 198 n.84; and laissez-faire, 4, 5, 115, 118; "modern paganism" of, 77, 78; and moral philosophy, 86–87; naturalism of, 77, 80, 85, 93; originality of, 92–93, 97, 98–101, 104, 106; place in history of economic thought, 75–76, 77, 107, 112–13; place in natural law tradition, 89, 92, 99–101; *Political Discourses*, 106–20; radicalism of, 77, 78; and "science of man," 74–114 passim; skepticism of, 77; *Treatise of Human Nature*, 81–106; views on: commerce, 75, 96, 107–20; essay writing, 102–4, 118; free trade, 77, 79, 107, 111–15; justice, 76, 88–92, 98–101, 115; merchants, 80; moral sense, 81–82; passions, 85, 90–91, 110; property, 90–92; public credit, 119–20; self-interest, 98; sympathy, 82; virtue, 86–87; Whig and Tory, 106, 119. *See also* Hutcheson, Francis; Smith, Adam
Hume, Joseph, 80
Hutcheson, Francis, 29–74; and antislavery writers, 54; and Barbeyrac, 68, 69; and Carmichael, 67, 73; and civic humanism, 72–74; and Cumberland, 67, 69, 73; and Grotius, 57, 65, 66, 67, 68; and Harrington, 72–73; and Hobbes, 67; and laissez-faire, 4, 5, 31; and Locke, 37, 66, 69–70, 71; and Mandeville, 38–39, 48, 55; place in history of economic thought, 31–32; place in natural law tradition, 32–34, 56–71 passim; and Pufendorf, 67–69; and Shaftesbury, 36–37, 38; views on: civil society, 55; commerce, 31, 47–49; division of labor, 67; justice, 56, 65; money-making, 48; moral philosophy, 44, 56, 57,

87; moral sense, 29, 33, 36–41, 70; morality of commerce, 47–49; natural liberty, 67–68, 70, 71; passions, 36, 48, 70; property, 65, 67–68, 69; right of resistance, 65; rights, 50–56; sociability, 69; virtue, 36, 42, 44–46, 49; writings: "Considerations on Patronage," 73–74; *Essay*, 35; *Inquiry*, 26, 29, 35–36, 37, 40, 50, 89; *Short Introduction*, 46, 56, 57, 65, 67, 72; *System*, 29, 31, 37, 56, 57, 65, 70, 95. *See also* Hume, David; Smith, Adam

Ignatieff, Michael, 180 n.13, 189 n.57, 202 n.76
Interest, 94–95. *See also* Self-Interest
Ireland, 34
ius, 22
ius ad rem, 22, 141
ius in rem, 23, 141
iustum, 23

Jurisprudence, 20. *See also* Smith, Adam
Justice. *See* Grotius, Hugo; Hume, David; Hutcheson, Francis; Smith, Adam

Kames, Lord Henry Home, 11, 79, 102, 126
Kelly, George A., 193 n.11
Killyleagh, 34
Kirk, Scottish, xiv, 11, 35; Hume and, 105; Hutcheson and, 73–74
Kirkcaldy, 125
Knox, John, 42
Krieger, Leonard, 61

La Bruyere, Jean de, 110
Laissez-faire, 1, 2, 13, 155; Adam Smith and, 4–6, 181 n.2; and free trade, 4–6; in history of moral philosophy, 10, 157; Hume and, 115; Hutcheson and, 5–6; Quesnay and, 4; view of politics, 8, 113–14
La Rochefoucauld, François, Duc de, 110
Latitudinarians, English, 11, 74, 184 n.18, 191 n.87
Leechman, William, 84
Letwin, Shirley, 78, 193 n.8
Letwin, William, 158
Levellers, 59
Liberality, 47–48
Locke, John, 37, 57, 108, 129, 131, 156; *Essay Concerning Human Understanding*, 37, 39; and Grotius, 59; on property, 63; *Two Treatises of Government*, 37, 63, 64. *See also* Hume, David; Hutcheson, Francis; Shaftesbury, Earl of; Smith, Adam
Louis XV, 4
Luther, Martin, 42

McCulloch, J. R., 170
Mackintosh, James, 173
Macpherson, C. B., 155–56
Magherally, 35
Malthus, T. R., 173
Mandeville, Bernard de, 108; on commerce, 48–49, 108; Hume and, 81, 110; Hutcheson and, 37–39, 55; Smith and, 128, 136; on virtue, 39
Marx, Karl, 2
Meek, Ronald, 143
Mercantilism, xv, 181 n.1; and free trade, 1, 18–19, 107–9. *See also* Hume, David; Hutcheson, Francis; Smith, Adam
Mill, James, 177, 183 n.16
Mill, J. S., 75
Millar, John, 11
Miller, David, 192 n.7, 193 n.11
Montchrétien, Antoine de, 108, 109, 197 n.66
"Moderates," Scottish, 11, 183 n.18
Moore, James, 69, 71, 76, 92
Monopolies, 7; Smith on, 153–54, 166–67
Montesquieu, Charles Secordat, Baron de, 11, 16
Moral philosophy, 10, 27. *See also* Hume, David; Hutcheson, Francis; Smith, Adam
Moral sense, ideological implications of, 26–28, 41–47; Hume on,

81–82; Hutcheson on, 12, 16, 29, 33, 36–41, 70; Smith on, 129–30
Mossner, Ernest, 105, 196 n.55
Murdoch, Alex, xiv, 180 n.10
Mure, William, of Caldwell, 84

Natural law, 20–21; view of politics, 21–26. *See also* Grotius, Hugo; Hume, David; Hutcheson, Francis; Smith, Adam
Natural rights: and natural law, 21–25; types of, 23–25, 50–53. *See also* Grotius, Hugo; Hume, David; Hutcheson, Francis; Pufendorf; Smith, Adam
Northy, Dudley, 108

Oswald, James, 11
Oxford, 34

Paine, Thomas, 172, 173
Passions, 10, 13; and commerce, 95–97; in Western Thought, 14–15, 93–95. *See also* Hume, David; Hutcheson, Francis; Smith, Adam
Petrarch, 42
Petty, William, 108
Phillipson, Nicholas, 196 n.54
Physiocrats, 4, 5, 29, 113; and Smith, 125, 186 n.1
Plato, 46
Playfair, William, 170
Pocock, J. G. A., 3
Polanyi, Karl, 204 n.95
Politeness, 17
Political economy, xii, xvi, 108, 197 n.66
Poynter, J. R., 173
Presbyterianism, 34
Profit, 7, 114
Property, 22, 24, 29. *See also* Grotius, Hugo; Hume, David; Hutcheson, Francis; Smith, Adam
Proprietas, 23–25
Propriety, 15, 135
Protestantism, liberal, 11, 74, 84
"Proto-industrialization," 6
Prudence, 17, 43, 134, 135, 136
Pufendorf, 20, 21, 25, 57, 143, 156;

Grotius and, 62, 63; Hutcheson and, 67–69; place in natural law tradition, 60–62; Smith and, 143

Quesnay, François: and laissez-faire, 4; and Smith, 125

Rae, John, 31
Reformation, 42
Reformation, Scottish, 105
Reid, Thomas, 11, 98, 99, 192 n.1
Renaissance, 3, 42–46
Rice, Duncan, 53
Robertson, John, 198 n.84
Robertson, William, 158, 170
Rousseau, Jean-Jacques, 128, 146

Schumpeter, Joseph, 157, 158, 162, 165, 189 n.49
Scotland, xiii, 11, 34, 80, 127; Smith and, xiv–xv, 125–27
Scott, W. R., 31, 187 n.6
Selden, John, 59–60
Self-interest, xi, 3, 9, 98, 111, 112; Smith on, 136–37
"Self-liking," 38
Self-love, xi, 38, 55
Shaftesbury, Earl of: Hume and, 81; Hutcheson and, 36–39, 49, 57; on Locke, 36–37; Mandeville on, 37–38
Simson, John, 35, 73
Skinner, Quentin, 188 n.25
Smith, Adam, ix–xvi, 121–78; and capitalism, 6–10, 139, 155, 172–75; cosmopolitanism of, 125, 127; *Das Adam Smith Problem*, xi, 200 nn.27 and 33; in Glasgow, 125–27, 128–29, 132, 138; and Grotius, 139, 143, 144, 145, 156–57, 176, 177; historical awareness of, 143–68 passim; and Hume, 121–54 passim; and Hutcheson, 121–54 passim; jurisprudence of, 137–38, 139–54, 155; and laissez-faire, 4–5, 124, 164, 166–68; *Lectures on Jurisprudence*, 139–54; and Locke, 129; and Mandeville, 128, 136; moral philosophy of, xi–xii, xiii, xvi, 4, 122, 123, 124, 126, 128–29, 133, 139, 155,

170, 177; originality of *Wealth of Nations*, 121–25, 156–79; place in history of economic thought, 157–58; place in natural law tradition, 138, 139, 142–54, 156–57, 179 n.7, 180 n.13; and Quesnay, 125; and Rousseau, 128, 146; *Theory of Moral Sentiments*, x, xi, xii, 43, 123, 126, 128, 129–38, 170, 171; views on: Athens, 150; commerce, 134, 136–37, 140, 143, 151, 155–56, 174–75; Corn Laws, 135, 156, 159–61, 162; division of labor, 165–66, 168; entail, 149, 152, 154; forms of government, 150–52; "four stages" of society, 142–47, 151–54; free trade, 5, 124, 127, 157, 158–69, 204 n.95; French Revolution, 171–73; inequality, 146–47; labor, 6, 182 n.12; mercantilism, 124–25, 161–63; monopolies, 153–54, 166–67; moral sense, 129–30; natural liberty, 5, 156; Navigation Acts, 204 n.98; passions, 131, 133, 135; primogeniture, 149, 152, 154; property, 140–47, 148–49, 152–53; propriety, 15, 135; prudence, 134, 135, 136; "public spirit," 171; rights, 123, 131–40 passim, 144; self-interest, 123–24, 135, 137; self-love, xi, 136; "spirit of system," 171; sympathy, x, xi, 123, 130–31, 134–36, 140, 143; vanity, 135–36; virtue, 123, 129–31, 133–35, 137. *See also* Hume, David; Hutcheson, Francis
Smith, N. K., 76, 87
Sociability, 17, 69

Steele, Richard, 102
Stephen, Leslie, 37
Sterne, Laurence, 42
Stewart, Dugald, 11
Stewart, John B., 195 n.51
Strahan, William, x
Stroud, Barry, 82, 87

Taylor, W. L., 31
Temperance, 43
Theology, Christian, 2
Thompson, E. P., 159, 160, 203 n.82
Townshend, Charles, 127
Treaty of Union (1707), xiv, 73
Tribe, Keith, 197 n.66
Trinity College, 34
Tuck, Richard, 23, 24, 190 n.65
Tully, James, 54, 58, 63, 190 n.65

Universities, Scottish, 64, 205
Utilitarianism, 177

Values, Christian, 3
Vanity, 135–36
Viner, Jacob, 166, 181 n.2
Virtue, xiii, 10; and capitalism, 9; and commerce, 3, 45, 47; in Western thought, 13–15, 42–46. *See also* Hume, David; Hutcheson, Francis; Smith, Adam
Voltaire, 2, 6

Weber, Max, 2
Wills, Gary, 191 n.70
Winch, Donald, 124, 138, 154, 177
Wolin, Sheldon, 79
Wollstonecraft, Mary, 173

About the Author

Richard F. Teichgraeber III was born in Houston, Texas, in 1950. He grew up in São Paulo, Brazil, and in Houston. He attended Amherst College and Brandeis University, where in 1978 he received his Ph.D. in the History of Ideas Department. His articles and reviews have appeared in a number of journals and magazines, including *Journal of the History of Ideas, Journal of British Studies, Eighteenth-Century Studies, University Publishing,* and *The Texas Observer.* He has also introduced and abridged the new Modern Library College Edition of Adam Smith's *Wealth of Nations.*

During 1977–79 he was a Teaching and Research Fellow in the History Department at Stanford University. Since 1979 he has taught in the Department of History at Newcomb College, Tulane University; in 1984 he was appointed Director of Tulane's Murphy Institute of Political Economy.